In this important new essay, Joseph Mali argues that Vico's *New Science* must be interpreted according to Vico's own clues and rules of interpretation, principally his claim that the 'master-key' of his *New Science* is the discovery of myth. Following this lead Mali shows how Vico came to forge his new scientific theories about the mythopoeic constitution of consciousness, society, and history by reappraising, or 'rehabilitating', the ancient and primitive mythical traditions which still persist in modern times. He further relates Vico's radical redefinition of these traditions as the 'true narrations' of all religious, social, and political practices in the 'civil world' to his unique historical depiction of Western civilisation as evolving in a-rational and cyclical motions. On this account, Mali elaborates the wider, distinctly 'revisionist', implications of Vico's *New Science* for the modern human sciences. He argues that inasmuch as the *New Science* exposed the linguistic and other cultural systems of the modern world as being essentially mythopoeic, it challenges not only the Christian and Enlightenment ideologies of progress in his time, but also the main cultural ideologies of our time.

THE REHABILITATION OF MYTH:
VICO'S *NEW SCIENCE*

THE REHABILITATION OF MYTH

Vico's 'New Science'

JOSEPH MALI

Tel Aviv University

CAMBRIDGE
UNIVERSITY PRESS

Published by the Press Syndicate of the University of Cambridge
The Pitt Building, Trumpington Street, Cambridge CB2 IRP
40 West 20th Street, New York, NY 10011–4211, USA
10 Stamford Road, Oakleigh, Victoria 3166, Australia

First published 1992

A catalogue record for this book is available from the British Library

Library of Congress cataloguing in publication data

Mali, Joseph.
The rehabilitation of myth: Vico's New science / Joseph Mali.
p.   cm.
Includes bibliographical references and index.
ISBN 0 521 41952 2
1. Vico, Giambattista, 1668–1744. Principi di una scienza nuova.
2. Myth. 3. Philosophy. 4. Social sciences. 5. Poetry.
I. title.
B3581.P73M35 1992
195 – dc20   91–41975   CIP

ISBN 0 521 41952 2 hardback

Printed and bound in Great Britain by
Woolnough Bookbinding Ltd, Irthlingborough, Northamptonshire

WD

To my parents – with love and gratitude

We are apt to think of civilization as something solid and external, but at bottom it is a collective dream. 'In so far as the soul is in the body', says Plotinus, 'it lies in deep sleep'. What a people dreams in this earthly sleep is its civilization. And the substance of this dream is a myth, an imaginative interpretation of human existence, the perception (not the solution) of the mystery of human life . . . The project of science, as I understand it, is to solve the mystery, to wake us from our dream, to destroy the myth; and were this project fully achieved, not only should we find ourselves awake in a profound darkness, but a dreadful insomnia would settle upon mankind, not less intolerable for being only a nightmare.

Michael Oakeshott, *Leviathan: A Myth*

Contents

Contents

Acknowledgements

In this study I offer a new interpretation of Vico's *New Science*, based on Vico's own interpretation of his work: it is inspired by his statement that the 'master-key' of his work was his discovery of myth. It took me several years to realize just what Vico could have meant by this statement, and even more years to elaborate its wider meanings and implications.

During these years I incurred many personal and professional debts. I would like to thank first and foremost two great teachers: Amos Funkenstein initiated me into this study as a graduate student at the University of Tel Aviv, and improved its first version with his insightful and critical observations; Sir Isaiah Berlin read and discussed with me subsequent versions of this study in Oxford, and was always generous with his time and comments; to him I owe not only my greatest scholarly debt, but also my deepest personal gratitude for his support during hard times. Saul Friedländer has been a most inspiring teacher – from whom I have learned most of what I know about myth. Warm thanks are due to Yehuda Elkana and Zvi Yavetz for their advice and encouragement over the years. I also wish to thank friends and scholars with whom I have had illuminating discussions about Vico and other modern ancients: Yehoshua Arieli, Miri Eliav, Rivka Feldhay, Michael Heyd, Ted McGuire, Ernst Schulin, Dorit Tanay, and Donald Verene. I am very grateful to the following institutions for their support: The British Council, DAAD, and The Cohn Institute for the History and Philosophy of Science, Tel Aviv University. Gabriella Williams was most helpful in preparing the manuscript for publication. Finally, I must express my grateful thanks to my wife Anya whose wise counsel and good cheer has kept me going from beginning to end, and to my daughters Maya and Daniella for providing happy and much needed distraction.

In chapter 4 of my book I have drawn on material which has previously been published in articles in *New Vico Studies*, 6 (1988), and in *History of Political Thought*, 10 (1989). I thank the editors of these journals for permission to use this material.

A note on Vico's texts

I am grateful to the following publishers for the permission to use the following English editions of Vico's works.

The New Science of Giambattista Vico, tr. Thomas Goddard Bergin and Max Harold Fisch (Ithaca, N.Y.: Cornell University Press, 1968). All quotations from this work are noted in the text by NS/ and standard paragraph numbers in parentheses.

The Autobiography of Giambattista Vico, tr. Thomas Goddard Bergin and Max Harold Fisch (Ithaca, N.Y.: Cornell University Press, 1963).

The First New Science, in *Selected Writings*, tr. Leon Pompa (Cambridge: Cambridge University Press, 1982).

On the Most Ancient Wisdom of the Italians, in *Selected Writings*, tr. Leon Pompa (Cambridge: Cambridge University Press, 1982).

On the Study Methods of Our Time, ed. Elio Gianturco (Indianapolis, Ind.: Bobbs-Merrill, 1965).

For all other works I have used the standard Italian edition. *Opere di G. B. Vico*, ed. Fausto Nicolini, 8 vols. (Bari: Laterza, 1911–1941).

Introduction

On 14 May 1825, Samuel Taylor Coleridge wrote a letter to a friend, describing his first impressions of Vico's *New Science*:

I am more and more delighted with G. B. Vico, and if I had (which thank God's good grace I have not) the least drop of Author's blood in my veins, I should twenty times successively in the perusal of the first volume (I have not yet begun the second) have exclaimed: '*Pereant qui ante nos nostra dixere*'.[1]

Coleridge's curse in disguise still haunts Vichian scholars, many of whom must have had felt the same ambivalent sensation of *déjà lu*, as if they had already read – if not actually written – Vico's words. Of all the legends surrounding the man and his work, the legend of Vico the forerunner, the sage who grasped and expressed many truths of the future, has proven the most attractive, though hardly the most constructive, to interpreters of his work. Like Coleridge, many modern readers of the *New Science* believe, genuinely enough, to have discovered in its cryptic formulations affinities, or even outright solutions, to their own research problems. If, as Isaiah Berlin has noted, there is 'a particular danger that attends the fate of rich and profound but inexact and obscure thinkers, namely that their admirers tend to read too much into them, and turn insensibly in the direction of their own thoughts',[2] then surely Vico and his interpreters have been particularly prone to it. The Vichian industry of recent years has produced some remarkable, if ever more bizarre, samples of comparative studies, all implying Vichian intimations of our modern, all too modern

---

[1] Quoted from Max H. Fisch, 'The Coleridges, Dr Prati and Vico', *Modern Philology*, 41 (1943), p. 114.
[2] Isaiah Berlin, *Vico and Herder* (London: Hogarth Press, 1976), p. 95.

theories.[3] Vico has been hailed and promoted as the discoverer of almost every major field of knowledge in the humanities and in the social sciences. He is commonly compared with modern thinkers whom he would never have understood and who, all too often, have never bothered to understand him. On the whole, Vico has been made to advocate ideas which he could not possibly have conceived.[4] My aim in this essay on Vico's *New Science* is to establish what Vico had actually argued for, and thereby to argue for him. And, as the title of this work suggests, my argument is that in his *New Science* Vico sought, and ultimately achieved, a *Rehabilitation of Myth*. In the following remarks I would like to make clear, first of all, what this title of the work means.

The Rehabilitation of Myth: I have borrowed this phrase and its principal connotations from Jean-Pierre Vernant's well-known essay on 'The Reason of Myth'. Vernant's thesis is that

the concept of myth that we have inherited from the Greeks belongs, by reason of its origins and history, to a tradition of thought peculiar to Western civilization in which myth is defined in terms of what is not myth, being opposed first to reality (myth is fiction) and, secondly, to what is rational (myth is absurd). If the development of the study of myth in modern times is to be understood it must be considered in the context of this line of thought and tradition . . . [which would ultimately result in] discovering the authentic and essential nature of that shadowy part of man that is hidden from him. This new attitude was eventually to lead, in various ways, to the rehabilitation of myth. Its 'absurdity' was no longer denounced as a logical scandal; rather, it was considered as a challenge scientific intelligence would have to take up if this other form of intelligence represented by myth was to be understood and incorporated into anthropological knowledge.[5]

My main claim in this work is that this *rehabilitation of myth* was first conceived by Giambattista Vico. Furthermore, I shall argue

---

[3] For a comprehensive survey of this secondary literature, see Andrea Battistini, 'Contemporary Trends in Vichian Studies', in *Vico: Past and Present*, ed. G. Tagliacozzo (Atlantic Highlands, N.J.: Humanities Press, 1981), pp. 1–47, esp. pp. 16–22 for some pertinent critical commentaries on the excessive 'comparativism' and 'presentism' of Anglo-American scholars.

[4] These methodological premises are further elaborated by Bruce Haddock, 'Vico: The Problem of Interpretation', in *Vico in Contemporary Thought*, ed. G. Tagliacozzo, M. Mooney, and M. P. Verene (Atlantic Highlands, N.J.: Humanities Press, 1979), I, pp. 145–62.

[5] Jean-Pierre Vernant, 'The Reason of Myth', in *Myth and Society in Ancient Greece*, tr. J. Lloyd (London: Methuen, 1980), pp. 186, 216.

that this was the main aim of Vico's work, and that in so doing he
initiated a seminal process of revisionism in various spheres of
knowledge. I trust that this perspective, which might seem at first
glance to be rather limited in its scope, will prove to be the ideal
vantage-point from which to view the enormous range of the *New
Science*. This work, then, is neither a comprehensive study of Vico's
works, nor even a conclusive commentary on all aspects of his *New
Science* (let alone on the vast critical literature about it!), but rather
an attempt to elaborate the full meaning and implications of one
singular notion that undergirds that work: the definition of myth
as 'true narration' (*vera narratio*).

I aim to demonstrate that in this positive definition Vico conceived not only a new theory of classical mythology, but a *New
Science* of humanity. Vico's definition is unique because in it he
takes *mythology* which had previously been considered as essentially
false – because its *poetic narrations* of facts seemed to be opposed to
either the *rational theories* of philosophy and science, or to the
revealed gospels of religion, or to the *critical reports* of history – to be
true in itself. This was the definitive conclusion of his inquiries into
the origins of 'the history of human ideas', in which he found out
that the archaic and anonymous *mythologein*, the discourse of
tradition which consists in repeating *what they say*, is the main
mode of knowledge in which men have actually constituted their
civil world (*mondo civile*). In his *New Science* Vico sought to discover
the *poetic logic* which permeates this kind of experiential-historical
knowledge, which he termed *coscienza*, and, by setting it over
against the *rational logic* of the experimental-mathematical knowledge, or *scienza*, of the new sciences of nature, was concerned to
establish upon it an equally valid, and ultimately superior, science,
a truly *scienza nuova*, of human history. He regarded the archaic
myths as the 'true narrations' of this history because he saw that in
our (and any other) civilization the fictions of mythology
illuminate the 'real world' by constituting or 'prefiguring' all its
human actions and institutions: unlike natural occurrences which
display law-like, repetitive regularities which are unknowable to
us because they are totally alien to our form of life, human
occurrences throughout history display forms of action which are
knowable to us insofar as we can recognize in them the coherent
narrative patterns of the mythical stories with their well-made
characters and plots. His comparative study of classical and

primitive myths had led him to believe that these had formed a 'mental language common to the nations' (*una lingua mentale comune a tutte le nazioni*), that is, a symbolic language composed of concrete figures or acts which initially served as vehicles for more abstract and general concepts not yet fully conceived. Vico thought that these archaic images, which he called 'poetic characters', were still embedded in a variety of modern cultural performances – as in linguistic common-places, religious beliefs, social customs, or political rites and institutions:

We find that the principle of these origins both of languages and of letters lies in the fact that the first gentile peoples, by a demonstrated necessity of nature, were poets who spoke in poetic characters. This dis-covery, which is the master-key of this Science, has cost us the persistent research of almost all our literary life, because with our civilized natures we cannot at all imagine and can understand only by great toil the poetic nature of these men. (NS/34)

In itself, Vico's 'discovery' is akin to what modern theorists of culture would eventually proclaim as their own major discovery, namely – to use Wittgenstein's words – that 'a whole mythology is deposited in our language'.[6] On a more fundamental level, this discovery suggests that Vico, like many modern interpretive social theorists, could establish his *New Science* only after he had taken a linguistic turn: he saw that inasmuch as the world in which men live is a world of institutions based on language, the task of the human sciences most resembles, and must be modelled on, the interpretation of texts. His concrete *New Science*, let us not forget, is an exercise in the old art of 'philology' – an art which tradition-ally entailed the formal interpretation of words in classical books, but which was elevated by Vico to a universal method of under-standing human beings in past or foreign cultures through their collective symbolic figures and myths. Hence my contention that the definition of myth as 'true narration' is the single most important notion in Vico's entire *New Science* – because this is its interpretive code: the notion, namely, which runs through and illuminates all the other notions in that work. As, in fact, did Vico himself see it: he regarded 'the discovery' of these 'poetic characters' to be 'the master-key of this Science' – because it

---

[6] Ludwig Wittgenstein, *Remarks on Frazer's Golden Bough*, ed. R. Rhees, tr. A. C. Miles (Retford: The Brynmill Press, 1979), p. 10.

enabled him to decipher the essentially mythopoeic constitution of humanity. Vico's discovery of a new science of the human world may thus be seen as akin to Galileo's discovery of a new science of the natural world in that both stem from the same *linguistic* conception of their respective worlds. For both authors perceived their worlds as 'books' which have been composed, and must be interpreted, according to their own immanent code, or *chiave maestra*: just as Galileo based his new science of physics on the discovery of its constitutive 'mathematical characters', so Vico based his new science of history on the discovery of its constitutive 'poetic characters'. Vico's 'master-key', however, has rarely been used to unlock his own *New Science*. How has the decipherment of ancient mythology enabled him to interpret the entire history of the modern civil world? This issue lies at the heart of this essay.

What I propose in this study, then, is an interpretation of Vico's *New Science* based on his own interpretive principles. In so doing, I follow the methodological advice of Hayden White, who has rightly observed that the main problem with Vico's great work is to decide what it is about. White notes that even though the subject-matter of the *New Science* can be quite clearly defined – it is, he says, 'literally about the ways men make societies and the proper way to comprehend these processes' – its category cannot be easily classified. White argues that Vico's *New Science* is 'one of those master texts of humanistic studies' like Hegel's *Phenomenology*, Nietzsche's *Genealogy*, or Freud's *Totem and Taboo*: these works, he says,

are neither exactly philosophy . . . nor quite literature . . . They are about historical subjects, but are not histories; they deal with problems that interest modern social science, but they are not scientific in method. What such master texts seem to be about, over and above their manifest subject, is interpretation itself . . . they serve as repositories of interpretive strategies by which to make sense of texts in general, themselves included.[7]

These are the basic thematic and methodic assumptions which govern this essay. In singling out Vico's notion of myth for such thorough – and seemingly exclusive – treatment, I do not mean to

---

[7] Hayden White, Review Essay on Leon Pompa, *Vico: A Study of the 'New Science'*, in *History and Theory*, 15 (1976), pp. 198–9.

suggest that other issues in that work are less important. Rather, I want to show how, in Vico's scheme, practically all human creations (*cose umane*) can, and indeed must, be traced back and reappraised according to their mythical components. Therefore, while I shall not treat in detail certain major topics in the *New Science* – such as, for example, Rhetorics or Law – in detail, I trust that the elaboration of Myth will clarify the basic heuristic principles and strategies by which to assess these and other matters in that work.

More generally still, I think that there is much truth in the astute observation of the French philosopher Henri Bergson, who once said that any great thinker conjures up one, and only one, original and inexhaustible idea, which he then spends his whole life coming to terms with: '*Et c'est pourquoi il a parlé toute sa vie*'.[8] This observation seems particularly apt in the case of Vico, if only for the reason that he himself perceived his life and work to have unfolded in that way. From around 1720, he tells us, his 'intellectual life' was totally dominated by one monumental attempt – to retrace the process of civilization among the gentiles in and through the minds of those who experienced and carried it out:

To discover the way in which this first human thinking arose in the gentile world, we encountered exasperating difficulties which have cost us the persistent research of a good twenty years. [We had] to descend from these human and refined natures of ours to those quite wild and savage natures, which we cannot at all imagine and can comprehend only with great effort. (NS/338)

These words reverberate throughout the *New Science*, as well as in the vast literature on that work – including this essay. It was this initial perception of the mental distance that separates us from our primitive ancestors which set Vico on his descent into what he called the 'deplorable obscurity of the beginnings of the nations and into the innumerable variety of their customs'. Having duly recognized the fact that because of this distance an immediate entry into their alien culture, by purely intuitive and merely 'imaginative' means, is impossible, he sought to discover in their cultural performances certain moral codes, or 'principles' of

---

[8] Henry Bergson, *Oeuvres*, ed. A. Robinet (Paris: Presses Universitaires de France, 1970), p. 1347.

behaviour, which are still understandable to us. These 'principled' modes of human life, when recognized as such in their cultures as well as in 'the modifications of our own human mind', could then point to what has become the truly 'common nature of the nations', that which unites, as it were, the ancient-primitive world of the pagans with the modern, 'human and refined' world of Christian Europe in one tradition of humanity. Where the other dominant cultural ideologies of his time – Christianity and the Enlightenment – saw only discontinuity between the false superstitions of the ancients and the true faith or correct reasoning of the moderns, Vico perceived a certain underlying community and continuity between 'the obscure and fabulous' times and the 'enlightened' age – that of the 'poetic speech', or *mythologein*: 'The poetic speech which our poetic logic has helped us to understand continued for a long time into the historical period, much as great and rapid rivers continue far into the sea, keeping sweet the waters borne on by the force of their flow' (NS/412).

Vico's theory of myth has long been recognized by scholars of myth as a major contribution to the modern science of mythology. And yet, on the whole, they have commonly waved it off with this gesture of recognition. Thus, for example, Ernst Cassirer, who repeatedly praised Vico as 'the real discoverer of the myth', did not deal with Vico's actual writings on the topic.[9] As for Vichian scholars, while most of them have paid due attention to the mythological inquiries in his work, they have generally dismissed them as fatuous and quite irrelevant to the more serious theories in his work.[10] Following Croce's idealistic method of distinguishing between 'what is living and what is dead' in masterpieces of the past – by which he sought, in the case of *New Science*, to disregard most of the philological (and least 'certain') assumptions in that

---

[9] Ernst Cassirer, *The Problem of Knowledge*, tr. W. H. Woglom and C. W. Hendel (New Haven: Yale University Press, 1950), p. 296.
[10] Of the many works which deal specifically with Vico's theory of myth, I found the following most valuable: Gianfranco Cantelli, *Mente corpo linguaggio: Saggio sull'interpretazione vichiana del mito* (Florence: Sansoni, 1987): Guido Dorfles, *L'estetica del mito; Da Vico a Wittgenstein* (Milan: Mursia, 1968); Frank Manuel, 'Vico: the "giganti" and Their Joves', *The Eighteenth-Century Confronts the Gods* (Cambridge, Mass.: Harvard University Press, 1959), pp. 149–67; David Bidney, 'Vico's New Science of Myth', in *Vico: International Symposium*, ed. G. Tagliacozzo and H. White (Baltimore: The Johns Hopkins Press, 1969), pp. 259–77.

work, and to concentrate solely on its refined – and genuinely
'true' – philosophical conclusions,[11] many interpreters have come
to completely ignore Vico's own proclamation that he had derived
his 'true' philosophical ideas from 'certain' philological facts.
The whole lot of mythological interpretations, etymological
associations, scriptural manifestations, and such like oddities
which Vico regarded as the 'philological proofs' of his philosophical and historical arguments, have thus been dismissed by
his modern interpreters as no more than those topical interests
which have since proved to be not just superficial in themselves,
but really unnecessary to the work in the first place. The *New
Science*, so runs their argument, just happens to be a work in which
the most insightful ideas and conclusions are often derived from
the most abstruse factual premises. This attitude is prevalent in
the much too limited way they have commonly treated the mythological stuff in this work. As Gianfranco Cantelli has recently
noted,

The common tendency of the majority of Vico's interpreters has been to
approach the problem [of myth] from a point of view too exclusively
aesthetic and linguistic, which has left obscured the perhaps decisive fact
that, for Vico, the investigation of the origins of poetry grew out of a
predominantly historical inquiry and that his true intention was less
to establish the manner in which poetic language was born than to
examine the function of myths, to clarify the origins of religion, and to
determine its role in the civil development of mankind.[12]

Why have all those scholars shown so little interest in, or understanding of, Vico's mythological inquiries? The reason, I think,
lies in Vico's peculiar 'philological' mode of interpretation, in his
baffling 'style'. It seems that, like most common readers of the *New
Science*, they too have found Vico's poetic elaborations of mythological idioms and images quite obscure, at best speculative, and
all too often just nonsensical. His philological style, indeed,
presents endless obstacles to a systematic study of his theory of
myth and yet, at the same time, this style in itself conveys a certain
message. In an era in which writers came to regard 'style' as an

---

[11] Benedetto Croce, *The Philosophy of Giambattista Vico*, tr. R. G. Collingwood (N.Y.: Russell and Russell, 1964).
[12] Gianfranco Cantelli, 'Myth and Language in Vico', in *Vico's Science of Humanity*, ed. G. Tagliacozzo and D. P. Verene (Baltimore: The Johns Hopkins University Press, 1976), p. 48.

expressive rather than merely decorative mode; and believed, in Buffon's famous words, that *Le style est l'homme même*, the literary form and rhetorical strategies of Vico – who was, after all, a Royal Professor of Rhetoric and Eloquence – were surely purposeful. Against the fashionable tradition of pure philosophical reasoning, highlighted in his time by Descartes' corroboration of 'clear and distinct ideas' only, Vico moulded his *New Science* in a different, and consciously contrarious, fashion: he not only thought out a new science but also worked it out in a new scientific style. The argumentative style of the *New Science* – its poetics – is an argument in – and about – itself; it is only when we know *how* Vico argues that we can fully understand *what* he argues for. Or, to make the point in Vico's own terms, it appears that although his first heuristic rule – in which he states that 'theories must start from the point where the matter of which they treat first began to take shape' (NS/314) – has been duly recognized by interpreters of the *New Science* as its most fundamental methodological postulate, it has not been properly applied by them to this work itself.[13] Concerned as they were with the *theories*, they have rarely if ever concentrated on the original raw *matter* from which Vico carved these theories – the archaic mythological texture. This, they assumed, was only the medium, not the message. My entire counter-argument is perhaps best summed up in Marshall MacLuhan's well-known dictum: 'The medium is the message'. The theoretical message of the *New Science* is already included in, and must therefore be elucidated directly from, its mythological examples and assertions: it consists in the activity of *mythopoeisis* itself, in the recognition that all our cultural creations, including the *New Science* itself, are recreations of myths.

Does this mean, then, that Vico consciously composed his *New Science* as a *New Myth*? This romantic hypothesis, provocative as it is (and is probably meant to be), must be considered, if only for the reason that some respectable interpreters of the *New Science*, from Francisco De Sanctis to Norman O. Brown, have seriously argued for it: as they saw it, this is what Vico must have meant to do were he loyal to his innermost convictions about the value of myth-making – not only in antiquity but also, and especially, in the

---

[13] The exception here is Donald Phillip Verene, *Vico's Science of Imagination* (Ithaca: Cornell University Press, 1981).

modern times.[14] Though I find this suggestion intriguing, I think it must be rejected for the simple reason that Vico perceived his work, as he actually defined it, as a 'science of mythology' (NS/51), and not as a mythology of science. Unlike his predecessors in the Renaissance and his followers among the Romantics, Vico did not seek to work out a new mythology, but rather to clarify the work of myth in our minds and cultures. His attitude might well be summed up in the words of Hans Blumenberg, who by way of explaining the title of his massive study – *Work on Myth* – says that 'only work *on* myth – even if it is the work of finally reducing it – makes the work *of* myth manifest'.[15]

In any case, the assumption that Vico has really come of age only in our time, when, luckily for him, his archaic philological concerns have been *aufgehoben*, is only half true. It is true, indeed, that he remained largely unknown in his life-time. But it would be more accurate to say that he was ignored rather than misunderstood or rejected by his contemporaries. His text baffled his contemporaries, as it still amazes us, because its subject matter – the distinctly 'poetic' way in which men both made their 'civil world' and 'could come to know it' – was worked-out in a most unusual, but very appropriate, poetic fashion. And if anything, the oddity of his 'philological proofs' has not been diminished, let alone resolved, by what we take to be our purer understanding of its intrinsic philosophical message. We simply do not pay as much attention or respect to them as did some old-fashioned 'philologist' readers in the past – readers like Coleridge and Michelet, Grote and Auerbach, and above all Joyce who did not believe in Vico's – or any other – science, but revelled in his linguistic fantasies. We think we understand better than earlier generations what this text is all about because we have taken far greater interpretive liberty to give a rational rendering of its poetic ideas, to recast its crude images and assertions in our own

---

14 Francesco de Sanctis likens Vico's *New Science* to Dante's *Divine Comedy*: 'Bristling with myths, with etymologies, with symbols, with allegories, and pregnant with presentiments and divinations, it is not less great than the "sacred poem" itself; it is the work of a fantasy excited by philosophical genius and fortified by erudition, and has all the physiognomy of a great revelation' (*History of Italian Literature*, tr. J. Redfern, (N.Y.: Harcourt, Brace and Co., 1959), II, pp. 807–8. In *Closing Time* (N.Y.: Random House, 1973), Norman O. Brown likens Vico's interpretation to Joyce's recreation of mythology.

15 Hans Blumenberg, *Work on Myth*, tr. R. M. Wallace (Cambridge, Mass.: MIT Press, 1985), p. 118.

enlightened terms and concepts. And in many cases, especially where Vico does not use facts or figurative examples merely to 'illustrate' his seemingly deeper and more conceptually refined ideas (as, in his view, Plato did), but really works his way through and infers his ideas from these materials (as, in his view, Tacitus did), when, in short, he reasons wholly philologically, not about words but, as it were, with and through them – then, it seems, our tendency to over-intellectualize him lets us down. By trying to read too much into his utterly superficial poetical musings we miss what was perhaps immediately and plainly legible to less sophisticated, but more finely-tuned, readers in the past. One of the guiding heuristic principles of this essay is that there are in Vico's work many hidden – or rather already forgotten – perspectives, such that had been more properly recognized and worked upon by readers in earlier generations, and very often more by wayward Vichian artists than by meticulous Vichian scholars. A major task of this essay will be to regain these lost perspectives on –and in – the *New Science*.

To sum up: All those modern scholars who have dismissed Vico's obsessive immersion in mythological examples and interpretations as antiquated, as no more than a 'medium', the merely material examples which Vico used to illustrate his deeper and more significant ideas, have, I think, missed the main point of the *New Science*. They did not ask themselves the simple question: why myth? Why would Vico spend so much energy – 'almost all our literary life' as he puts it (NS/34) – trying to make sense of this massive repository of archaic images and tales? The answer, as I have indicated above, must be, that Vico believed that modern man, being the inheritor of former modes of thought, speech, and behaviour, still lives by these examples. In his *New Science* Vico expressed this notion in one memorable and eminently revealing oration, surely the most famous passage and the one that has been quoted and interpreted more than any other in that work, but rarely, I would argue, in its right – and only meaningful – context:

But in the night of thick darkness enveloping the earliest antiquity, so remote from ourselves, there shines the eternal and never failing light of a truth beyond all question: that the world of civil society has certainly been made by men, and that its principles are therefore to be found within the modifications of our own human mind. Whoever reflects on this cannot but marvel that the philosophers should have bent all their energies to the study of the world of nature, which, since God made it, He alone knows; and that they should have neglected the study of the world of nations, or civil world, which, since men made it, men could come to know. (NS/331).

Typically enough, most commentators who have elaborated on this passage concentrated on its seminal epistemological conclusion, on what has become known as 'Vico's principle of knowledge' – the *verum ipsum factum* – and its significance for the foundation of the human sciences. Clearly, however, the 'truth' about the autonomous self-making of man, society and history, that which Vico and his interpreters celebrate as his 'great discovery', is rather trivial, and certainly not new. In fact, as Vico himself hints, it is in many ways as old as philosophy itself. Its basic principle of humanism was first intimated by certain pre-socratic philosophers, and was thereafter reiterated time and again in various forms by many ancient, medieval, and Renaissance theories concerning the 'dignity' of man and civic society. During the seventeenth century, with the eclipse of the Christian world view, this theory of human self-making acquired greater vigour through better epistemology and more accurate anthropo-history. Allowing that Vico's 'truth' was rather common – both in itself, and among his contemporaries, one must ask, in what sense, then, if any, Vico could seriously claim to have discovered it, and whether his discovery rendered it especially important. This is precisely the point: I think that the significance of Vico's 'truth' lies not so much in *what* Vico claims, but rather in *why* and *how* he does so. In other words, Vico's 'lesson' still merits consideration but less for itself, than for the means and materials from which he drew it. Like any other general philosophical discovery in the *New Science* this too becomes fully meaningful only in its concrete philological context-of-discovery.

And so, when we turn again to the above-quoted passage, it becomes clear that what is so patently lacking in those modern attempts to explicate its message is a consideration of its formal and imagistic reasoning. It is clear, to begin with, that Vico here construes his entire argument syllogistically, i.e., he infers its major philosophical conclusion – 'that the world of civil society has certainly been made by men' – from certain philological observations he had made about its origination in 'the earliest antiquity' of mankind. He strongly implies that he has actually discovered something in their crude way of making and knowing *their* world which is crucial to our refined way of knowing and making *our* world. Our ability to understand *how* these men 'had made' their world in the first place guarantees that 'we could come to know' *what* our world is. We can do it insofar as we are the inheritors of their archaic patterns of knowing and making things. In order to know the human world we must know its constitutive myths. And this is precisely what Vico did and instructed us to do:

Truth is sifted from falsehood in everything that has been preserved for us through long centuries by those vulgar traditions which, since they have been preserved for so long a time and by entire peoples, must have had a public ground of truth. The great fragments of antiquity, hitherto useless to science because they lay begrimed, broken, and scattered, shed great light when cleaned, pieced together, and restored. (NS/356–7)

The 'Truth' referred to in this passage is that which is most essential to the work as a whole, the truth namely about *how men had made their civil world and why, therefore, men could come to know it.* Vico repeatedly says what this truth is, but here, rather enigmatically, he goes further by specifying precisely how and where he had found it. He claims to have discovered this 'truth' in those 'fragments of antiquity' – the ancient myths – which enabled the ancients, 'who were all by nature poets', to create the human world, as they might still enable us, the new scientists, to come to know it – inasmuch as these myths still persist in our minds and cultures.

Such views as I ascribe to Vico are nowadays labeled 'revisionist'. In view of the fact that this adjective has been so commonly – and variably – applied to all kinds of political and historical theories, it is hard to know whether the *New Science* deserves to be so praised or condemned. If revisionism means merely 'going back to the sources' and a re-evaluation of orthodox views according to new facts or theories, then Vico's work might well be considered revisionary, but then so too could countless other works, including those which Vico opposed. It seems, therefore, that in order to get the true meaning of revisionism as a methodico-ideological theory of interpretation we have to adhere more closely to its etymological connotations, and to accentuate its conservative, and even reactionary, premises. The first and

most common assumption of all the revisionists is that human
affairs are intricate and uncertain because they are always liable to
be disrupted by chance, ignorance and error of egotistical desires,
so that what happens in history is often unforeseen and undesired.
This inevitable heterogeneity-of-ends defies, in principle, all kinds
of rigid logical, and especially teleological, schemes of social
evolution, whether those of the politicians' foresight or those of
the historians' hindsight. They thus oppose the rational-liberal
theories of humankind and society and their concomitant pro-
gressivist accounts of history with narratives which reveal religious
beliefs and moral values, social practices and political institutions
to be subservient to historical events and processes. Revisionism
thus entails a re-evaluation of apparently scientific explanations by
more casual considerations, the reduction of universal theories to
local practices and accidents, the elevation of poetical sensibilities
over against logical ratiocinations – both among the historical
agents as among those who study them. Seen in this way revisionism would imply not so much a modern view of the past but a view
of modernity from past perspectives. For the revisionist considers
human beings to be essentially traditional, living in immemorial
and largely impersonal structures of meaning, of which they are
only dimly aware, and which they cannot, nor should, change by
radical intellectual or political acts. Believing thus that behind all
the forms of modern rationalism there lurk past and continuous
traditions of belief, the revisionist scholars attempt to expose in
them the poetic images and habitual practices which resist progressive, never mind revolutionary, categories; they seek, as a rule,
to read historical documents as if from the point of view of those
who were immersed in the very process which later scholars
describe in their own modern terms and theories.

Vico's critical expositions of all kinds of conceptual anachronism, the fallacy which he neatly termed as that 'conceit of the
scholars . . . who will have it that what they know is as old as the
world' (NS/127) – renders him a 'revisionist' in that sense –
though, of course, a revisionist in all but name. His deconstruction
of rational modern theories of mind, man, and society – such as,
for example, the Cartesian *cogito*, neo-Epicurean atomism, or
social contract – into their poetical components, further confirms
this view. As does his socio-historical narration of the evolution of
mankind from barbarism to civilization 'out of ferocity, avarice,

and ambition, the three vices which run throughout the human race' and 'which could certainly destroy all mankind on the face of the earth' (NS/132), a narration which does not display civilization as a linear and always progressive process of enlightenment through Revelation or Reason, but as a cyclical and occasionally regressive process of courses and recourses from and to barbarism, through Myth. It is for these and similar reasons, and according to these terms, that I present Vico's *New Science* as a series of 'revisions' of four modern theories – of Science, Civilization, Mythology, and History – which cover those spheres of knowledge on which he sought to establish his new science of humanity. In his revision of all these theories Vico followed the principal rule which he set for all students of humanity, whose 'theories must start from the point where the matter of which they treat first began to take shape', and which I, in my theory of his theory, follow as well.

CHAPTER I

The revision of science

> If natural philosophy, in all its parts, by pursuing this method,
> shall at length be perfected, the bounds of moral philosophy
> will also be enlarged.
>
> Isaac Newton, *Opticks*, 31st Query

> Indeed, were you to apply the geometric method to life, 'you
> would succeed only in trying to be a rational lunatic', steering
> in a straight line amid life's curves, as though caprice,
> rashness, chance and fortune held no sway in human affairs.
>
> Vico, *On the Most Ancient Wisdom of the Italians*, ch. v

I

In his well-known and influential essay, *The Divorce between the
Sciences and the Humanities*, Isaiah Berlin argues that although
there have always been disputes about method and distinctions
with regard to these spheres of knowledge (Berlin effectively
discards the common notion of 'two cultures'), it was only in the
eighteenth century that there emerged a 'sense of contrast'
between the two. Berlin concludes that 'the great cleavage
between the provinces of natural science and the humanities was,
for the first time, made, or revealed, for better or for worse, by
Giambattista Vico. Thereby he started a great debate of which the
end is not in sight.'[1] Similarly, in his *Newtonian Studies*, Alexander
Koyré touches upon the same problem, and points to Newton as
the culprit responsible for 'the splitting of our world in two'.
Newton, he says, was 'responsible . . . for substituting for our world
of quality and sense perception, the world in which we live, and

---

[1] Isaiah Berlin, 'The Divorce between the Sciences and the Humanities', repr. in *Against
the Current* (Oxford: Oxford University Press, 1980), p. 110.

love, and die, another world – the world of quantity, of reified geometry, a world in which, though there is place for everything, there is no place for man'.[2]

With regard to the 'splitting of our world in two' Vico may be said to have conceived in theory what Newton did in practice: he made us more aware of what Newton had done – to us. Vico tried to regain for us that 'world of quality and sense-perception', the truly human world, which the Newtonians had discarded, or had been willing to accommodate only in terms of their own mechanical world. Thus, already in his inaugural lecture of 1709, *On the Study Methods of Our Time*, Vico declared that

Since, in our time, the only target of our intellectual endeavours is truth, we devote all our efforts to the investigation of physical phenomena, because their nature seems unambiguous; but we fail to inquire into human nature which, because of the freedom of man's will, is difficult to determine. A serious drawback arises from the uncontrasted preponderance of our interest in the natural sciences . . . When it comes to the matter of prudential behaviour in life, it is well for us to keep in mind that human events are dominated by chance and choice, which are extremely subject to change and which are strongly influenced by simulation and dissimulation (both pre-eminently deceptive things). As a consequence, those whose only concern is abstract truth experience great difficulty in attaining their ends.[3]

When Giambattista Vico wrote these words in 1709 he was already aware of the main task of his life: to construe an alternative 'science' to the new sciences of Descartes, Galileo, and Newton, one that would be primarily concerned with 'prudential behaviour in life' and its related truths, that is, those truths which men have made about and for themselves. A science like this, Vico believed, would be a human science in the full sense of the term since it would expose all truths, and particularly those of the privileged physico-mathematical sciences – as merely human truths. Like all other truths, these too would turn out to be essentially fictive conceptions of reality that men have always devised in order to control and determine their new and unbearably contingent experience. The rational conceptions of modern man might well be more sophisticated than those of the *primi*

[2] Alexander Koyré, 'The Significance of the Newtonian Synthesis', in *Newtonian Studies* (Cambridge, Mass.: Harvard University Press, 1965), p. 23.
[3] Vico, *On the Study Methods of Our Time*, p. 33.

uomini, and yet, at bottom, Vico felt, they are substantially the same: modern sciences, like ancient mythology and like all our cultural endeavours, would be seen as a primarily conservative mechanism, in which man, by fixing boundaries to and within natural reality and by subjecting the phenomena to various laws of nature, creates to himself a measure of reliability and orientation in his world.

These notions, which are already implicit in Vico's criticism of Descartes' physico-geometrical method, mark, as Eugenio Garin has noted, 'the return to the humanistic "declamations" on the vanity of the sciences'.[4] The renewed debate about literature and the sciences, or about the literary (i.e. fictive) aspects in science, motivated him to reflect in depth upon the foundations of contemporary natural science. Vico's growing awareness of the epistemological crisis of the scientific revolution is most evident in the words quoted above, where, while not yet opposing the mechanical conception of nature, he nevertheless questions its applicability to the study of man and society. It was, indeed, the failure of the new mechanical sciences to provide convincing hypotheses, let alone successful solutions, to practical problems encountered by scientists of man – in medicine, education, politics, and the like – which made many scholars in Naples antagonistic towards the absolutist pretensions of the exact mechanical sciences.[5] And yet, even the most severe critics of the mechanical philosophy accepted, as a rule, its own basic definitions of 'science'. This mechanical philosophy with its objective assumptions, experimental method of inquiry and proofs thus established the model or, to use Kuhn's famous idiom, the 'paradigm' of what scientific reasoning was all about. One of the most fortunate insights of Vico's early work, and one which was later to form the foundation of his entire *New Science,* was his realization that the key question in the study of human affairs is not only what constitutes their scientific 'knowledge', but rather what do we want to know about them. Eventually, as we shall see, he came to the conclusion that what we want to know about

---

4 Eugenio Garin, 'Vico and the Heritage of Renaissance Thought', in G. Tagliacozzo (ed.), *Vico: Past and Present* (Atlantic Highlands, N.J.: Humanities Press, 1981), p. 105.
5 Paolo Casini, *Introduzione all'Illuminismo: Da Newton a Rousseau* (Bari: Laterza, 1973).

human beings is not 'The Truth' but rather their many different 'truths', or, as he put it, just 'the true' (*il vero*). The latter is synonymous with what we know as certain and what we know for certain (*il certo*) – a conclusion which entailed also a different conception of scientific 'knowledge' in the human sciences. Our first step, therefore, will be to elucidate these key terms in Vico's *New Science*.

Vico's claim, that the knowledge espoused in his work is 'scientific' in the strong, positivistic sense of the word, has been much debated.[6] And yet, surprisingly little has been written on his main argument – that his 'New Science of Humanity' is truly scientific because it lays down 'universal and eternal principles, such as every science must have' (NS/332). In his view, any valid *scientia*, in the natural as well as in the human sciences, is, or must be, an *archaeology* – namely an inquiry into the first origins, or *principles*, of the phenomena. This belief was, in Max H. Fisch's apt words, 'the controlling methodological postulate of Vico's new science', and it posits 'that genesis, or becoming, is of the essence of that which the new science treats: that, at least for the new science, nascence and nature are the same'.[7]

And thus, as Vico set out to construe a new science of humanity he attempted to discover in the primitive ideas, customs, and institutions of the *primi uomini* those normative rules which generated, and still sustain, our modern civil world (*mondo civile*). There are certain archaic rules, Vico would eventually claim, which are not just regulative but constitutive to social life, such that form and govern any civil association. For Vico these rules constitute the very *principles of humanity* – those on which mankind 'at all times and in all places has based its practices'.[8] It was on these archaic origins of humanity that Vico sought to establish a new *science* of humanity – precisely as Newton had done in his new science of nature. In what follows I shall argue, indeed, that not only was Vico very much aware of the topical issue of knowledge-in-principles, but, furthermore, that like many other scientists of man in his time he too believed that the Newtonian method alone would lead him

---

[6] Leon Pompa, 'Vico's Science', *History and Theory*, 10 (1971), pp. 49–83.
[7] Max H. Fisch, Introduction to *The New Science of Giambattista Vico*, tr. T. Bergin and M. H. Fisch (Ithaca, N.Y.: Cornell University Press), p. xx.
[8] Vico, *The First Science*, par. 10, *Selected Writings*, pp. 82–3.

to the 'principles of humanity'. I shall seek to show that in entitling his work *Principi di scienza nuova* Vico was not only alluding to the similarities between his work and the natural new sciences, but, more specifically, that he used the term 'principles' in its distinctly Newtonian meaning. After a brief discussion of the Newtonian method and its impact on social theorists at the time, my main task in this chapter will be to elaborate the way in which Vico's key notion of principles of humanity grew out of, but ultimately turned against, Newton's principles of nature.

Now, the demand to 'know in principles' (*scire per principes*) is as old as philosophy itself. Its *locus classicus* is in Aristotle's *Metaphysics* 1003a, where it means to grasp matters at their root. This particular notion enjoyed a long and fruitful career through the Stoic and the medieval Christian theories of Natural Law. In the Christian approach, the universal principles and the operational laws of all things were ultimately equated with the Divine Reason and Commands, which man, a being naturally endowed with intelligence and piety, could perceive. This, as A. H. Whitehead explained, was 'the greatest contribution of medievalism to the formation of the scientific movement', as it established 'the inexpungable belief that every detailed occurrence can be correlated with its antecedents in a perfectly definite manner, exemplifying general principles'.[9]

This view still permeated the thought of the seventeenth century, and it can be detected even among exponents of 'mechanical' theories like Hobbes or Newton. For the human scientists in the Enlightenment this assumption was crucial: as secular observers of human reality they were eager to liberate their object of study from the old metaphysical-theological conception of Natural Law, and yet were equally committed to the prescription to know this reality 'in principle'. Newton's new and neutral conception of principles supplied them with the perfect method. The reason being that Newton, while still retaining the possibility – for him, a certainty – that the principles of nature were ultimately Divine Commands, nevertheless prescribes that in the practical study of nature we must reason about these principles in strictly operational terms, not in any essential ones. Newton's

---

[9] Alfred N. Whitehead, *Science and the Modern World* (New York: Mentor Books, 1948), p. 13.

reasoning 'in principles' about natural motions thus became a paradigm for reasoning 'in principles' about human actions.[10]

In entitling his great work *Mathematical Principles of Natural Philosophy*, Newton inveighed not only against Descartes' *Principles of Philosophy* but against the entire Aristotelian-Christian tradition of reasoning from 'first principles'. Newton's new conception and rules of reasoning 'in principles' both retained yet radically changed this tradition.[11] For Euclid or Descartes, a 'principle' was an *a priori* true and self-evident proposition, predicated on logical necessity. Whether it was, for Euclid, a geometrical statement about relationships holding between abstract mathematical quantities, or, for Descartes, a clear and distinct concept, the 'knowledge of which is naturally implanted in our minds' – a principle had to be, by definition, an axiomatic assumption: an unproved formula or a postulate from which one could draw, in an uninterrupted chain of deduction, the logical conclusions implicit in it, without, as it were, any recourse to factual evidence.[12] Descartes' theory of 'space' exemplified this method: Descartes first defines the concept of 'space' from which he then derives the conclusions about physical space. For Newton, on the other hand, the term 'principle' meant a statement about empirical relationships between the forces that actually form and govern physical phenomena. The Newtonian principle had to be obtained directly from observations of the phenomena, preferably under experimental conditions, so as to separate factual from merely normative or metaphysical principles. This line of thought converged with the anti-Aristotelian sentiments of Bacon and his followers in the Royal Society. They all regarded Aristotle's belief in the ability of human reason to penetrate the subtleties of nature as being too ambitious and arrogant. Bacon thought that the quest for 'first principles' was not only hopeless in itself but also dangerous to scientific practice, as it focused attention on 'the quiescent principles, *wherefrom*, and not the moving principles, *whereby*, things are produced', and therefore led only 'to discourse' and not 'to

[10] Koyré, *Newtonian Studies*, pp. 30–40, 264–72.
[11] Ernst Cassirer, *The Philosophy of the Enlightenment*, tr. F. Koelin and J. P. Pettegrove (N.J.: Princeton University Press, 1951), pp. 21–2, 54–5.
[12] Descartes elaborates on his conception of innate principles in *Principles of Philosophy*, esp. in the Preface (letter to translator) and in art. 203, pt. 4.

works'.[13] It was, however, Hobbes who fully realized what these considerations implied for the new human sciences:

Of arts some are demonstrable, others indemonstrable; and demonstrable are those the construction of the subject whereof is in the power of the artist himself, who, in his demonstration, does no more but deduce the consequences of his operation. The reason whereof is this, that the science of every subject is derived from a precognition of the causes, generation, and construction of the same; and consequently where the causes are known, there is a place for demonstration, but not where the causes are to seek for. Geometry therefore is demonstrable, for the lines and figures from which we reason are known and described by ourselves; and civil philosophy is demonstrable, because we make the commonwealth ourselves. But because of natural bodies we know not the construction, but seek it from effects, there lies no demonstration of what the causes be we seek for, but only of what they may be.[14]

Hobbes further elaborates his notion that we can know what is true only in those 'arts' which we ourselves make by pointing out the essentially social (or what he would call 'nominal') constitution of truths in such cases: namely, that they are based on (merely) common agreement and *a priori* evaluation of certain norms as absolutely correct. Of those which pertain to ethics and politics, for example, he says, 'we ourselves make the principles – that is, the causes of justice (namely laws and covenants) – whereby it is known what justice and equity are, and their opposites injustice and inequity, are. For before covenants and laws were drawn up, neither justice nor injustice, neither public good nor public evil, was natural among men any more than it was among beasts.'[15] As we shall see, Vico largely followed Hobbes in defining and seeking the 'principles of humanity' as those definitive 'civil institutions' which have been agreed as such and practised by all known societies, but, in contrast to Hobbes' rationalistic and a-historical account, he conceived these principles as customs which were both natural and historical, and utterly a-rational. In any case, his debt to the empirical tradition of knowledge-in-principles is evident.

13 Francis Bacon, *Novum Organum*, in *The Philosophical Works of Francis Bacon*, ed. J. Spedding, R. L. Ellis and D. D. Heath (London, 1857), IV, p. 67.
14 Thomas Hobbes, *Six Lessons to the Professors of Mathematics*, in *The English Work of Thomas Hobbes*, ed. W. Molesworth (London: 1839–45), VII, pp. 183–4.
15 Thomas Hobbes, *On Man*, in *Man and Citizen*, tr. C. T. Wood, T. S. K. Scott-Craig and B. Gert (N.J.: Humanities Press, 1978), p. 42.

Newton shared these views. He regarded his 'principles' as truly scientific, whereas those of old or rival schools were discarded by him as merely hypothetical. His concept of 'scientific principles' may thus be said to have curbed the absolutist claims of the Cartesian principle. Whereas Descartes' principle was a final and logically necessary conclusion about what things were, with an absolute authority to exert knowledge on the phenomena, the Newtonian principle was a temporal and empirical conclusion, indeed an 'assumption', about how the things operated, but an assumption based on observation and calculation. Newton reiterates the fact that although his principles are, in themselves, only inductive generalizations of specific phenomena, they are 'very nearly true' with regard to all other phenomena – by virtue of the mathematical formulation of the relationships holding between the forces and motions of these phenomena. This abstract formulation secures the superior objectivity and universality of his statement over against the mere subjective descriptions of these phenomena. As against other abstract and objective descriptions, such as the geometrical ones, Newton emphasizes the empirical sense-experience and strict 'phenomenalism' implied in the derivation of his own principles. This experimental base guarantees that his merely 'mathematical' principles do correspond to actual forces in nature, and ensures that they are statements neither about metaphysical forces 'only geometrically demonstrated' (as in Descartes), nor about 'occult' pseudo-forces which cannot be demonstrated at all:

These Principles [such as Inertia, Gravity, Cohesion of Bodie] I consider, not as occult Qualities, supposed to result from the specifick Forms of Things, but as general Laws of Nature, by which the Things themselves are form'd; their Truth appearing to us by Phaenomena, though their Causes be not yet discover'd . . . to derive two or three general Principles of Motion from Phaenomena, and afterwards to tell us how the Properties and Actions of all corporeal Things follow from those manifest Principles, would be a very great step in Philosophy, though the Causes to those Principles were not yet discover'd: And therefore I scruple not to propose the Principles of Motion above-mention'd, they being of very general Extent, and leave their Causes to be found out.[16]

---

[16] Isaac Newton, *Opticks* (1728), repr. of the 4th edn (London: G. Bell & Sons, 1931), pp. 401–2.

Now, Newton's conception of 'principles' as (no more than) those inductive generalizations about the actual forces which form and govern the physical operations of bodies in space was, at once, both liberating and challenging to contemporary scientists of man and society. It required them to reason about human phenomena 'in principles', yet without recourse to all the old 'hypothetical', i.e. theological, metaphysical, essential, etc. – preconceptions about human nature. It relegated the search for the 'principles of humanity' to new, purely empirical–mechanical patterns of reasoning: the goal was to find equivalent actual 'forces' in man, which could be proven to have formed his society and to govern his actions therein.

And so, when we cast a glance at Newton's *Mathematical Principles of Natural Philosophy* and then at the various attempts of his contemporaries to construe equivalent 'principles of human philosophy' we are at once struck by the apparent success of the 'Newtonian Philosophy', that is, by what its practitioners took to be Newton's 'knowledge-in-principles'. This latter notion had a widespread impact, so much so, indeed, that even those thinkers in the Enlightenment who were otherwise opposed to Newton's world view – like Montesquieu or Hume – adhered to this method.[17] His method proved particularly persuasive among the Enlightenment's 'scientists of man'.

For Newton's fellows in the Royal Society the scientific study of man did not seem a feasible or urgent task. Thomas Sprat all but dismissed it entirely from their agenda:

In men, may be consider'd the Faculties, and operations of their Souls; The constitution of their Bodies, and the works of their Hands. Of this the first they omit: both because the knowledge and direction of them have been before undertaken, by some Arts, on which they have no mind to intrench, as the Politicks, Morality, and Oratory; and also because the Reason, the Understanding, the Tempers, the Will, the Passions of Men are so hard to be reduc'd to any certain observation of the Senses; and afford so much room to the observers to falsifie counterfeit: that if such discourses should be once entertain'd they would be in danger of falling into talking, instead of working, which they carefully avoid. Such Subjects therefore as these, they have hitherto kept out. But yet, when they shall

---

17 On Newton's reputation in the Enlightenment, see Peter Gay, *The Enlightenment: An Interpretation*, vol. II: *The Science of Freedom* (London: Weidenfeld and Nicholson, 1970), pp. 126–66.

have made more progress, in material things, they will be in a condition, of pronouncing more boldly on them too ... there, without question, be very near guesses made, even at the more exalted, and immediate Actions of the Soul.[18]

This strictly physiological approach to the study of man prevailed in the Enlightenment, but its cautious and rather dismissive tone now gave way to an impassioned plea: ' 'Tis evident', wrote Hume, 'that all the sciences have a relation, greater or less, to human nature', so that 'there is no question of importance, whose decision is not compriz'd in the science of man; and there is none, which can be decided with any certainty, before we become acquainted with that science'.[19] Diderot, in his acclaimed article on man in the *Encyclopédie* set the tone and the goals of his age by declaring that 'Man is the single place from which we must begin and to which we must refer everything'.

Generally speaking, the Enlightenment view of humanity was that it was thoroughly natural and that in order to study human nature, it was necessary, or indeed enough, to study nature itself. The *philosophes* sought to mould their treatises on man in Newton's mechanical style, but alas against Newton's deeper spiritual beliefs. Their scientific observations on man were to be devoid of any theological explanations, metaphysical entities, and aesthetic considerations. Such observers as D'Holbach, Condorcet, or Hartley prided themselves on having established facts, not values. They believed that human affairs, however irregular and variant they seem to be, are, at bottom, uniformly regular and as invariable as the physical occurrences which Newton discovered in the universe. And the same was true of society: if the social scientist could only subject such 'manifest phenomena' as religious rites, laws, political institutions and the like to the empirical tests and objective assignment of causes, then he would find behind them certain universal 'springs of action' (as Hume called them), that is, the elementary and utterly natural 'propensities' and 'aversions' common to all mankind. They surmised that these 'springs of action' are to humanity and its

18 Thomas Sprat, *The History of the Royal Society*, ed. J. I. Cope and H. W. Jones (London: Routledge and Kegan Paul, 1959), pp. 82–3.
19 David Hume, *A Treatise of Human Nature*, ed. L. A. Selby-Bigge (Oxford: Oxford University Press, 1888), pp. xix–xxiii.

actions what Inertia, Gravity or Cohesion of Bodie are to bodies and their motions: they constitute their 'principles'. As Hume put it in some well-known phrases: 'It is universally acknowledged that there is a great uniformity among the actions of men, in all nations and ages, and that human nature remains still the same, in its principles and operations. The same motives always produce the same actions.'[20]

Of course, the principles which form and govern human actions are seen here as qualitatively different from those which form and govern physical motions, but the main idea was that such principles exist. Conceiving of human society as analogous to natural reality, the Enlightenment philosophers regarded communities as collections of individual particles, each one of them possessing and operating according to the same physical properties, and thus aimed to discover the principles and laws which govern their interaction. A social science, so ran the Enlightenment argument, was possible on the following premises: (a) human beings, unique as they seem to be in this world, are none the less as natural as any other bodily-intelligent being in their obedience to Newtonian laws; they are like any body which 'endeavours to persevere in its present state' – in this case that of living; (b) the forces of self-preservation function as the 'principles' of his nature, and also make up the science of man; (c) the method to discover these principles must consequently be a Newtonian one, that is, that of social physics. This meant that from the observation of actual social phenomena, on the diverse 'secondary qualities' of cultures, the social scientist must infer the 'primary qualities' of human nature, that is, those which seemingly do not vary across time and space; and (d) the language used in accounting for human nature must be likewise 'natural' rather than 'human'. The assumption here was that the language of everyday life is vague and value-laden, expressive rather than designative, and that it must be replaced by a more precise, scientific language. Since in this instance it is clearly impossible to use mathematical characters, and as long as there is no more suitable *mathesis universalis*, the effort should be to avoid all anthropomorphic characters. This of course means that metaphors and other poetic fictions are

---

[20] David Hume, *An Enquiry Concerning Human Understanding*, ed. L. A. Selby-Bigge (Oxford: Oxford University Press, 1902), p. 83.

definitely out of the question since they project human emotions and terms onto nature; instead, a reverse strategy must be used: namely, that of imposing natural terms on human emotions.

Here, then, much like in Newtonian science, metaphysical hypotheses and terms were not to be allowed, whereas all kinds of natural analogies were welcome. Newton's well-known, though ambiguous, *Third Rule of Reasoning in Philosophy* – which asserts that 'We are certainly not to relinquish the evidence of experiments for the sake of dreams and vain fictions of our own devising; nor are we to recede from the analogy of Nature, which used to be simple and always consonant to itself'[21] – was aimed primarily at natural scientists, but, during the eighteenth century, it had been applied to human philosophy with as much vigour and conviction. As Arthur Lovejoy put it:

Assuming human nature to be a simple thing, the Enlightenment also, as a rule, assumed political and social problems to be simple, and therefore easy of solution. Rid man's mind of a few ancient errors, purge his beliefs of the artificial complications of metaphysical 'systems' and theological dogmas, restore to his social relations something like the simplicity of the state of nature, and his natural excellence would live happily ever after.[22]

Newton himself, as we already noted, did not take any part in these attempts to make bed-fellows of science and human philosophy. His deep religious beliefs allowed him a certain view of man, society, and history, which was not challenged by his or any other scientific discovery. Other philosophers, however, wayward Newtonians or rigorous followers, who lacked his moral and theological convictions, ultimately created such a new Human Philosophy by taking his critical positivism to an extreme and applying it to the study of the human sphere. Newton's method in the demystification of nature served as their paradigm in the demystification of human society and history, from which they were now willing to ban such 'occult qualities' as the 'Fallability of

---

[21] Isaac Newton, *Mathematical Principles of Natural Philosophy*, tr. Andrew Motte, rev. by F. Cajori (Berkeley: University of California Press, 1934), p. 399.

[22] A. O. Lovejoy, *The Great Chain of Being* (Cambridge, Mass.: Harvard University Press, 1964), p. 23. On the epistemological premises of this view, see the brilliant analysis of Michel Foucault in *The Order of Things: An Archaeology of the Human Sciences* (New York: Vintage Books, 1973), pp. 62–3, where he presents the Enlightenment *épistème* as thoroughly obsessed by the idea of uniformity and one objective and universal method in all the spheres of knowledge.

Man', 'Divine Right of Kings', or even 'Providence'. Alexander
Koyré sums up the issue poignantly: 'So strong was the belief in
"nature", so overwhelming the prestige of the Newtonian (or
pseudo-Newtonian) pattern of order arising automatically from
interaction of isolated and self-contained atoms, that nobody
dared to doubt that order and harmony would in some way be
produced by human atoms acting according to their nature, whatever this might be'. According to Koyré, the ideas of Newton and
Locke were united in such a way as to produce, on the one hand,
'an atomic psychology, which explained (or explained away) mind
as a mosaic of sensations and ideas linked together by laws of
association (attraction)' and, on the other hand, 'atomic
sociology, which reduced society to cluster of human atoms,
complete and self-contained each in itself and only mutually
attracting and repelling each other'.[23]

David Hume may well serve as our guide here. In his youth he
was a professed Newtonian, and in his main philosophical works
he set out to apply Newton's methods to moral subjects. And
although his commitment to the Newtonian philosophy receded
in later years, along with his faith in philosophy, he remained loyal
to its main methodological rule of reasoning 'in principles'.[24] In
subtitling his *Treatise of Human Nature* 'an attempt to introduce the
experimental method of reasoning into moral subjects' Hume
made clear that his Human Philosophy was to be predicated on a
Newtonian model of rigorous mechanical necessity and causality.
In the *Introduction* to this work he concedes that:

Moral philosophy has, indeed, this peculiar disadvantage, which is not
found in natural, that in connecting its experiments, it cannot make
them purposely, with premeditation, and after such a manner as to
satisfy itself concerning every particular difficulty which may arise . . . We
must glean up our experiments in this science from a cautious observation of human life, and take them as they appear in the common
course of the world, by men's behaviour in company, in affairs, and in
their pleasures. Where experiments of this kind are judiciously collected
and compared, we may hope to establish on them a science which will
not be inferior in certainty, and will be much superior in utility to any
other of human comprehension.[25]

[23] Koyré, 'The Significance of the Newtonian Synthesis', p. 22.
[24] On Hume's intellectual debt to Newton, see Norman Kemp Smith, *The Philosophy of
David Hume* (London: Macmillan, 1949), pp. 53ff.
[25] Hume, *Treatise*, pp. xxii–xxiii.

Hume thus set out to 'anatomize human nature in regular manner', which, for him, meant to explain how human beings act, think, perceive and feel the way they do. Rooted in the belief that every human action is an event that has a mechanical cause, his 'moral philosophy, or the science of human nature' seeks these causes according to the Newtonian guidelines: Hume does not allow any primal hypotheses about essential human qualities, nor does he seek any ultimate reasons as to why human beings are what they are – he merely wants to account for their actions in strictly causal terms: 'Any hypothesis, that pretends to discover the ultimate original qualities of human nature, ought at first to be rejected as presumptuous and chimerical . . . original qualities of human nature, I pretend not to explain'.[26]

Hume differed, however, from other Newtonian philosophers in the human sciences, like D'Holbach, Condillac, or Hartley, in that he was much more attentive to, and respectful of, what he referred to as Newton's 'modesty' in the derivation and characterization of his 'principles'. In fact, he was more sceptical than Newton about the prospects of scientific discovery. While Newton believed that science was progressing steadily, however modestly, towards the discovery of ultimate causes, Hume thought that Newton's discoveries must not be thought of as pertaining to the real causes of nature, but only as the actual limits of our reasoning about nature, as 'probably the ultimate causes and principles which we shall ever discover in nature; and we may esteem ourselves sufficiently happy, if, by accurate inquiry and reasoning, we can trace up the particular phenomena to, or near to, these general principles'. Hume could thus conclude that Newton enabled us to account for the apparent contingent regularities, not for the ultimate causal connections, of natural phenomena, so that even 'the most perfect philosophy of the natural kind only staves off our ignorance a little longer'.[27] Newton's professed 'agnosticism' with regard to 'first causes', it seems, helped Hume combine his empiricism with his radical scepticism, as it allowed him to retain the scientific ideal of 'objective assignment of causes', while rejecting its claim to be an absolute law of nature. In his *Dissertation on the Passions* he writes:

[26] Hume, *Treatise*, pp. xxi, 13.   [27] Hume, *Enquiry*, pp. 30–1.

I pretend not to have here exhausted this subject. It is sufficient for my purpose, if I have made it appear, that in the production and conduct of the passions, there is a certain regular mechanism, which is susceptible as accurate a disquisition, as the laws of motion, optics, hydrostatics, or any part of natural philosophy.[28]

Hume's method in his search for the principles of human nature is a modified version of what is nowadays referred to as 'applied individual psychology'. This method purports to explain and ultimately justify general moral and social principles by showing that there are physical individual inclinations ethically acceptable and shared by most members of most groups. Hume used it in neutral terms in order to explain how the natural dispositions of man produced rule-governed actions and social institutions in history. Hume thought that all the different normative judgements of individual agents in their various cultures are reducible to common and universal natural desires. And it was this naturalistic streak in his thought which hampered his historical and anthropological efforts 'to glean up our experiments' from 'observation of human life . . . in the common course of the world'. His plea to 'collect and compare' manners and institutions was misguided by the belief that local experience was insignificant in itself; that it merely attested to one universal and unchanging nature:

It is universally acknowledged, that there is a great uniformity among the actions of men, in all nations and ages, and that human nature remains still the same, in its principles and operations . . . Would you know the sentiments, inclinations, and course of life of the Greeks and Romans? Study well the temper and actions of the French and English: You cannot be mistaken in transferring to the former most of the observations which you have made with regard to the latter. Mankind are so much the same, in all times and places, that history informs of nothing new or strange in this particular . . . Its chief use is only to discover the constant and universal principles of human nature, by showing men in all varieties of circumstances and situations, and furnishing us with materials from which we may form our observations and become acquainted with the regular springs of human action and behaviour.[29]

---

[28] David Hume, 'Dissertation on the Passions', in *Essays, Moral, Political and Literary*, ed. T. H. Green and T. H. Grose (London: Longmans, 1875), II, p. 166.
[29] Hume, *Enquiry*, p. 84.

This clearly means, then, that what humankind in ancient Greece or Rome actually felt, thought, and did; what, nowadays, French or English people actually feel, think, and do – is not really essential in determining what Man is. In Hume's view, moral values, aesthetic tastes, religious beliefs, national traditions, ethnic customs, in short – all the merely 'cultural' aspects of human life, because they are temperamental, local, or accidental, cannot possibly indicate the 'principles' of human nature: 'all these operations', Hume remarks, 'are a species of natural instincts, which no reasoning or process of the thought and understanding is able to produce or to prevent'.[30]

Now, Hume's assertions that what counts in the study of man are not culture but nature, not reason but feelings and instincts, not historical development and diversity but psychological constancy and unity – these assertions were, and still are, most attractive to the practitioners of the sciences of man. But, in the eighteenth century there were also many philosophers who grew increasingly suspicious of purely mechanical-deductive reasoning on things human. Human behaviour, it was now argued, displays complexities which cannot be reduced to the mechanical models, the natural analogies, and the deductive mathematical patterns of Newtonian physics. Even if it were true, as Hume thought, that human beings were mainly impelled by 'passions', it was felt that this was rarely – if ever – a case of 'simple' desires. As a modern critic of Hume put it, in any act of seemingly 'physical desire' there are always tacit considerations and conventions at work, and so such an act must be understood 'in a wider context of beliefs and conceptions'.[31]

These critical observations about the efficacy of Hume's Newtonian project for the humanities became clear to Hume himself later in his life, as he became more and more sceptical of the cognitive foundations of the new natural sciences, and eventually realized that in order to account for human affairs it was necessary to concentrate not on man's nature but on what he called man's 'second nature', namely the particular socio-historical conditions

[30] Hume, *Enquiry*, pp. 46–7.
[31] H. A. Walsh, 'The Constancy of Human Nature', in H. D. Lewis (ed.), *Contemporary British Philosophy* (London: Allen & Unwin, 1976), pp. 281–2. For a radical revision of these common views of Hume, see Donald W. Livingston, *Hume's Philosophy of Common Life* (Chicago: The University of Chicago Press, 1984).

and narratives within which human beings are bound by their common moral conventions. In his *History of England* (1754–62) he reflected on Newton's achievements and legacy, and observed that

In Newton this island may boast of having produced the greatest and rarest genius that ever rose for the ornament and instruction of the species. Cautious in admitting no principles but such as were founded on experiment; but resolute to adopt every such principle, however new and unusual . . . While Newton seemed to draw off the veil from some of the mysteries of nature, he shewed at the same time the imperfections of the mechanical philosophy; and thereby restored her ultimate secrets to that obscurity in which they ever did and ever will remain.[32]

Thus, according to Hume, Newton's ultimate claim to glory lies in his 'modesty', and not only in personal terms ('ignorant of his superiority above the rest of humankind'), but also, and primarily, in scientific terms: Newton was modest enough to recognize that his new principles of Natural Philosophy, successful as they were in laying bare the operations of bodies, could achieve only a better, but by no means absolute, knowledge of these operations; the principles considered these operations, in Newton's words, 'not physically, but mathematically'.[33] Hume took seriously Newton's own admission that his principles could 'either be made more accurate, or liable to exceptions', namely that they were only provisional points of departure for further and possibly divergent enquiries. He noted a certain tension in Newton's natural philosophy, regarding those principles which are statements about the things, but not, as it were, their own; that is, such that are man-made, or dependent on man's power of experimentation and calculation, and therefore liable to be temporary. This tension, Hume thought, could never be resolved. We may call this awareness the 'agnostic moment' in the process of scientific inquiry, the moment at which the scientist realizes the impossibility of penetrating the essential matter and composition of nature. I shall not dwell further on this issue here, but only suggest, that it was precisely this enlightened 'agnostic moment' in the evolution of the modern science of nature which liberated and gave new hope to the not yet fully crystallized science of humanity:

---

[32] David Hume, *The History of England* (Edinburgh: 1754–62), VIII, p. 326.
[33] Newton to Cotes, 28 March 1713, in *Correspondence of Sir Isaac Newton and Professor Cotes*, ed. J. Edelston (London: John W. Packer, 1850), p. 155.

here, it was now argued, we can have a better access to and knowledge of the essential matter and composition of the human world, and a real grasp of its principles at work, because we ourselves make these principles. The elements which make up the human world can be not only knowable to us through observation and calculation, but also intelligible to us – through some inner knowledge, through participation in the process itself.

My main task now will be to show how, out of Newton's conception of principles of nature, yet eventually against it, there emerged, in the singular thinking of Giambattista Vico, a new conception of the principles of humanity. Vico, I shall argue, was responsible for changing the terms and the course of the quest for the 'principles of humanity' – by a simple, yet daring claim. He held that human beings are initially driven by 'natural instincts', but that gradually, as they become more submissive to 'social rules', it is the latter which prevail in whatever they do. These social rules become, as it were, the 'principles' by which we can and must understand man. In what follows I will try to show why and how Vico advanced this new search. Before that, however, I would like to comment briefly on a preliminary question which has caused much controversy among Vichian scholars – namely, whether and to what extent Vico was aware of the scientific culture of his time?

Now, in the vast literature on his work, Vico is not normally credited with any genuine knowledge of the natural sciences. Isaiah Berlin, for example, writes that 'Vico was not interested in mathematics or in the natural sciences as such' and that he 'was remote from the scientific revolution of his time'.[34] These harsh remarks are quite correct and rightly counter Vico's own pretentious claims in these fields. This assessment, however, overlooks certain crucial aspects of his work, above all his declared intention to be as truly 'scientific' in his field as the natural sciences were, and even more so, by virtue of the equivalent, yet different, 'scientific principles' he postulated. These intentions, of course, do not suffice to credit Vico as a natural philosopher of any importance, but they suggest, at least, that Vico was genuinely interested in the methodology of the new natural sciences, and,

---

[34] Isaiah Berlin, *Vico and Herder* (London: The Hogarth Press, 1976), pp. 9, 117ff.; see also Casini, *Introduzione all'Illuminismo*, p. 316.

furthermore, that he was quite informed about their new trends and achievements.

Vico was for many years a fellow in various learned academies in Naples, where he probably became acquainted with the main names, theories, and discoveries relevant to the natural sciences. According to his contemporary, the historian Pietro Giannone, the Neapolitan intellectuals at that time were well-informed about the developments in the scientific centres of Europe, mainly through visits of such illustrious scholars as Mabillon, Burnet, Leibniz, Montfaucon, Shaftesbury, Berkeley, and Montesquieu, and of travellers and commercial agents who supplied their book-stores, libraries, and salons with books, pamphlets, and other unauthorized works: 'By means of the great number of journals which are published in these countries, everybody may have an account of the books that are printed in Europe, of the matters they contain, and of the news of the commonwealth of learning', and many were using them 'to shake off the heavy yoke which the philosophy of the cloisters had put upon the necks of the Neapolitans'.[35] As a son of a bookseller Vico surely knew how and where to get every book he needed. And though his own means were modest, he was a regular guest at the literary salon of Giuseppe Valleta, and could find in Valleta's library the most important philosophical, historical and scientific publications. More significantly still, as Eugenio Garin has argued, the truly important matter is not what and how much Vico knew about the new sciences of physics, biology, or chemistry, but rather 'how he translated the profound contemporary problems [in those sciences] into his own language'. Garin is certainly right to point out that Vico's interest in the sciences was 'foundational': 'he was able to tackle, perhaps with less grace but always with greater depth, the great questions of the foundations of science, and of the sense of man and of history'.[36]

[35] Pietro Giannone, *The Civil History of the Kingdom of Naples*, tr. J. Ogilvie (London: 1729–31), ii, pp. 840–2.
[36] Garin, 'Vico and the Heritage of Renaissance Thought', p. 108. On Vico and the scientific community in Naples, see the authoritative account of Nicola Badaloni, *Introduzione a G. B. Vico* (Milan: Feltinelli, 1961), esp. chs. 1–2. For the earlier and more general background, see M. H. Fisch, 'The Academy of Investigators' in E. H. Underwood (ed.), *Science, Medicine, and History: Essays in Honour of Charles Singer* (London: Oxford University Press, 1953), I, pp. 521–63.

As for Vico's actual knowledge of Newton's theories, it must be noted, first of all, that, luckily for Vico, his intellectual development was not disrupted by any religious or political interventions. He spent his formative years as a tutor to the Rocca family at Vatolla from 1686 to 1695, and was thus able to pursue his studies and to compose his first literary and scholarly works in relative freedom. It was during that period, from 1686 to 1693, that the Inquisition persecuted the 'atheists' in Naples, and some of Vico's friends and colleagues were harshly treated in that process. Later on, however, the Inquisition withdrew from the city, and the Papal censorship, though always intimidating, was not very active or effective in suppressing heretical views. During those years the Neapolitan intellectuals retained the reformative momentum of the first age of the 'modernists' – of men like Tommaso Cornelio, Lionardo di Capua and Francesco d'Andrea – and were able to conduct, under the guise of *libertas philosophandi*, their own scientific research as well as discuss the scientific theories of Bacon and Galileo, Boyle and Gilbert, Gassendi and Hobbes. The foundation of the Academy of the Medinaceli in 1698, which was to convene twice a month in the Royal Palace till 1701, signalled the triumph of modernism in the town. Its founders and leaders were modernist scholars like Giuseppe Valletta, Lucantonio Porzio, Nicola Caravita, Giorgio Caloprese and others, who were all committed to the 'new sciences'. The proceedings of their sessions reveal that they raised and discussed the major contemporary issues in the natural sciences and history. Later on during the early decades of the eighteenth century, there was a widespread diffusion of Newtonian ideas in Naples. Some of the city's leading men of letters – Agostino Ariani, Nicola Cirillo, Giambattista Galiani, Antonio Genovesi and other *novatores*, who were intent on constructing a new 'science of politics' along empiricist and utilitarian guidelines – openly endorsed Newtonian and Lockean ideas and posited them against the Cartesian and Platonic ideas of men like Doria and other *veteres*.[37]

[37] D., Carpanetto and G. Ricuperati, *Italy in the Age of Reason 1685–1789* (London: Longman, 1987), pp. 78–137; Vincenzo Ferrone, 'Galileo, Newton, e la *libertas philosophandi* prima meta del xviii secolo in Italia', *Rivista storica italiana*, 93 (1981), pp. 143–85. On the diffusion of the Newtonian philosophy in Naples, see Paola Zambelli, 'Antonio Genovesi and Eighteenth Century Empiricism in Italy', *Journal of the History of Philosophy*, 16 (1978), pp. 195–208; Franco Palladino, 'La formazione scientifico-matematica di Celestino Galiani', *Bolletino del centro di studi Vichiani*, 17–18 (1987–8), pp. 263–62.

Vico constantly wavered between the two sects: while his social and political ideals aligned him to the conservative sect, his philosophical ideas, which were motivated by strong anti-Cartesian sentiments, were closer to those of their opponents. He did not endorse the Newtonian philosophy openly, but, as I shall argue below, he was quite susceptible to some of its positivistic ideas and methods. Finally, there is also a tenuous personal connection which lends weight to the affinity I am suggesting: one of Vico's first readers was the Abbé Antonio Conti, a leading Newtonian on the Continent, who had been made a member of the Royal Society in London at the recommendation of Newton. In 1725, upon the publication of Vico's major work, the first edition of *New Science*, Conti urged Vico to send a copy to Newton, who, Conti thought, would appreciate such a work and help it reach a wider public. Vico sent the copy, but Newton, who died a few months later, probably never saw it.[38]

In order to illustrate Vico's affinity to the Newtonian philosophy in his own profession note, for example, his treatment of the topical issues of the battle of the Ancients against the Moderns – a battle in which he did not participate, nor even mentioned, but one that he must surely have been aware of as it was constantly reported on in the learned journals and books. Vico supported wholeheartedly the modernists' claims regarding the superiority of modern science over ancient science, but he rejected their concomitant claims for the superiority of modern arts and letters over those of the ancients' – because, in his (distinctly Newtonian) view, in both sciences and arts superiority was achieved and determined in exactly the same way: by concrete observations and representations of nature. Hence his conclusion that the moderns are superior in science, where the Newtonian method was much more concrete than that of Aristotle, but inferior in arts: while contemporary neo-classicists were mannerists who either copied examples from antiquity or played with abstract ideas and their ever more intricate stylistic formulations, the artists in antiquity, though certainly more primitive in their outlook, were, for that reason, more attentive and responsive to nature. The same criteria of concreteness in observation and description serve Vico

---

[38] For Conti's life and connections with Newton and Vico, see Nicola Badaloni, *Antonio Conti: Un abate libero pensatore tra Newton and Voltaire* (Milan: Feltinelli, 1968).

to posit the philosophical style of ancient thinkers like Socrates or Cicero over against that of Descartes – for where they argued from and by means of concrete lively everyday cases, the modern rationalist argued from and with ideas which, however clear and distinct they might be – were sterile and unpersuasive. I do not want to argue that Vico owes this commitment to reasoning in concrete examples and inductive generalizations to Newtonian philosophy, but only that it is likely that he developed them in the intellectual context where this philosophy was pervasive and very effective. Like most of his contemporaries he had no real knowledge of Newton's scientific ideas, but could have had a fair notion of their philosophical meaning and implications. After all, the 'Newtonian Philosophy' was not synonymous with Newton's own natural philosophy. It was, as Carl Becker has shrewdly observed, the work of the 'popularizers, who could find in the *Principia* more philosophy than the common man could, very often more . . . than Newton himself did'.[39] And, as I have indicated above, like practically all his contemporaries, what Vico could, and must, have got from this philosophy was a new notion of 'principles'.

In his *New Science* Vico hails Newton as one of 'the two foremost minds of our age', the other being Leibniz (NS/347), and there are many indications that this praise is not vacuous but substantial. This can be seen already in Vico's earliest thoughts on scientific method in the inaugural orations which he delivered at the University of Naples from 1701 onwards, namely while he was still engaged in the discussions on the topic in the Academy of the Medinaceli. In these public lectures Vico sought, among other things, to defend the new physical sciences against both its 'metaphysical' enemies – the Aristotelian and Cartesian scientists, whom he dismissed as being equally 'dogmatists'. In his view, the worst sin of Aristotelian science was its 'arrogance' in the treatment of nature: he argues that the Aristotelians, because of their pride in their own rational ability to know, and in order to control, the empirical 'innocent objects' in nature through their *a priori* 'theoretical propositions', attributed to these objects human 'faculties' and 'virtues' like intentions, desires, attractions, aversions and other 'occult qualities' that rendered nature more

---

[39] Carl H. Becker, *The Heavenly City of the Eighteenth Century Philosophers* (New Haven: Yale University Press, 1932), p. 61.

susceptible to human appropriation. Furthermore, Vico is indignant at the very attempt to subject living beings of any kind to the conceptual rules and schemes of 'scientific theory'.[40] Vico, like Newton, called for 'modesty' in scientific inquiry and mastery of nature:

It is our task to study physics in a speculative temper of mind, as philosophers, that is, curbing our presumption. Let us surpass the Ancients: they pursued researches in nature in order to match the gods in happiness; we should, instead, cultivate the study of physics in order to curb our pride. Intensely ambitious as we are to attain truth, let us engage upon its quest. Where we fail in this quest, our very longing will lead us as by the hand towards the Supreme Being, who alone is the truth, and the Path and Guide to it.[41]

Vico's 'modesty', like that of Newton, was deeply religious, for he knew that ultimately and 'in truth, everything that man is permitted to know is finite and imperfect, like man himself'.[42] He therefore confined the natural sciences to probabilistic, or latitudinarian, standards of truth, to what Newton called 'very nearly true' – or, to use Vico's terminology, to 'certain' rather than 'true' – knowledge. The term 'certain' in Vico's writings is significant, because it indicates the latitudinarian-Newtonian origins of Vico's definition of truth in the natural sciences as being only a highly probably inductive generalization and not yet – not, in fact, ever – so absolute as the Aristotelian and Cartesian 'dogmatists' believed their truths to be. In fact, it can be shown that the discovery of Newton helped Vico distance and eventually liberate himself from his early Cartesian infatuations.

For in his early work on the *Study Methods of Our Time*, Vico's image of the new natural science was still more Cartesian than Baconian, let alone Newtonian. In that work he declares:

What cannot be denied is the fact that leading investigators have available to them a science enriched by a number of new and extremely ingenious discoveries. Modern scientists, seeking for guidance in their exploration of the dark pathways of nature, have introduced the geometrical method into physics. Holding to this method as to Ariadne's thread, they can reach the end of their appointed journey. Do not consider them as groping practitioners of physics: they are to be viewed,

---

40 Vico, *On the Most Ancient Wisdom of the Ancients*, in *Selected Writings*, pp. 56–69.
41 Vico, *On the Study Methods of Our Time*, pp. 23–4.
42 Vico, *On the Study Methods of Our Time*, p. 7.

instead, as the grand architects of this limitless fabric of the world: able to give a detailed account of the ensemble of principles according to which God has built this admirable structure of the cosmos.[43]

Gradually, however, this physico-geometrical science of Descartes (and the physico-mathematical science of Galileo) became the object of his severest criticism, and his predilection for the Newtonian method became more and more obvious. And again, as in the case of Aristotelian science, it seems that what set him against the scientific method of the Cartesians were primarily moral reasons: he found their absolutistic claims for 'true' knowledge of nature utterly immodest: as human beings all we could ever know about the natural world were only its phenomenal, merely 'certain', facts and laws. In fact, already in the first inaugural lecture Vico argued, against the Cartesians, that the Law of Gravity is 'certain', but its certainty is more real than the apparent truths of the 'dogmatists', because it has been deduced through inductive-experimental procedures, and not through application of geometrical laws to physical phenomena. Whereas the Cartesians believed that the application of geometrical methods to physics can bestow on it the absolute veracity of their axiomatic truths, Vico acknowledged that mathematical and geometrical truths are absolutely certain, but drastically qualified their value by arguing that they are true (*verum*) because they are merely made (*factum*) and calculated in our minds, and are not given nor can be discovered in nature. Hence his famous dictum that 'the true is what is made', and the Newtonian conclusion that we can only 'demonstrate' but never really 'prove' physical truths 'by causes', because 'the elements of natural things are outside us'.[44]

For the rest of his life Vico held to these fundamental convictions, and, moreover, he turned their seemingly negative epistemological conclusions into new, positive premises for a new kind of science – of humanity, not of nature. As he worked towards his own new science of humanity, Vico came to regard the new sciences of nature as idle exercises in *a priori* constructions of merely possible and ideal pictures of the world, not real ones, and so he deemed their 'principles' to be no more than fictive entities.

[43] Vico, *On the Study Methods of Our Time*, pp. 9–10.
[44] Vico, *On the Most Ancient Wisdom of the Ancients*, in *Selected Writings*, pp. 51, 65.

It was this insight into the utterly 'fictive' nature of the principles in the construction of the physico-mathematical science that alerted him to the very different principles in the mathematico-physical science of Newton, which, he saw, offered a much more reliable and realistic picture of the world. Its mathematical principles were not just abstract figures invented by man, but rather quantified real forces, such that have been drawn, as it were, directly from experimental observations of concrete phenomena.

Thus, in 1720, while he was at work on *The One Principle of Universal Law*, a work in which he introduced for the first time the phrase *nova scientia*, Vico remarked that, contrary to the natural sciences and their newly-established *Principia* – *Historia nondum habet sua principia*: 'History has not yet got its own principles'.[45] This statement marks his first cautious wish for, though as yet not a concrete attempt at, turning history into a science. And this problem, as Vico well knew, has been more or less removed from the agenda of philosophy since Aristotle. The latter's declaration in the *Nichomachean Ethics* (VI.7.1141) that a science (*épistéme*) of human things was impossible, for these are contingent and governed by time, circumstances, and chance – and 'of chance there can be no science' – is retained, and yet sublated, by Vico. Vico alludes to the Aristotelian maxims by reiterating 'that property of every science, noted by Aristotle, that science has to do with what is universal and eternal' (NS/163), but nevertheless ponders how one could still make a science out of the concrete and particular human affairs. This was the main methodological obstacle in the long road towards a science of humanity, and one which, in Vico's view, all his predecessors had failed to clear. Upon the completion of his own work Vico reflected on the causes of this failure:

Philosophy contemplates reason, whence comes knowledge [*scienza*] of the true; philology observes that of which human choice is author, whence comes consciousness [*coscienza*] of the certain . . . This axiom shows how the philosophers failed by half in not giving certainty to their reasonings by appeal to the authority of the philologians, and likewise how the latter failed by half in not taking care to give their authority the sanction of truth by appeal to the reasoning of the philosophers. (NS/138, 140)

---

45 Giambattista Vico, *Il Diritto universale*, in *Opere*, II, p. 95.

Vico distinguishes between two kinds of knowledge: *scienza*, or true science, which is the knowledge of the causes and laws by which things are governed; and *coscienza*, or a certain consciousness, which is the knowledge of things as they merely appear to us in our everyday, commonsense experience. In the key concept and title of his work *scienza nuova*, Vico claims to have formed a new kind of knowledge. The *coscienza*, that knowledge of things we have by virtue of our human, all too human capacities, can be transformed into *scienza*, and thereby be a true knowledge, if we apply it to the right object: to ourselves. Philological propositions, Vico says, can only 'give us the foundations of the certain', namely, concrete yet occasional information about what people did and how they behave and so on. But such observations obviously lack scientific validity. If the study of human nature is to become truly scientific it cannot just 'observe' and record human phenomena in the way they appear to be, as 'philology' does; nor can it indulge in mere 'contemplation' and definitions of what this nature is all about or should be, as 'philosophy' has hitherto done. It must combine both methods so as to produce 'philosophical' inductive generalizations, or 'principles', from sound 'philological' observations of human phenomena. Just as the modern physical sciences replaced philosophical speculations about the matter and composition of the nature of the universe with more heuristic, empirical descriptions, so too, Vico argued, philosophical reflection on the nature of man had to be superseded by the more concrete and accurate methods of philology. Vico thus moved away from a 'philosophy' devoted to analyzing metaphysical concepts and consciousness toward a 'philology' of linguistic and social practices.

II

The attempt to establish a new science of man on the cultural customs of 'the nations' rather than on the physical nature of man; to derive the principles of humanity from the concrete and particular modes of human beings' common sense rather than from 'what is eternal and universal' in them – namely, their reason, marked a radical change in the methodology of the human sciences at the time. By his appeal to the convictions of 'common sense', Vico challenged the basic rationalistic and positivistic assumptions of social scientists in the Enlightenment who, as a rule, dismissed all ordinary modes of thought, speech, and behaviour as merely 'wrong' descriptions of social reality, rather than seeing them as constitutive of it. As Descartes has put it in his *Discourse on Method*, 'so long as I gave thought only to the manners and customs of men, I met with nothing to reassure me, finding almost as much diversity in them as I had previously found in the opinions of the philosophers'.[46] Manners, customs, and opinions were not to be trusted, nor seriously researched, because what they seemed to manifest was only the superficial diversity of people, and not their deeper psychic unity, on which alone, these scientists believed, a science of man could be founded.

This belief in some pre- or a-cultural homogeneity of human nature, in a perfectly natural and a-historical humanity which consists, as it were, in principles innate in the human psyche, hampered even the most enlightened effort at a new cultural science of man – Voltaire's *Essay on the Manners and Mind of Nations* (1756). In this remarkable exercise in anthropological history Voltaire fails to achieve a truly pluralistic definition of the human world because, while summing up his inquiries into various cultures, he felt compelled to appeal to what lies behind the plethora of customs – namely, the more basic unity of nature:

As a result of this presentation of the subject, it is clear that everything which belongs intimately to human nature is the same from one end of the universe to the other; that everything that depends on custom is different, and it is accidental if it remains the same. The empire of custom is much more vast than that of nature; it extends over manners and all usages, it sheds variety on the scene of the universe; nature sheds unity there; she *establishes everywhere a small number of invariable principles.* Thus the basis is everywhere the same, and culture produces diverse fruits.[47] (italics mine)

Voltaire's last appeal to the natural principles of humanity typifies the Enlightenment's Newtonian philosophy of man. And it is, I would say, precisely on this issue that Vico's ambiguous stance in – and against – the Enlightenment can best be illustrated. His ambiguity with regard to the great ideals of the time

---

[46] Descartes, *Discourse on Method,* in *Descartes' Philosophical Writings,* tr. N. Kemp Smith (N.Y.: The Modern Library, 1958), p. 99.

[47] Voltaire, *Essai sur les moeurs,* quoted in Cassirer, *The Philosophy of the Enlightenment,* p. 219.

has been much discussed. It seems, however, that many interpreters of his thought, especially the Idealists, were much too hasty in concluding that he was a champion of the anti-Enlightenment movement, a romantic *avant le lettre.* Isaiah Berlin is more cautious. He admits that Vico was 'opposed to the central stream of the enlightenment', and yet qualifies this judgement by showing that Vico was also much attracted to many of the ideals of the age. Vico's position, according to Berlin, was not that of anti-Enlightenment, but rather that of counter-Enlightenment: he worked, as it were, from within the movement of the age – but against it.[48] This dialectic attitude enabled him to revise the Newtonian philosophy of man so as to forge a counter-theory of the 'principles of humanity'. The 'humanity' of man, Vico would conclude, cannot be found in what man is by nature, that is in his biological properties, but rather in what he has made of them in history, namely in his 'civil institutions'. Hence, while for the thinkers of the Enlightenment the focal issue in the science of man was that of fixed human *nature,* for Vico, in contrast, it is that of evolving *human* nature. Whereas Hume and Voltaire sought to explain how natural 'passions' in man became conventional in society, Vico sought instead to explain how cultural customs in society become natural to man. And consequently, the scientific principles by which Hume and Voltaire explained man, society, and history – were considered as utterly 'natural instincts' in individual man, while for Vico, as we shall see, these principles were seen to be secondary, man-made conventions and 'civil institutions' of entire nations.

The full title of Vico's work, *Principles of a New Science concerning the Common Nature of the Nations,* bears this out most clearly. Vico introduces a slight yet significant change in the terms and concerns of the search for principles of the common human nature – 'nations' takes the place of 'man'. Vico's 'new science' of man would not, properly speaking, concentrate on man, but on the group: the nation, the society, the class, the family. It would shift the focus of interest from the a-historic individualism of the social theorists of the Enlightenment (which, as Koyré noted, owed its inspiration to Newton's atomistic theory) by suggesting, instead, that it is not man that makes society, but rather society that makes

---

[48] Berlin, 'The Counter-Enlightenment', in *Against the Current,* pp. 1–24.

man – through its historical institutions and traditions. Thus, contra Hume, the 'common nature' which Vico was to glean from his observations would be the secondary, made-up, and collective nature of man: namely, culture. Ultimately, the 'principles' of human nature would have to be 'cultural', not 'natural'.

Modern historians of science have repeatedly called our attention to the fact that from around the middle of the eighteenth century there has been a significant shift of metaphors in the scientific jargon: instead of the mechanical-physical terms there is recourse to generic-biological ones. This change in the terms and ideals of scientific explanation has been particularly noticeable in the human sciences. Here, it seems, the 'organicist' jargon implied more than just a 'metaphoric redescription': it also conveyed new ideas and theories about man. While the universe of the Counter-Enlightenment and Romantic thinkers was still safely Newtonian, their human world and the means by which they came to terms with it, were quite new. This terminological and thematic change in the discourse of the human sciences owes its inception to a general discontent with the mechanical, artificial, and stereotyped forms of reasoning about things human. The revival of Aristotelian ideas of entelechy in the natural as well as in human world signified a new awareness that this mode of describing things – in terms of their natural-historical growth rather than in terms of their mechanical operations and laws – is much more appropriate. Vico's employment of the term 'principle' bears this out most clearly, as he combines the generic-teleological Aristotelian conception (*Metaphysics*, 1013a) with the new mechanical-Newtonian one.

Vico derives the meaning of the term from its etymological root: a 'principle' is that which exists *pre-incipium*, the set of properties and conditions which generate the phenomenon. The same meaning holds for 'principles' in nature as well as in the historical 'world of nations':

The nature of institutions is nothing but their coming into being (*nascimento*) at certain times and in certain guises. Whenever the time and guise are thus and so, such and not otherwise are the institutions that come into being ... In reasoning of the origins of institutions, divine and human, in the gentile world, we reach those first beginnings beyond which it is vain curiosity to demand others earlier; and this is the defining character of *principles*. We explain the particular guises of their birth, that is to say their nature, the explanation of which is the distinguishing mark of science. (NS/147, 346)

Vico thus set out to discover 'in the deplorable obscurity of the beginnings of the nations and in the innumerable variety of their customs' (NS/344) certain regular and recurrent patterns of behaviour, not, it should be noted, those qualities which are merely natural and common to all men as normal living beings (like fear, sexual desire, maternal instincts, etc.), but those which could be proved to have been absolutely necessary for them to exist – and be identifiable – as human beings. The new science of man had to go beyond the 'philological observation' of the merely 'physical' in the nature of man, as well as beyond the 'philosophical contemplation' of the apparently 'metaphysical' in him, in order to find the distinctly 'human' in man. And for Vico the term 'human' was synonymous with 'social'. Already in the opening paragraph of his work he inveighs against 'the philosophers who have not yet contemplated' on that 'which is most proper to men, whose nature has this principal property: that of being social [*socievole*]' (NS/2). In Vico's view, their 'philosophical contemplations on Man' lacked, as it were, historical observations of people.

Vico's general charge against 'the philosophers', here as elsewhere, is directed against a particular school – the Natural Law theorists of society, those who, in the words of Otto Gierke, have been 'engaged in the general study of all forms and phases of human society which were capable of developing a law or of being regulated by law'.[49] Though the general search for the basic natural-rational laws of civil association has been paramount among philosophers since Plato and Aristotle, it acquired greater significance and urgency during the sixteenth and seventeenth centuries, as European rationalists became increasingly critical of the old mythical and historical theories of the state, and sought to explain it on common rational grounds. The 'classical' sources of such Renaissance political theorists as Machiavelli and Bodin enabled them to replace the organicist notions of their medieval predecessors with new, thoroughly artificial, notions about 'the state as a work-of-art'. They duly realised that no civil society in his-

[49] Otto Gierke, *Natural Law and the Theory of Society, 1599 to 1800*, tr. E. Barker (Cambridge: Cambridge University Press, 1958), p. LIII.

tory was an organic natural or divine creation, but rather a
thoroughly arbitrary, legal and authoritarian, construction of its
members.[50] Though Vico generally agreed with their basic
assumptions and methods he was more concerned with the moral
implications of their inquiries.

The discovery of America and the growing awareness of the
diversity of human societies raised the question as to whether
there was an inherent morality common to them all. For modern
sceptics like Montaigne and Charron, as well as for the various
proponents of Libertinism, the multiplicity of beliefs and practices
around the world proved that there were no universal moral codes
of civility, but rather that each society was held together by laws
which were neither divine nor natural but human, positive,
customary. This relativistic attitude towards human values and
norms of civility, as exemplified in Montaigne's observation that
'we have no other test of truth and reason than the example and
pattern of the opinions and customs of the country we live in',[51]
was liable to undermine any attempt to establish an absolute
moral – and political – authority in society, since it ruled out the
possibility of absolutely abiding norms of justice, and hence of
laws. And this was precisely what the modern sceptics and
libertines sought to achieve: to liberate the individual from the
oppressive authority of such civil norms and laws so as to allow him
to live freely, in what they perceived to be a happy state of nature
– ruled, as Montaigne claimed, 'by the laws of nature, and very
little corrupted by ours'.[52]

Now, there were many objections to these antinomian notions.
Those advanced by the modern theorists of Natural Law proved
particularly effective.[53] For these thinkers accepted the actual
observations of their opponents – particularly that which posited

---

[50] On the origin and connotations of the concept of 'the state as a work-of-art' in the
Renaissance, see the classic account in Jacob Burckhardt, *The Civilization of the
Renaissance in Italy*, tr. S. G. C. Middlemore (London: George Allen & Unwin, n.d.),
pp. 1–69; for a modern account, see Quentin Skinner, *The Foundations of Modern
Political Thought* (Cambridge: Cambridge University Press, 1978), II, pp. 352–8.

[51] Michel de Montaigne, 'On Cannibals', in *The Complete Works of Montaigne*, tr. D. M.
Frame (London: Hamish Hamilton, 1957), p. 152.

[52] Montaigne, 'On Cannibals', p. 153.

[53] Richard Tuck, 'The "Modern" Theory of Natural Law', in *The Languages of Political
Theory in Early Modern Europe*, ed. A. Pagden (Cambridge: Cambridge University Press,
1987), pp. 91–119.

the natural impulse of self-preservation as the main, or even the sole, motive in all man's activities – but used these same observations to undermine the foundations of the theory built on them. Their basic strategy was to show that the primal urge to survive engenders certain necessary rules of 'civil' behaviour by which all men must abide. The modern theorists of Natural Law thus deviated from the classic Platonic-Christian tradition because they did not normally speak of *Reason* as divine illumination of the mind that unites man with God, but rather as *reasoning*, by which they connoted all the human faculties which rule and dictate social behaviour, such as passion, fear, or pride. According to Grotius, Pufendorf, and their followers, human beings have survived the difficulties and dangers encountered in the state of nature, because they have always been guided by some prudential lessons of self-preservation, that is by some moral and social norms which they naturally deduced from their common experience of life in the state of nature. Grotius thus defined natural law (*ius naturale*) in relation to the essential nature of man, which he perceived to be rational and social, as 'a dictate of right reason which points out that an act, according as it or is not in conformity with rational nature, has in it a quality of moral baseness or moral necessity; and that in consequence, such an act is either forbidden or enjoined by the author of nature, God'.[54] This innate rational ability to grasp certain universal and eternal rules of social life, be they, for the theologians, the explicit Commands of God, or, for the philosophers, the implicit 'Dictates of Reason' seemed to ensure that these rules obtain (in Pufendorf's words) 'the Power and Dignity of Laws'.[55] During the sixteenth and seventeenth centuries, this ancient Aristotelian notion with its later Stoic and Thomistic modifications became the focus of a lively controversy, one which echoes throughout Vico's work.[56]

Vico rejected these doctrines and their underlying conception of Natural Law because, in his view, they were all too narrowly rationalistic. They all required that men in the state of nature be

[54] Hugo Grotius, *The Law of War and Peace*, tr. F. W. Kelsey (Oxford: Oxford University Press, 1925), Prolegomena, sec. 10.
[55] Samuel Pufendorf, *The Law of Nature and Nations*, ed. J. Barbeyrac, tr. B. Kennet (London: 1794), p. 134.
[56] Luigi Bellofiore, *La dottrina del diritto naturale in G. B. Vico* (Milan: Giuffrè, 1954); Bruce A. Haddock, *Vico's Political Thought* (Swansea: Mortlake Press, 1986), pp. 81–105, 162–9.

enlightened, or at least prudential enough, to deduce and behave according to some rational 'law'. Such expectations, he thought, were quite unrealistic with regard to 'the first men of the gentile humanity', who, being 'the children of nascent mankind', were not as yet able 'to form intelligible class concepts of things' – such as, for example, the abstract concept of justice. Vico did not deny, however, the ability of these men to grasp such concepts in a different, pre-rational and poetic form. As we shall see, Vico's theory of the 'natural law of the gentes', was an attempt to mediate between the two rival classical-Christian and the modern-secular theories of Natural Law, and to transcend both: for while he accepts the anthropo-historical premises of the modern-secular theorists about the emergence of civilization 'out of ferocity, avarice, and ambition' of each individual man, he rejects their conclusions about the ability of man to redeem himself solely by his natural-rational capacities; and while he accepts the theistic premises of the classical-Christian theorists about 'weak and fallen mankind' that needs divine illumination, he rejects their conclusion about the ability of man to redeem himself by sharing in the divine Reason or even – in the case of the gentes – by Revelation. His mediative solution would be to relate the process of civilization, as exemplified by the history of the gentes, not to reason or revelation – but to the human imaginative, or 'poetic logical', capacities, to divination, in sum – to Myth. In the *New Science* he thus shows (on shaky etymological grounds) how the gentiles arrived at a rational concept of justice (*ius*) through the mythical image of *Jove* (NS/14). And this, in his view, was the pattern in keeping with which all the nations developed from bestiality to humanity.

The Natural Law theorists, on the other hand, depicted the process of humanization as thoroughly natural, because so absolutely necessary, to man, a process through which, as it were, man must go by force of a law-of-nature; this was thus clearly inimical to what Vico regarded as the *raison d'être* of man's life – his 'human authority' to create and live by his own man-made law. He duly saw that these theorists, while seeking to refute the extreme conventionalist views of the sceptics and the libertines about the sheer contingency and relativity of all moral values, reached the opposite extremity, that of naturalism, and ultimately reduced the multiplicity of all moral values to certain basic utilitarian instincts and rational considerations of self-preservation in man. In so doing they reduced all the cultural activities of man to mere tactics of a defence mechanism (as, in Vico's view, Hobbes did), and worse still, by turning man's capacity for self-preservation into a kind of natural law which regulates all human affairs – they removed from their system the necessity for supernatural guidance. Grotius' hypothetical remark that the natural laws of civil association guarantee the preservation of mankind 'even if we grant, what without the greatest wickedness cannot be granted, that there is no God, or that he takes no care of human affairs' outraged Vico so much that he repeatedly referred to it as a proof of the dangers of Epicureanism even among the most learned and pious Christians – as Grotius certainly was.[57] What these philosophers failed to see was that law was not really natural to or in man; that is to say, it did not just arise in him due to some natural impulses of self-preservation, but rather that it was, like any other human creation, a counter-natural act, a conscious – albeit not rational, but poetical – effort of man to transcend his state of nature. Religious beliefs and myths were the first and most effective means by which man could do it, and hence any suggestion (as hinted by Grotius, and openly asserted by Bayle) that atheists could create and live in civil society seemed to Vico implausible. The real danger with this modern-secular version of Natural Law was not its explicit realism, but rather its implicit idealism: it betrayed the excessively optimistic belief of the Enlightenment in the capability of man to be equally passionate and rational, or, to render it in Vico's own terms, that it combined the incompatible Epicurean and the Stoic views of man, allowing him, as it were, to possess both strong healthy physical desires and strong rational capacities to control them. Vico thought that this seemingly coherent view was not just wrong about, but ruinous to, modern men: it misled them to believe that they could do whatever they desires as long as they were able to rationalize it.[58] As

---

[57] According to Alexander Passerin d'Entreves, Grotius 'proved that it was possible to build up a theory of laws independent of theological presuppositions. His successors completed the task. The natural law which they elaborated was entirely "secular"' (*Natural Law* (London: Hutchinson, 1951), p. 55.

[58] For a full exposition of this Stoic-Epicurean core of Hobbes' philosophy, see Michael Oakeshott, *Hobbes on Civil Association* (Berkeley: University of California Press, 1975), pp. 1–74.

Vico put it in some poignant phrases

To be useful to the human race, philosophy must raise and direct weak and fallen man, not to render his nature or abandon him in his corruption. This axiom dismisses from the school of our Science the Stoics, who seek to mortify the senses, and the Epicureans, who make them the criterion . . . Both should be called monastic, or solitary, philosophers. (NS/129–30)

On the whole, then, Vico opposed the modern theories about the efficacy of the natural Dictates of Reason in the process of civilization as both historically implausible and philosophically dangerous. The problem, as he saw it, was not to establish what man is, or could be, by nature, but rather, what he had actually made out of his very nature. Henceforth, in his search for the 'principles of humanity', Vico would concentrate only on the social behaviour of man, which is as natural to human beings as their physical make-up:

In view of the fact that the human race, as far back as memory of the world goes, has lived and still lives comfortably in society, this axiom alone decides the great dispute still waged by the best philosophers and moral theologians against Carneades and the skeptic and Epicurus – a dispute which not even Grotius could set at rest – whether law exists by nature, or whether man is naturally sociable, which comes to the same thing. (NS/135)

Ultimately, then, Vico's main quibble with the Enlightenment theorists was, that the 'principles' in question, that is, those which form and govern human affairs, are not to be thought of as natural forces in human beings, believed to be operating through and even regardless of them, according to some rational-physiological 'laws' of self-preservation; rather, these principles must be seen as human ideas, customs, and institutions - wholly dependent on man's pre-rational, distinctly 'poetic', character. Vico turned away from the fashionable psychological reductionism which pegged human actions to some ultimate intrinsic forces working within man – be they the Grotian *inclinatio ad societam*, the Hobbesian 'Fear and Vain Glorie', the Neo-Epicurean 'enlightened self-interest' or the variety of Humean 'passions'. Instead, Vico concentrated on man's secondary, counter-natural conventions. The 'principles of humanity', he concluded, are not philosophical or theological truths, but rather poetic fictions, created by the spontaneous and collective common sense of the 'entire human race'. Humanity, in short, had been created by and sustains itself through very fragile and contingent forms of 'poetic wisdom'.

Having thus defined man as primarily a cultural being rather than just a natural one, and, as such, more poetic than rational, Vico was finally able to free himself from the vogue of the fashionable mechanical theories about man-in-society. The attempt of Newtonian social philosophers to derive the truth about man from what he is by nature rather than from what he has made of himself in history, to establish, as it were, an absolute truth *about* man (his principles of nature) without recourse to the truths *of* man (his principles-of-humanity), was thus not just futile, but fundamentally misconceived, because ultimately what mattered in human life and history was not what human beings are made of – their *physis* – but rather what they have made of and against this nature – their *nomos*.

Generally speaking, throughout his work Vico strives to overcome the age-old dichotomy between *physis* and *nomos*, between the truly 'natural' and merely 'cultural' in man. He thus rejects a central paradigm of the Enlightenment theorists of man and society. Because the latter thought of human nature in mechanical-physical terms, they saw only opposition and an eternal conflict of essential forces within man: human life and history presented to them a struggle of the modern-civil-rational over against the ancient-primitive-irrational. Vico, instead, thought of human nature in organic-historical terms: he thus perceived the two apparently contradictory forces in complementary terms, as continuous and generative phases in one process of growth and decay which he termed (in the title of the work) the 'common nature of the gentes'. He established thereby a 'natural law' of psychological-historical transformation, in which the irrational-primitive in human mind and culture evolved into the rational-civil, and vice versa. In so doing, he dissolved the very conception of Human Nature itself, or at least the one most cherished by the Enlightenment, to wit, the belief in an intrinsic, primary, and fixed 'nature' which exists behind and apart from all the temporal manifestations of cultural species.

Vico did not believe that there is an ideal and perfect 'nature' of human beings which resides, or comes to fulfilment, in any specific stage of their life or history. He repeatedly rejects the claims of the modern Natural Law theorists who purport to have found the 'truest' nature of man in what is absolutely common and ideal in all people – namely, as Hobbes put it, their ability to derive out of their different experiences in social life the same rational conclusion, to deduce 'a Precept, or a general Rule, found out by Reason, by which a man is forbidden to do that which is destructive to his life'.[59] As we shall see later on, Vico opposed the Hobbesian and similar theories which sought to explain the constitution of society by virtue of Natural Law, because he found their basic assumptions and universal claims about the natural rationality of all people at all times – the rationality which led people to create and maintain the social contract – most inadequate, both psychologically and historically. He repeatedly inveighed against the 'princes of natural law' and their failure to visualize and interpret the behaviour of people in the state of nature because they imputed to them their own modern charac-teristics: what they took to be Reason, he thought, was only *their* reason. They present, in short, a typical case of what he calls 'the conceit of the scholars', namely, the egocentric and wishful thought 'that what they know is as old as the world' and therefore abides in all times and places (NS/127). Vico, instead, allowed for as many kinds of reason as there are nations to develop and hold to them. Similarly, he rejected the modern notion that there is a certain practical reasoning at work in everyday matters which is valid everywhere, be it the French *le bon sens* or the English *common sense*. Instead, he developed his notion of *senso comune*, a term which implied, as did the other terms, an intuitive and popular knowledge, and yet attributed and confined it to members of specific social and linguistic constituencies. What is true and common among all people, what finally constitutes the 'common nature of the nations', is only the immanent process of 'being social', a truly universal process which indeed produces many kinds of human nature and reason and society; and yet, as Vico tries to show, this production process passes through the same general stages of growth:

[59] Thomas Hobbes, *Leviathan*, ed. M. Oakeshott (N.Y.: Collier Books, 1962), p. 103.

This New Science or metaphysic, studying the common nature of nations in the light of divine providence, discovers the origins of divine and human institutions among the gentile nations, and thereby establishes a system of the natural law of the gentes, which proceeds with the greatest equality and constancy through the three ages . . . The age of the gods . . . The age of the heroes . . . The age of men, in which all men recognized themselves as equal in human nature . . . (NS/31)

Elsewhere Vico elaborates the more precise states of mind and culture through which all peoples and nations must go in their circular-spiral movement from age to age: 'The nature of peoples is first crude, then severe, then benign, then delicate, finally dissolute' (NS/242). These states conform to the general process of natural growth and decay, which Vico calls the 'ideal eternal history' of humanity. As I shall deal with this notoriously ambiguous notion later on, I should like here to note only that in Vico's scheme the two first ages of mankind – which make up its 'mythical' stage – are far more potent than the last 'rational' one, and they dictate the rhythm and course of the entire 'eternal and ideal' (yet very real) cyclical process of the 'rise, progress, maturity, decadence, and dissolution' of nations and civilizations. In short, what Vico sought to do was not to explain history by human nature, but human nature by history.

Vico's quest for the 'principles of humanity' then, turned out to be an ambitious exercise in comparative social anthropology. Its aim was to find in the habitual manners of primal groups (he singles out primitive peoples, children, and village-men) those customary routines and rules of association, which could be shown to have been the necessary and sufficient conditions for the generation of human social life. 'Humanity', for Vico, is not only a field of practical interaction between people, but, above all, a field of rule-guided and rule-governed association. It is primarily a moral association of peoples, organized, rather arbitrarily as they went along, into certain rules, or 'civil institutions', which specify right and wrong, and prescribe obligations. Vico finally narrows down these ruling ideas to three:

Now since this world of nations has been made by men, let us see in what institutions all men have perpetually agreed and still agree. For these institutions will be able to give us the universal and eternal principles (such as every science must have) on which all nations were founded and on which they still preserve themselves. We observe that all nations, barbarous as well as civilized . . . keep these three human customs: all have some religion, all contract solemn marriages, all bury their dead. And in no nation, however savage and crude, are any human actions performed with more elaborate ceremonies and more sacred solemnity than the rites of religion, marriage, and burial . . . from these three institutions humanity began among them all. (NS/332–3)

Further on Vico makes clear that he opted for these three 'civil institutions' because, in the whole range of habitual civil manners, these are unique in that they are 'natural customs' (*i naturali cotumi*).[60] In this term Vico effectively mediates between and supersedes the traditional dichotomy between the 'natural' and the 'customary' in human nature. He suggests thereby, that the appearance of these rule-governed routines, which are manifestly morally principled, is the most crucial, as well as the final, moment in man's natural evolution: it marks the beginning of human history. The moment in which humanity no longer obeys its natural instincts, but rather submits itself to its own rules, it not only becomes a proper 'human being', but, to use Ayer's famous phrase, it becomes a proper 'subject for science'.[61] All the more so because, as Vico would have it, it is only under such conditions, that is, when man lives 'in principles', that he can be recognized and understood 'in principle' by other human beings.

Vico contends that 'there is nothing more natural (for there is nothing more pleasant) than observing natural customs . . . [and hence] human nature, in which such customs have had their origin, is sociable' (NS/350). The term 'observation' here, and elsewhere in Vico's work, is significant. Vico intentionally manipulates its dual meaning. Whereas in the Newtonian vocabulary observation stands for absolute empirical neutrality and detachment in the 'inspection' of phenomena, here it implies and calls for a subjective involvement in 'keeping' the customs – both on the part of those who actually perform them, as well as on the part of those who study them. Vico intimates here that a cross-cultural understanding of primitive or foreign cultures is possible only if we can observe in their alien forms of life those few elementary 'natural customs' being observed. He makes it clear

---

60 For a lucid elaboration of this notion, see James C. Morrison, 'Vico's Doctrine of the Natural Law of the Gentes', *Journal of the History of Philosophy*, 16 (1978), pp. 47–60.
61 A. J. Ayer, 'Man as a Subject for Science', in *Philosophy, Politics and Society*, Series III, ed. P. Laslett and W. G. Runciman (Oxford: Basil Blackwell, 1967).

that these 'natural customs' are not just communal 'practices', but must be – or rather have become – 'social institutions', namely more formal and legally-binding conventions that are to be strictly observed by all members of the community and their rulers. Once we discern 'in the deplorable obscurity of the beginnings of the nations and in the innumerable variety of their customs' (NS/344) this morally-principled behaviour, which is absolutely necessary to all human beings, and therefore immanently familiar to us from our own experience of being human, only then can we make sense of their strange yet essentially 'human' world. It is for this reason that in his work Vico refers, in a rather confusing fashion, to these 'civil institutions' as being the 'principles' of both the social world and its 'new science'. He sums up Book I of the *New Science*, aptly entitled 'The Establishment of Principles', with a resounding moral, as well as scholarly, warning:

From all that has been set forth in general concerning the establishment of the principles of this Science, we conclude that, since its principles are 1) divine providence, 2) marriage and therewith moderation of the passions, and 3) burial and therewith immortality of human souls, and since the criterion it uses is that what is felt to be just by all men or by the majority must be the rule of social life . . . [then] these must be the bounds of human reason. And let him who would transgress them beware lest he transgresses all humanity. (NS/360)

Now, the validity of Vico's concrete 'principles' may easily be contested on logical and empirical grounds. Vico was not a cultural relativist who would allow that any society has its own principles which underly whatever moral rules and civil institutions it chooses to observe. Nor was he a methodological formalist who would just put forth ideas and lay down guidelines to be filled by whatever concrete examples. What Vico did do was insist on the absolute necessity of his three concrete 'civil institutions', and these three only. In this he perhaps leaves himself most open for criticism. In fact, when he made his principal claim that religion is absolutely necessary to the constitution of society, he knew that his claim had already been refuted on empirical grounds by Pierre Bayle who, relying on new anthropological evidence, contended not only that there are non-religious societies, but that they are even more humane than religious societies! But to argue that this empirical refutation renders Vico's theory false – is, I think, to miss his more basic claim. For what Vico says, in fact, is that any cross-cultural understanding, to be possible at all, must assume and pursue certain absolute 'principles of humanity'. What is really novel and important in Vico's theory of the 'principles of humanity', then, is not its actual choice of these three particular institutions – though, this too is quite instructive; it is rather the very conception of how 'understanding in principles' is possible in and indispensable to the human sciences.

Vico's anti-relativistic position here can, perhaps, be termed 'moral realism' if that term is understood in its rather loose meaning, namely as a claim that our moral beliefs, practices, and institutions are real insofar as they grow out of the same real biological, ecological, and historical conditions in which all people have always lived. When Vico argues that religion, marriage, and burial embody the definitive values of our humanity, he in fact claims that we must recognize them as real moral facts in the world, regardless of what we or other performers or critical observers like Bayle think of their moral value. We can argue about their particular characteristics in each society, their origins, functions, and other factual forms, as we normally do when we inquire about possible objects of human knowledge which exist out there in the world, but we cannot ignore or doubt their moral necessity and utility for human life. As moral practices they are, as it were, beyond our beliefs about what is right and wrong. This is why Vico argues, time and again, that even the most primitive and brutal religions, which so offend our moral sensibilities and beliefs, must not be judged as morally wrong, but rather must be seen as part of merely a different, even if inferior, moral form of life (NS/10, 14, 177, 265, and passim). Historical experience – in which alone morality is to be found and judged – has taught him that 'if religion is lost among the peoples, they have nothing left to enable them to live in society: no shield of defense, nor means of counsel, nor basis of support, *nor even a form by which they may exist in the world at all*' (NS/1109).

Vico's original notion that in order to understand human beings in an alien culture the human scientist must grasp their 'principled' behaviour, and that this is feasible only insofar as he can relate it to his own experience, has been carried over, and much advanced, by modern social theories of understanding. One of the leading exponents of this theory in modern social science, Peter Winch, has, in fact, evoked Vico's conception of 'principles of humanity' to develop his own conception of similar 'limiting notions' (birth, death, sexual relations) in social life. In his classic essay *Understanding a Primitive Society* Winch seeks to overcome a common objection to the Wittgensteinian notion of the incommensurability of different 'forms of life', which might seem to imply also incomparability of moral values, and thereby to undermine any possibility of moral judgement. Winch thus points out that

the very conception of human life involves certain fundamental notions – which I shall call 'limiting notions' – which have an obvious ethical dimension, and which indeed in a sense determine the 'ethical space', within which the possibilities of good and evil in human life can be exercised . . . Their significance here is that they are inescapably involved in the life of all known human societies in a way which gives us a clue where to look if we are puzzled about the point of an alien system of institutions. The specific forms which these concepts take, the particular institutions in which they are expressed, vary very considerably from one society to another; but their central position within a society's institutions is and must be a constant factor. In trying to understand the life of an alien society, then, it will be of the utmost importance to be clear about the way in which these notions enter into it.[62]

In so far as Vico saw that the world in which people live is a world of cultural meaning which they themselves have created, and that in order to understand them the observer must grasp this meaning *for* them and *in* himself, Vico may well be said (as Isaiah Berlin has claimed) to have 'virtually invented the concept of the understanding – of what Dilthey and others call "Verstehen"'.[63] But, as we can see from our discussion of his concept and method of understanding 'in principle' Vico did not really indulge in Dilthean feats of intuition or intimate modes of *Miterlebnis*. Vico certainly believed that any act of understanding requires us to 'enter into' the minds of other people, to discover their thoughts, emotions, and projects, an act which impels us, as he puts it, 'to descend from these human and refined natures of ours to those quite wild and savage natures, which we cannot at all imagine and can comprehend only with great effort' (NS/338). Here and elsewhere Vico claims that in order to determine the nature of an

---

[62] Peter Winch, 'Understanding a Primitive Society', *The American Philosophical Quarterly*, 1 (1964), p. 322.
[63] Berlin, *Vico and Herder*, p. 107.

historical event or a social situation, the observer must know what
it meant to the participants involved; and in order to do that, he
must discover what these agents thought they were doing, what
their cultural propositions were. But, as Pompa and others have
pointed out,[64] Vico is definitely quite explicit in his rejection of
purely or even partly 'imaginative' attempts of understanding,
saying that because

the nature of our civilized minds is so detached from the senses, even in
the vulgar, by abstractions corresponding to all the abstract terms our
languages abound in, and so refined by the art of writing . . . that it is
naturally beyond our power . . . to enter into the vast imagination of
those first men, whose minds were not in the least abstract, refined, or
spiritualized, because they were entirely immersed in the senses,
buffeted by the passions, buried in the body. (NS/378)

What Vico proposed, instead, is to discern in any alien society
those few 'elaborate ceremonies' which disclose a general framework of social attitudes, categories and concepts which fundamentally are the same for all peoples at all times. Such are, he
believed, the metaphysical ideas which constitute the three basic
civil institutions of humanity – they are always and everywhere the
same because they arise, as it were, out of the human condition
itself. He has found them, he says, 'by a severe analysis of human
thoughts about the human necessities or utilities of social life . . .
our Science is therefore a history of human ideas, on which it
seems the metaphysics of the human mind must proceed'
(NS/347). While he agreed that the ceremonial practices of
marriage or burial may differ due to the local and temporary
features of particular cultures, he contended that because they all
originate from a common human predicament, they must disclose
the same notional meaning: 'Uniform ideas originating among
entire peoples unknown to each other must have a common
ground of truth' (NS/144). The main aim of his inquiries into the
particular 'laws and deeds of the Romans or the Greeks', he says
in his concluding remarks, was precisely this – to prove the universal 'identity of the intelligible *substance* in the diversity of their
modes of development', and it was due to this achievement that 'we
could not refrain from giving this work the invidious title of a *New
Science* (NS/1096).

[64] Leon Pompa, 'Imagination in Vico', in *Vico: Past and Present*, 1, pp. 162–70.

The key to Vico's humanistic 'understanding in principles', then, is the fact, that the 'human ideas' which pervade the 'principles' in question are not just personal experiences of belief in God, respect for parents, fear of death, and so on. They are, at the same time, the collective historical experience of the social group, of all social groups, in which similar yet different personal experiences of other people have been embedded and objectified into common ideas, customs and institutions. Any recourse to them implies, then, a certain knowledge of and participation in the motives, goals, and means of other people. The experience we have in observing these civil institutions is, by its very nature, different from that in observing natural phenomena. Because scholars are themselves human beings they interpret these civil institutions by using their own experience of mental life and human action in similar institutions. This means, for example, that in order to understand a religious institution 'in principle', the observer cannot just 'follow its rule' in a mechanical way; this, Vico would say, may provide sufficient and valid knowledge 'in principle' – but only in the natural sciences, and in the specific Newtonian sense of the term. In the case of humanistic under-standing 'in principle' the observer must have a certain self-knowledge of the thing observed. When observing, for example, religious institutions, he or she must know what it is 'to believe', to take part in a religious rite, etc.; similarly, the observation of burial rites will be meaningless unless the observer shares the implicit 'universal belief in the immortality of human souls' (NS/512). In short, observers of social affairs of this kind must make their own personal experience bear on and give meaning to what they observe. The impartial observation and mechanical description of what is going on in the performance of rites then clearly fall short of understanding the rite 'in principle'. It seems, then, that Vico was in fact somewhat more 'positivistic' than portrayed by his Idealist followers. Indeed, as we saw above, his search for certain concrete, common, and well-defined 'civil' rules in the seemingly 'wild and savage' natural behaviour of totally alien people suggests that he sought to forge some more accurate and practical means by which to approach, observe and compare other human beings. He thought that 'understanding' other human beings was possible 'in prin-ciple' because of our ability to make sense of the 'civil institution' we observe – to discover, as it were, its 'principle' in and for ourselves.

Such interpretive procedures between the self and the other are possible as long as they are conducted on some common ground of concepts and practices, around a 'principle of humanity', which enables the observer to engage in what Clifford Geertz calls the interplay of experience-near and experience-distant concepts. This interplay is a dialectical oscillation between the particular and the general, which brings the 'exotic minutiae' which we observe in another form of life – say, a specific burial rite – into the range of our general, more theoretical conception of what 'burial' is all about. This back-and-forth movement between the 'whole conceived through the parts that actualize it and the parts conceived through the whole that motivates them' is generally known as the 'hermeneutic circle',[65] a movement which Vico would have understood, and sought to solve, by referring it to the central axle upon which it turns – the three 'principles of humanity'. And this kind of understanding others through some common practices is a way, perhaps the best way, for understanding ourselves. As Winch points out, 'we may learn different possibilities of making sense of human life, different ideas about the possible importance that the carrying out of certain activities may take on for a man, trying to contemplate the sense of his life as a whole'.[66]

In his quest for the principles of humanity Vico thus reaches the final stage: he now turns inwards, to humanity itself, but not, as Hume did, to the ultimate physiological 'springs of human actions' in human beings (which, like other natural phenomena, we cannot claim to know), but rather to what 'men had made' in history, to their 'civil institutions' which we know in as much as we still make them ourselves, 'within the modifications of our own human minds'. This is the message of the best-known oration in the *New Science*.

But in the night of thick darkness enveloping the earliest antiquity, so remote from ourselves, there shines the eternal and never failing light of a truth beyond all question: that *the world of civil society has certainly been made by men, and that it is in our ability to retrieve its principles from within the*

---

[65] Clifford Geertz, ' "From the Native's Point of View": On the Nature of Anthropological Understanding', *Bulletin of the Academy of Arts and Sciences*, 28 (1974), p. 43.
[66] Winch, 'Understanding a Primitive Society', p. 319.

modifications of our own human mind. Whoever reflects on this cannot but marvel that the philosophers should have bent all their energies to the study of the world of nature, which, since God made it, He alone knows; and that they should have neglected the study of the world of nations, or civil world, which, since men had made it, men could come to know. (NS/331)

Vico's contention that true knowledge is identical with construction, so that 'the rule and criterion of truth is to have made it', was, in itself, a rather commonplace notion among ancient and medieval philosophers. This ergetic or, as we would nowadays call it, 'constructivist' conception of knowledge has been often employed by the proponents of the *vita activa* in their polemics against the ideal of *vita contemplativa*, because it depicts knowledge as a creative, not merely a receptive, appropriation of the world. Bacon, Hobbes, Locke and the modern empiricists gave it, in their conception of reason as primarily a practical experience, a more positivistic flavour. Likewise, social and political theorists since antiquity have commonly predicated their notions of *homo sapiens* on a particular image of man as *homo faber.* Aristotle's philosophical anthropology of the *zoon politikon* was carried through and further developed by Stoic (Ciceronian), patristic (Augustinian) and Renaissance (Machiavellian) schools to meet their respective ideals of human beings as communitarian beings, namely as creatures who create, and thus can (and must!) know, the world in which they live.

In all these theories we can find intimations (though never clear formulations) of the Vichian notion, that we can know the human world because we have made it. Vico's concomitant view, the sceptic conclusion – that such 'true knowledge' of the essential matter and composition of things is impossible to man in the natural world, was also rather common. It informed the professed 'agnosticism' of the natural scientists themselves – notably, as we have seen, even that of Newton. The argument itself had been used already by the Sceptics against the Stoics, or, in a different context, by the practitioners of 'negative theology' in the middle ages. What is novel and liberating in Vico's rendering of these ideas is, therefore, not so much its agnosticism with regard to the natural sciences, as its vote of confidence in the human sciences. This is reflected in the assertion that we can have true knowledge of any human form of life only by virtue of our *reflective* 'ability to retrieve its principles from within the modifications of our own human mind' (*ritruovare i principi dentro le modificazioni della nostra medesima mente umana*). This seems to be the new message of the *New Science*, a message which is intimated already in Vico's early works, and is captured in the phrase which has become Vico's trademark: *verum et factum convertuntur sunt* – we can know as true only that which is made by us and other human beings.

The *verum et factum* dictum has been given much, perhaps too much, attention in the secondary literature;[67] Vico himself, it is worth remembering, refers to it only briefly, and with significant modifications, in the *New Science*, where he speaks of knowing (*conoscere*) through making (*fare*) in terms of *certainty* (rather than *verity*) (NS/331, 349, 376). In any case, since the general philosophical history, meaning and significance of this topos have been thoroughly, albeit very differently, elucidated by many interpreters, I shall focus only on an aspect of this notion which has been largely ignored – its importance for Vico's distinctly social theory of knowledge.

Vico first formulated this idea of our ability to know only those things which we have made ourselves, or can recognize in ourselves, in his early work *On the Most Ancient Wisdom of the Italians* (1710). He used it there as an anti-Cartesian argument, claiming that the 'cogito' starting-point is invalid because the mind cannot be the criterion of mind: 'for while the mind perceives itself, it does not make itself, and because it does not make itself, it does not know the genus or mode by which it perceives itself'.[68] This charge, however, is commonly misinterpreted as an early Vichian claim against the very possibility of human self-understanding, while, in fact, Vico used it to undermine what he regarded as the most outrageous aspect of the Cartesian method – its extreme rational individualism. In order to understand the full polemical meaning of this utterance, and of the *verum et factum* principle in general, we must follow and elaborate on Michael Mooney's insightful comment that 'Vico's objection to Descartes was not scientific, and only derivatively epistemological. In the first

---

[67] For comprehensive reviews, see Rodolfo Mondolfo, *Il 'verum-factum' prima di Vico* (Napoli: Guida, 1969), and Karl Löith, *Vicos Grundsatz: Verum et factum convertuntur: Seine theologische Prämisse und deren säkulare Konsequenzen* (Heidelberg: C. Winter, 1968).

[68] Vico, *On the Most Ancient Wisdom of the Ancients*, in *Selected Writings*, p. 55.

instance it was "moral" or "civil" – applied beyond the narrow realm of in which it was helpful, Cartesian analysis would wreck public life.'[69]

The basic assumption of the Cartesians was that the world consists of facts, and that knowledge of the world rests in ideas and propositions which represent these facts. The best way for us to gain knowledge is to let the world act causally on our senses, that is to experience its objects immediately and methodologically. The principle of knowledge as a controlled personal experience was established by Descartes in his *Rules for the Guidance of our Native Powers*. According to Descartes, however, real knowledge or 'science' must not only be 'evident', by which he meant a congruence between ideas in the mind and the objects of reality, but also 'certain': that is, critically tested and demonstrated by the individual by means of a reliable method. The important point for our concern is that the new 'certainty' was based on the personal experience and reasoning of the individual, not on traditional authorities. This is the message of the Third Rule: 'In treating of the objects for investigation what we have to examine is not what others have opined, nor what we ourselves may conjecture, but what we can clearly and evidently intuit, or can deduce with certainty: knowledge is not obtainable in any other way'.[70] The introduction of experimental and inductive methods seemed to ensure, contra the sceptics, that the new scientist would indeed be freed from beliefs presented by authority and rely only on his own observation, on his own senses, and on his own powers of ratiocination. Reason, the possession of every man, is all that is needed to derive general knowledge from personal experience of objective reality. It was ultimately this rationalistic-individualistic conception of the nature and growth of knowledge, or 'mind', which so offended Vico: and he opposed it not only because he found it wrong in theory but also because he found it wrong for practice, the practice of a religious and political conservative which was based on entirely different premises of what is true knowledge. Vico, in other words, found the 'rationalist' conception of

[69] Michael Mooney, *Vico in the Tradition of Rhetoric* (N.J.: Princeton University Press, 1985), p. 108.
[70] Descartes, *Rules for the Guidance of our Native Powers*, in *Descartes' Philosophical Writings*, p. 8.

knowledge dangerous because he identified it with the Protestants' conception of knowledge. Both were equally critical of the Catholic 'traditionalist' conception of knowledge: 'tradition', so ran the argument, could not be a genuine source of knowledge, because real knowledge was gained by an immediate personal experience, not through historical collective experience.

By positing his collective-historical *mente* (which is roughly synonymous with what we mean by mentality) over and against Descartes' solitary *cogito*, Vico thus forged a new epistemological model of the nature and growth of knowledge. And it was by virtue of this new theory that he could eventually transcend both the Cartesian claims for knowledge and his own early objections to it: he now postulated that it is precisely due to the ability of the human mind to apprehend itself through 'its form or modes' – by reflection on primal patterns of thought, through recognition of conventions embedded in culture – that we can claim a 'true knowledge' in the human sciences.

As we saw, in his earlier writings Vico had argued that such 'true knowledge' through conventions was possible only in mathematics, wherein we deal with definitions, axioms, and postulates – all artificial objects that we have made; there, however, this true knowledge is of little significance beyond its own formal rules. Similarly, we can have true knowledge in physics, to the extent that we can recreate in experiments the process by which things are made and operate in nature. But here, too, Vico qualifies the value of this knowledge by arguing, that since we do not create the matter and laws of physical objects, our knowledge of their intrinsic nature and composition is rather vacuous. As against these insufficient forms of 'true knowledge' he now posits the knowledge of 'the world of nations, or civil world, which, since men had made it, men could come to know':

For the first indubitable principle posited above is that this world of nations has certainly been made by men, and its guise must therefore be found within the modifications of our own human mind. And history cannot be more certain than he who creates the things also narrates them. Now, as geometry, when it constructs the world of quantity out of its elements, or contemplates that world, is creating it for itself, just so does our Science, but with a reality greater by just so much as the institutions having to do with human affairs are more real than points, lines, surfaces, and figures are. (NS/349)

It was in that way then, by transposing the principle *verum et factum convertuntur sunt* from pure conventions (such as geometrical figures) to 'more real' cultural and social conventions (like myths, laws, states, and the like) that Vico was able to proclaim his new science of society. He came to realize that practically all our 'civil institutions' are as artificial and conventional as are the geometrical forms, and that consequently our knowledge of the human world results from what is equally an essentially constructive activity: we know this world because, and only in as much as, we still make or share its constitutive ideal fictions. And as I shall argue at length later on, Vico identified these constitutive elements of the human world with the classical myths, *i grandi frantumi dell'antichità*, which have persisted in our civilization.

Vico, then, was certain that a scientific knowledge of humanity was possible, in so far as it was, much like in Newtonian science, a knowledge 'in principle', that is, a knowledge of the primal forces which form and govern 'this world of nations, the civil world'. It was, however, his new conception of 'humanity' itself which ultimately brought a change in his conception of its 'principles'. If, as he now realized, the forces which formed and govern the world of humanity were manifestly different from those of the world of nature, in that they were utterly contingent and poetic (literally fictional creations of man himself) then, he reasoned, they must also be understood differently. Having concluded that in 'the world of nations, the civil world' the primal forces we are looking for are man-made rules, those commonsensical 'human ideas' which have generated and still sustain certain universal 'civil institutions' in all known societies, he ultimately concluded that in the human sciences we are dealing not just with forces of a different kind, but also with a qualitatively different kind of knowledge; for the knowledge of 'religious belief' is different from the knowledge of 'Cohesion of Bodie' not only in its degree of exactitude, but in the kind of comprehension it involves. And so, while Vico's notion of scientific knowledge ('scienza') still remained the same, he developed, as it were, a new conception of what it is that we want to know, and how to achieve it. Having established the fact that human beings can exist, and be understood as such, only by following their particular principles-of-humanity, he then concluded that the Newtonian model of understanding human beings as obeying general principles-of-nature was inadequate.

During the period which witnessed 'the mechanization of the world picture', the immediate problem which faced divergent thinkers like Vico, was how to break the spell of the pervasive naturalistic reasoning and language. As a professional rhetorician Vico was more qualified than others to know that it was not enough to think differently about human affairs; one had to find alternative patterns of discourse, to invent better analogies and more adequate vocabularies with which to convey the new insights. My final remarks in this section will concern Vico's attempt to reformulate the discourse of the human sciences.

III

As we have seen, the so-called Newtonian Philosophers took the natural sciences to be the most adequate – indeed, the only relevant – model for the human sciences. Their contention that all scientific explanations must conform to the same deductive model of Newtonian physics prescribed a certain mode of analogical reasoning and vocabulary. The requisition to transfer methods and terms from the 'body natural' to the 'body politick' seemed quite reasonable in view of the success of the natural sciences, and in any case was very pervasive not only in academic discourses but also in everyday speech. Vico saw this clearly:

Indeed I recall that when Aristotelian philosophy and Galenic medicine flourished, illiterate men were frequently heard using the phrases 'abhorrence of a vacuum', 'the repulsions and attractions of nature', 'the four humours', 'qualities', and many others of a similar kind. But now that the new physics and medicine have prevailed, one hears the common man everywhere talk of the 'circulation' and 'coagulation of the blood', or 'useful and harmful ferments', and of the 'pressure of air', etc.[71]

This new, physical-mechanical jargon proved to be irresistible. Even sceptical thinkers like Hume, who questioned the capability of the natural sciences themselves to live up to their own image of perfectly objective and rational methods, succumbed to this

---

[71] Vico, *On the Most Ancient Wisdom of the Italians*, in *Selected Writings*, p. 49.

temptation. For a while Vico too was quite enchanted by 'the growing prestige of experimental physics', but, as he related in his *Autobiography*, 'profitable as he thought it for medicine and spagyric, he desired to have nothing to do with this science. For it contributed nothing to the philosophy of man and had to be expounded in barbarous formulas, whereas his principal concern was . . . the philosophy of human customs.'[72]

Vico's starting point was to ask himself, why his fellow human scientists were so impressed with this kind of naturalism, why they 'should have bent all their energies to the study of the world of nature [and thereby] neglected the study of the world of nations'. He then observed that

this aberration was a consequence of that infirmity of the human mind by which, immersed and buried in the body, it naturally inclines to take notice of bodily things, and finds the effort to attend to itself too laborious; just as the body eye sees all objects outside itself, but needs a mirror to see itself . . . only with great difficulty does it come to understand itself by means of reflection. (NS/331, 236)

In this curious but typical passage, Vico hints that the problem of the human sciences is a lack of self-reflection. The human scientists are compelled to account for subjective human affairs in objective physical terms and analogies because they have not yet found 'the mirror', or device with which to reflect on their own world in its own terms, by its own analogies. Vico's *New Science* offered them that mirror. His most notable achievement in the human sciences resulted from his attempt to change the very terms and categories used by their practitioners in accounting for their observations and actions. In his choice of new terms and categories, Vico did not return to the old theological and metaphysical vocabularies, nor did he turn to the new physical-mechanical ones. He chose, instead, to replace both the old metaphysical and the new physical analogies with ones taken directly from the human world itself.

Now, natural analogies in the discourse of the humanities are not wrong in themselves; perhaps they are even necessary in cases where physical motives and conditions are discussed, or when we

---

[72] Vico, *The Autobiography*, p. 128.

use them in well-defined and controlled experiments.[73] What Vico and modern humanists have objected to, however, is the absolute demand to account for all human phenomena solely in Newtonian categories of rigorous mechanical objectivity in the assignment of causes, description of operations, and determination of laws. Vico rejected the idea that any account of human action, in order to be scientific at all, should be rendered in the terms of naturalistic discourse, that it be reduced to phrases like 'determining its causes', 'measuring its forces', 'predicting its effects', 'deducing its laws', and so on. Such terms offended his humanistic sensibilities and clashed with his conviction that human beings must be understood in performative rather than mechanical terms, namely as active agents who, consciously or not, are not so much obeying laws as following rules which they themselves have made. Vico's originality lies in his claim that the 'civil world' (or what we nowadays call 'culture') was not only created by the poetic fictions of the first men, but that it still consists in them – insofar as these fictions permeate all our social practices: they persist in linguistic metaphors, religious myths, marital and burial rites, national feasts, and in all the anonymous and collective customs we live by. Indeed, we 'can come to know' the 'civil world', but not as scientists, whose knowledge applies, as far as it is possible, only to the 'world of nature', but rather as 'poets', insofar as we still share in the traditional fictions which have constituted it.

The modern scholars who adopted for the humanities the new rational discourse, namely, that which substituted natural terms and analogies to human ones, not only countered the original poetic process of concept-formation – the anthropomorphic process in which, as Vico put it, 'When men are ignorant of the natural causes producing things, and cannot even explain them by analogy with similar things, they attribute their own nature to them' (NS/180) – but in fact reversed it in a way which was equally fallacious, and, in a deeper moral sense, more harmful to man. For the rationalist attempt to explain 'their own nature' solely by 'natural causes', to draw analogies to 'similar things' in the world

---

[73] Konrad Lorenz, in his Nobel Prize speech, 'Analogy as a Source of Knowledge', *Science*, 185 (July 1974), pp. 229–34, draws a set of contrasts and affinities between biological and cultural changes; he contends that innovations in our knowledge of human nature stem almost exclusively from the proper use of analogy.

of nature, was bound to deprive man of what Vico termed, very suggestively, man's 'human authority' – by which he meant, quite literally, the ability of people to be 'authors' of their lives, or creators of their own 'humanity', by virtue of their poetic, not rational or merely natural, capacities. This poetic ability, he declared, constituted 'the human authority in the full philosophic sense of the term; that is, the property of human nature which not even God can take from man without destroying him . . . This authority is the free use of the will, the intellect on the other hand being a passive power subject to truth' (NS/388).

This recognition of the essentially poetic nature of man, the idea that man is first and above all an 'author', a being who constitutes the 'civil world' by authorizing its own rules, is the fundamental postulate of the *New Science* for Vico. It meant that his – and any– account of human beings must be interpretive rather than mechanical science, a science based on a 'new critical art' (*nuova arte critica*) whose task is to make sense of the way in which people have made sense of their world. Scientists of humanity can come to know other, even alien, human beings insofar as they share the world of meaning within which they constitute themselves. And because people have always made their world as 'authors', and not as 'scientists', we must, when we seek to understand their world rationally, respond to their poetic modes of reasoning and making in adequate terms, which, for Vico, meant in 'philological' rather than in strictly 'philosophical' ones. And therefore, instead of illuminating human phenomena by drawing analogies from natural occurrences, Vico used analogies from other cultural performances, in which this peculiar poetic impulse of 'human authority' was most evident.

Vico realized that the best example for the poetic evolution of human mind, society and history is language. Throughout his work Vico used his considerable knowledge of rhetorics to point out, that the linguistic categories by which we order and define the distinct forms of speech – the master tropes of metaphor, metonymy, synecdoche, and irony – are generally descriptive of the stages of mental growth through which all peoples and nations must go in their *nascimento,* or coming-into-being human. Following his axiomatic assumption that 'the human mind is naturally inclined by the senses to see itself externally in the body, and only with great difficulty does it come to understand itself by means of reflection' (NS/236), Vico established 'the universal principle of etymology in all languages: [that] words are carried over from bodies and from the properties of bodies to signify the institutions of the mind and spirit' (NS/237); this principle, in turn, rendered the entire process of humanization as a gradual liberation from immersion in bodily-natural associations. The development of language from the metaphorical association of man with nature towards the ironical dissociation of man from nature is a process in which human beings have come to see themselves (and their language) as distinctly human, namely artificial and conventional. The development of language thus resembles that of humankind at large in that it was neither a natural, nor arbitrary, process of transformation from bestiality to humanity, but rather a combination of both necessary and free creativity: like all human institutions (*cose umane*), linguistic forms too originated in necessity and remained in convention. Vico's entire *New Science* was an attempt to find out how, and by what means of signification, human beings have constituted their world by imposing meaning on it. He postulated that this meaning constitutes human existence to such an extent that it cannot be reduced to prior, more elemental, natural causes.

Vico did not deny that human beings are prompted by biological impulses, nor did he ignore the impact of such material conditions as climate and geography on their thoughts and behaviour. He also noted that human reactions and manners often resemble those of animals. And yet, much as he was attracted to the sheer physical aspects of human existence, he was even more fascinated by the way in which these 'bodily movements' have been transformed by the peculiar 'civil institutions' of a culture based on language. He duly saw that language created a distinctly human domain, an elaborate framework of rules and norms and concepts without which it was impossible to make, let alone to understand, the realities of the *mondo civile*. 'To sum up, a man is properly only mind, body, and speech, and speech stands as it were midway between mind and body' (NS/1045). This apprehension of the sublimative and communicative functions of speech enabled him, I would argue, to tackle the major hermeneutical difficulty in his new science of philology, a problem which his 'first indubitable principle' – *that this world of nations has certainly been made by men, and its guise must therefore be found within the modifications of our own human mind* – only hints at, but does not solve: Can we ever fully surpass the circle of meaning within which we find ourselves? Because if, as he now postulated, we can come to know other human beings only by sharing the linguistic meanings within which they constitute themselves, how can we distinguish our meanings from theirs; how, in other words, are we to understand ourselves in the historical process of signification? Vico's answer would be that the only way we can come to know ourselves is by realizing how, and to what extent, we are caught, as it were, in the web of symbols and significations which has been woven into our own minds and cultural systems by our ancestors since the times of 'earliest antiquity, so remote from ourselves'. Yet this approach posed the most serious hermeneutical problem with regard to the original 'authors [*autori*] of the nations, among which more than a thousand years had to pass in order to bring forth the writers [*scrittori*] with whom criticism has hitherto been concerned' (NS/7): how can we possibly know what they really meant to say in their works, what kind of signification they introduced into the world? While we may still recognize the verbal forms of many archaic words we can hardly recover their original meaning for the *primi uomini*, because, both mentally and physically, we are not the same men as they were. Vico himself admits that

the nature of our civilized minds is so detached from the senses, even in the vulgar, by abstractions corresponding to all the abstract terms our languages abound in, and so refined by the art of writing, and as it were spiritualized by the use of numbers, because even the vulgar know how to count and reckon, that it is naturally beyond our power to form the vast image of this mistress called 'Sympathetic Nature'. Men shape the phrase with their lips but have nothing in their minds; for what they have in mind is falsehood, which is nothing; and their imagination no longer avails to form a vast false image. It is equally beyond our power to enter into the vast imagination of those first men, whose minds were not in the least abstract, refined, or spiritualized, because they were entirely immersed in the senses, buffeted by the passions, buried in the body. (NS/378)

Vico, then, had to find a way beyond the merely linguistic modes of the formation and transmission of meanings. He had to go, as it were, to the original existential experience of those men, whose words reached us, but whose meaning still eludes us. What

Vico suspected was that underlying all the different languages and
their articulate moral and social messages there exists a prior and
wider terrain of common human predicament, or some basic
social conditions to which all human beings react in more or less
the same way. His intuition was similar to what Nicolas Rescher has
noted:

By now, some four thousand natural languages have evolved on the
planet, and the remarkable thing about them is not so much that it is
difficult for the speakers of one language to penetrate the thought
framework of another, but that it is possible to do so. And this is so, in the
final analysis, not because their inherent conceptual schemes are
identical, but because their users, endowed with a common biological
heritage, face the same sorts of problems in making their way in the
world.[74]

This realization allowed Vico, as we saw, to establish certain
common reactive attitudes as the three universal 'principles of
humanity'. Vico called these pre-verbal means of discourse a
'mental language' (*lingua mentale*), and said that one of the main
aims of his work was to establish a universal 'mental dictionary
[*dizionario mentale*] for assigning origins to all the diverse articulated languages' (NS/145):

There must in the nature of human institutions be a mental language
common to all nations [*una lingua mentale comune a tutte le nazioni*], which
uniformly grasps the substance of things feasible in human social life and
expresses it with as many diverse modifications as these same things may
have diverse aspects. A proof of this is afforded by proverbs or maxims of
vulgar wisdom, in which substantially the same meanings find as many
diverse expressions as there are nations ancient and modern. This
common mental language is proper to our Science, by whose light
linguistic scholars will be enabled to construct a mental vocabulary
common to all the various articulate languages living and dead.
(NS/161–2)

Vico's belief in the possibility of a universal discourse based on a
common human predicament seems to have anticipated a view
which has become widespread among post-Wittgensteinian
philosophers of language. For philosophers like Peter Winch or
Karl-Otto Apel oppose the extreme relativistic conclusions which
have commonly been drawn from Wittgenstein's famous notion of

---

[74] Nicholas Rescher, *Empirical Enquiry* (London: Rowman, 1982), p. 37.

language as a particular social game. This notion, they argue, must not necessarily mean (as many Wittgensteinians assert) that all languages, and the societies which they sustain, are closed to each other; on the contrary, beyond all language-games we can detect some more fundamental (or, in Apel's term, 'transcendental') norms of intersubjective relations like, for example, 'telling the truth' or 'fair play' which are constitutive to all forms of social communication, and can thus form the common ground for universal understanding.[75] In sum: we must assume what David Lewis calls a 'convention of truthfulness' among the people whose alien ideas, beliefs, and practices we are seeking to understand.[76]

Vico's attempt to reach the 'common mentality' of all the nations through their languages and beyond them, required him to recover their deeper and more primordial 'reactive attitudes' to their natural and historical environments, to lay bare what he called their utmost 'necessities and utilities', those which prompted them to create their first and most enduring myths – of their gods and heroes:

To discover the way in which this first human thinking arose in the gentile world, we encountered exasperating difficulties which have cost us the research of a good twenty years. [We had] to descend from these human and refined natures of ours to those quite wild and savage natures, which we cannot at all imagine and can comprehend only with great effort. (NS/338)

In order to understand the Vichian answer we must follow his method and course of inquiry. Thus, before dealing with the specific case of 'our' classical mythology and the way in which Vico explained its origins and diffusion in our civilization, a topic which will concern us in the third and fourth sections, it may be useful to look first at Vico's treatment of the more general psychological-historical conditions for the creation of myth.

---

[75] Fred R. Dallmayr, 'Hermeneutics and Historicism: Reflections on Winch, Apel and Vico', *Review of Politics*, 39 (1977), pp. 60–81.
[76] David Lewis, *Convention* (Cambridge, Mass.: Harvard University Press, 1969), pp. 148–52.

CHAPTER 2

The revision of civilization

What life have you if you have not life together?
There is no life that is not in community,
And no community not lived in praise of GOD
                    T. S. Eliot, *Choruses from 'The Rock'*, II

To sum up, from all that we have set forth in this work, it is to
be finally concluded that this Science carries inseparably with
it the study of piety, and that he who is not pious cannot be
truly wise.
                    Vico, *The New Science*, par. 1112

I

*Principles of New Science of Giambattista Vico concerning the Common
Nature of the Nations*: As the full title of his work indicates, Vico's
aim was to lay down the universal principles of the *comune natura
della nazioni*.[1] Alas, as any reader of the work could see, Vico confined his range of meditations and investigations mainly to the
profane history of gentile nations, and repeatedly emphasized the
fact that his discoveries and conclusions about the ferine origins
and growth of humanity should not be applied to the sacred
history of the Hebrew-Christian nations. In his account, the
Hebrews, upon receiving the revealed truths directly from God,
began to live a kind of hidden life, isolated from all other nations,
and so were able to retain and safeguard their true beliefs, customs, and records for themselves. Hence, Vico's conclusion that
their entire development was radically different from that of all
other peoples. In his work Vico often criticizes those Biblical

---

[1] On the various titles of the *New Science*, see Benvenuto Donati, *Nuovi studi sulla filosofia
civile di G. B. Vico* (Florence: Le Monnier, 1936), pp. 412–21.

scholars who, in their attempts to construe a truly universal
science of history, have ignored, or sought to compromise, the
central notion which traditionally kept the two histories apart,
namely the anthropo-historical belief in the superiority of the
Hebrews over the Gentiles, a superiority which they sustained by
keeping intact their knowledge of the true God; this they did by
means of laws and rites of racial purity, and with the aid of their
linguistic and literary traditions (NS/165–9, 369–73, 527–33, 734–7).
Vico, indeed, rejected all the fashionable attempts to mediate
between the sacred history of the Judaeo-Christian nations and
the profane history of the Gentiles in a way which could undermine the absolute validity of the first, either by limiting the
relevance of Biblical events, laws, and prophecies only to the
particular case of the Hebrews (as La Peyrère and Spinoza seemed
to do), or, conversely, by universalizing them beyond this specific
case (as did, in his view, John Selden, Daniel Huet, and Samuel
Bochart). Vico's historical theory, however radical it may seem to
us, was thoroughly orthodox, and on all the crucial issues of the
day he sided with the teaching of the Catholic Church.[2]

And yet, Vico's professed adherence to this age-old dualistic
scheme of sacred and profane histories has always been doubted
and debated. On the whole, commentators on the *New Science* have
conveniently ignored this aspect of the work, arguing that if,
indeed, its celebrated observations and laws are applicable only to
those ancient and long-deceased civilizations, then Vico's own
claim to have erected a universal science of the whole *mondo civile*
would be invalidated. And since most of these commentators
regard this latter claim to universality to be much more crucial to
the work, they commonly reason that its more limited and limiting
demand to keep the separation of the sacred and the profane
must be superseded. On such grounds Vico's strictures have all
too often been simply dismissed or reasoned away as no more than
a gesture that Vico was making towards the religious authorities of
his time – a tactic of elusion which perhaps necessary for the
author, but is quite irrelevant for his readers. As Momigliano has
rightly pointed out, 'Vico was hailed as their predecessor by those
who did not share his concern with a clear separation between

---

[2] Vico's Catholic orthodoxy is a major theme in Franco Amerio, *Introduzione allo studio di
G. B. Vigo* (Turin: Società editrice internazionale, 1947).

profane and sacred history, but who accepted his view of profane history as the true view of history as such'.[3] Furthermore, it seems, that on this issue Vico himself was rather ambiguous, and perhaps purposefully so, as on numerous occasions he seems to have given enough clues and tacit instructions for this unitarian approach. Thus, for example, as he comes to conclude his preliminary 'notes on the chronological table' (in which he resets the major events in the history of the pagan nations so that they fit the history of the Hebrews) he says that

all that has come down to us from the ancient gentile nations . . . is most uncertain. So that in all this we have entered as it were into a no man's land where the rule of law obtains that 'the [first] occupant acquires title' [*occupanti conceduntur*]. We trust therefore that we shall offend no man's right if we often reason differently and at times in direct opposition to the opinions which have been held up to now concerning *the principles of the humanity of the nations*. By so doing we shall reduce them to scientific principles, by which the facts of certain history may be assigned their first origins, on which they rest and by which they are reconciled. For until now they have seemed to have no common foundation or continuous sequence or coherence among themselves. (NS/118)

As this passage indicates, Vico appears to have predicated his entire theory of history of the *mondo civile* on the history of the gentile nations. The fact that some Catholic interpreters of the work in the 1760s did indeed find Vico's theories about the feral state of nature and the largely autonomous emergence of human norms and institutions among the gentile too far fetched, and his claims on behalf of these norms too inclusive and universal, is often mentioned by modern commentators as a further proof of the subversive content of his work.[4] Such attempts to liberate Vico's work from its self-imposed constraints are, as we have noted above, partly justified by Vico's own treatment of his work. The problem facing the reader of the work, then, is how to account for Vico's seemingly contradictory claims, on the one hand, his

---

[3] Arnaldo Momigliano, 'Vico's *scienza nuova*: Roman "bestioni" and Roman "eroi"', *History and Theory*, 5 (1966), pp. 6–7.

[4] The attack on Vico's theory of the *ferini* was led by the Dominican Gian Francesco Finetti in his *Difesa dell' Autorità della Sacra Scrittura contro Giambattista Vico*, ed. B. Croce (1768; repr. Bari: Laterza, 1936). On the theological-historical background of this controversy see Paolo Rossi, *The Dark Abyss of Time: The History of the Earth and the History of Nations from Hooke to Vico*, tr. L. Cochrane (Chicago: University of Chicago Press, 1983), esp. pp. 251–61.

insistence on the radical difference in nature between the Judaeo-Christian and the gentile nations and the incommensurability of their respective sacred and profane histories, and, on the other hand, his claim to have found the universal principles of humanity and to have forged a science of the whole historical *mondo civile?* What, if any, of his discoveries and conclusions about the ancient pagan civilization could be applied to his own modern Christian civilization? So far, most commentators on his work have either eschewed these issues, or given unsatisfactory explanations.

Thus, for example, Paolo Rossi, who has dealt with these issues more thoroughly than any other scholar, maintains that Vico's main aims in the *New Science* were of a primarily critical and polemical nature.[5] Vico, suggests Rossi, set out to disprove the claims of both the ancient pagan *autori*, as well as those of their modern interpreters and propagators, regarding the *sterminata antiquità* of various pagan nations. And this was to be achieved by exposing the false nature of pagan customs over against the absolutely true claims of the Hebrews. Above all, Vico opposed, and sought to refute, those scholars who claimed to have found the origins of true religious beliefs, moral notions, arts and sciences among ancient pagan nations, and who, furthermore, dared to argue that the Hebrews had merely derived their sacred beliefs, rites, and laws from these pagan origins. Vico vigorously attacked Biblical scholars such as John Marsham, who tried 'to prove that the Egyptians preceded all the nations of the world in government and religion, and that their sacred rites and civil ordinances, transported to other peoples, were received with some emendation by the Hebrews' (NS/44). Other theorists preferred other nations – the ancient Chaldeans, Phoenicians, Chinese, and so on. Yet, much as they differed from each other in their respective theories, they all shared the same erroneous and dangerous belief in 'the matchless wisdom of the ancients', a belief which Vico himself had once succumbed to and propagated in his tract on *The Most Ancient Wisdom of the Italians*, but then gradually came to doubt and finally, in the *New Science*, set out to demolish.[6] 'In this work', he writes in the *Autobiography*,

---

[5] Rossi, *The Dark Abyss of Time*, pp. 168–92.
[6] Emanuele Riverso, 'Vico and the Humanistic Concept of *Prisca Theologia*', in *Vico: Past and Present*, I, pp. 52–65.

he finally discovers in its full extent that principle which in his previous works he had as yet understood only in a confused and indistinct way. For he now recognizes an indispensable and even human necessity to seek the first origins of this science in the beginnings of sacred history. And because philosophers and philologians alike acknowledge their despair of tracing the steps of its progress in the first founders of the gentile nations . . . he discovers this new science by means of a new critical method for sifting the truth as to the founders of these nations.[7]

'That principle' of humanity which Vico had sought in his previous works, and particularly in the *Universal Law* of 1722, was that of *honestas*, which was, in his words, a *vis veri* in man, an active principle which had not been lost in the Fall (NS/310).[8] Hence, his attempt to look for the origins of the humanity of the gentile nations 'in the beginnings of sacred history' and to relate how certain truths that the Hebrews had once known but then lost in the catastrophes of the Tower of Babylon and the Deluge were nevertheless retained, however weakly, by their pagan descendants and eventually regained. Vico, however, was careful to distinguish this kind of innate sense of justice from that of the classical-Christian Natural Law theorists by accentuating its common-sensical, not rational, characteristics, and, more generally, by claiming that its origin and diffusion in all men was an historical, not entirely natural, process. It was only in the first edition of the *New Science*, therefore, that he realized that

just as within us lie buried a few seeds of truth, which are cultivated gradually from childhood until, with age and through studies, they develop into the fully clarified notions which belong to the sciences, so, as a result of sin, within mankind were buried the eternal seeds of justice which, as the human mind develops gradually according to its true nature from the childhood of the world, developed into demonstrated maxims of justice. The following difference must, however, always be observed: that this occurred in one distinctive way among the people of God, and in a different, ordinary way among the gentile nations.[9]

And yet, having thus restated his belief in the primacy, authenticity and superiority of the revealed wisdom of the Hebrews, Vico still had to explain the efficacy of paganism, to solve the Baconian riddle of the *Wisdom of the Ancients*. He had to explain how it could

---

[7] Vico, *The Autobiography*, pp. 166–7.
[8] *Il Diritto universale*, in *Opere*, ii, pp. 44–6, 54ff.
[9] Vico, *The First New Science*, par. 48, *Selected Writings*, p. 106.

be that the pagan nations in antiquity, deprived, as they were, of both Revelation and Reason, nevertheless managed to reach such high standards of civility. His ultimate answer to this problem, I shall argue in this chapter, was simple and yet highly original: he postulated that these *primi uomini* were able to become human because they were 'by nature sublime poets', namely 'persons who by imagining did the creating' (NS/376). In what follows I shall try to explicate the exact meaning of this rather unusual claim.

According to Vico's own testimony, his theory about the poetic constitution of mankind was inspired by some famous lines in Horace's *The Art of Poetry*, in which the poet relates how

While men still roamed the woods, Orpheus, the holy prophet of the gods, made them shrink from bloodshed and brutal living; hence the fable that he tamed tigers and ravening lions; hence too the fable that Amphion, builder of Thebes' citadel, moved stones by the sound of the lyre, and led them whither he would by his supplicating spell. In days of yore, this was wisdom, to draw a line between public and private rights, between things sacred and things common, to check vagrant union, to give rules for wedded life, to build towns, and grave laws on tables of wood.[10]

Indeed, these Horatian verses impressed Vico so much that, in a way, his whole work on the origins and growth of civilization can be seen as an attempt to elaborate their meanings and implications. As, in fact, he himself admitted, 'the *New Science* [of 1730], and especially its second book [on poetic wisdom], is an extended commentary on this Horatian passage':[11] a commentary, that is, on the mythopoeic constitution of humanity. Following up on these Horatian premises, Vico's main effort in the *New Science* was to elaborate the general psychological and historical conditions which determined this process of self-creativity by means of spontaneous and collective fictions.

My main argument in this chapter will thus be that Vico concentrated on the ancient pagan *gentes* because it was principally through their history, rather than through that of the Hebrews,

[10] Horace, *The Art of Poetry*, 391–401, tr. H. Rushton Fairclough, The Loeb Classical Library (Cambridge, Mass.: Harvard University Press, 1928).

[11] Quoted in Michael Mooney, *Vico in the Tradition of Rhetoric* (New Jersey: Princeton University Press, 1985), p. 172. On Vico's unpublished commentary on Horace's *Ars Poetica*, see Salvatore Grasuolo, 'L'inedito vichiano sull' Arte Poetica di Orazio', *Bollettino del Centro di Studi Vichiani*, 4 (1974), pp. 36–50.

that he could demonstrate his major claim that 'this world of nations has certainly been made by men, and its guise must therefore be found within the modifications of our own human mind'. Their emergence from barbarism exemplified precisely those aspects which Vico considered most pertinent to the creation of 'human authority in the full philosophic sense of the term' – it was spontaneous, anonymous, collective, and poetic. It was, in other words, distinctly mythopoetic. Paradoxically, then, precisely because the post-deluvian *gentes* were largely (though never entirely) left on their own, and thus condemned, or privileged, to find a separate and independent route out of the feral state of nature, their achievement in raising themselves up to humanity seemed to Vico far more instructive than the divinely guided and thus fully guaranteed achievement of the Judaeo-Christian peoples. Compared with sacred history the profane history was simply and inevitably more human, all-too-human perhaps, and therefore, though less enlightened, it was much more revealing and instructive to the major historical issue of the *New Science*. What this issue amounted to, I shall endeavour to delineate in what follows.

As a work of historical scholarship, Vico's *New Science* abounds with all kinds of seemingly unrelated historical matters. Yet, underlying them all there is one meta-historical dilemma, a dilemma which originated in the early Christian historiography of paganism and then resurfaced in a new form in the historiography of the Enlightenment, when it became, in Dilthey's words, 'the real problem for the historiography of the eighteenth century' – this was the problem of the origins and nature of 'civilization'.[12] Now, though the term 'civilization' itself became fashionable only towards the end of the eighteenth century, its sense and conception had been known and expressed earlier in the century by various thinkers in equivalent organicist terms, one of the most notable of these terms being Vico's 'civil world' (*mondo civile*).[13]

---

[12] Wilhelm Dilthey, 'Das 18. Jahrhundert und die geschichtliche Welt', in *Gesammelte Schriften* (Stuttgart: Teubner, 1927), III, p. 231.

[13] Lucien Febvre, '"*Civilisation*": Evolution of a Word and a Group of Ideas', in *A New Kind of History*, tr. K. Folca (London: Routledge & Kegan Paul, 1973), pp. 219–57. On the scientific and ideological meanings of the term in the eighteenth century, see R. L. Meek, *Social Science and the Ignoble Savage* (Cambridge: Cambridge University Press, 1976), and Jean Starobinski, 'Le mot civilization', *Temps de la Réflexion*, 4 (1983), pp. 13–51.

The sensitivity of European observers in the era of the Enlightenment to the problem of 'civilization', and their attempts to define
it, signified a growing realization on their part that the traditional
religious criteria by which they had hitherto judged and compared the progress of societies had now become inadequate, and
that new, much more objective, comparative, and distinctly
cultural criteria were needed, which would determine the civility
of society by the degree of its autonomous progress in manners
and in the arts and sciences. As François Furet writes: 'The word
"civilization" itself, which dates from this period in both French
and English, was invented to express this drive of enlightened
society toward what ought to be, the conviction of being on the
right road, the certitude that the future was in fact infinite and
that history had a purpose'.[14] These ideas and criteria were
employed by practically all the leading scientists of man in that
age, who thereby widened their psychological, anthropological,
and historical perspectives on what man was, or, more accurately,
on what man has become during the ages. And Vico must surely
have been familiar with the term and its modern connotations,
as these informed, for example, Giannone's *Civil History of the
Kingdom of Naples* (1723).

The proponents of 'civilization' objected to the holistic
Aristotelian-Christian theory that attributed the progressive
refinement of humanity to some innate divine illumination, as
well as, and more fiercely, to its secular, excessively rationalistic
and individualistic version of thinkers like Hobbes, who let man
advance – or, as Rousseau would have it, fall – from the state of
nature to the state of civility solely on account of individual
natural-rational capacities. Thus, Adam Ferguson in his *Essay on
the History of Civil Society* (1767), argued against the latter that 'not
only the individual advances from infancy to mankind, but the
species itself from rudeness to civilization', and that an adequate
account of the growth of man must relate it to the general conditions and processes within which it occurs. In order to explain
how men in the pre-social condition, who were 'possessed of mere
animal sensibility, without any exercise of the faculties that render
them superior to brutes, without any political union, without any

---

[14] François Furet, 'Civilization and Barbarism in Gibbon's History', *Daedalus*, 105 (1976),
p. 209.

means of explaining their sentiments', nevertheless managed to civilize themselves – it was necessary to rethink the very notion of man from deeper and wider socio-historical perspectives, so that the 'disposition to friendship or enmity, his reason, his use of language and articulate sounds be retained in his description, as the wing and the paw are in the eagle and the lion'. Noting that 'art itself is natural to man', Ferguson thus considered man as being a widely 'artistic' rather than narrowly 'rationalistic' creature, one that is 'destined from the first age of his being to invent and to contrive'.[15]

As we shall see, in his theory of civilization Vico too emphasized the 'poetic' rather than the 'rational' characteristics of man – the ability to speculate rather than calculate in thought, to express rather than designate in language, to invent rather than imitate norms and means in practical life. He differed, however, from his contemporary theorists of civilization in one crucial aspect: he considered the *mondo civile* to be the last but not the final, let alone the perfect, stage in the socio-historical development of man. The ıact that modern society was technically more advanced in its manners, laws, arts and sciences did not necessarily imply that modern people have become more civil in their religious, moral, and aesthetic dispositions. For, as Vico well saw, the process of civilization which led to the refinement of human behaviour also caused what we nowadays call more repression, alienation, and – to use Vico's term – 'intellectual barbarism'.

Following Vico, we may perceive a different, rather negative, reason as to why 'civilization' became such a topical issue in the age of the Enlightenment: it indicates that the definitive criteria for distinguishing the civil from the barbarous had become more problematic than ever before; it implies that the Europeans were no longer sure about their own civility and its progress; and that in a way they had become aware of what Freud would call the *discontents* of civility, sensing that modern society was incompatible with, and even destructive to, their innermost human necessities and aspirations. According to Stuart Hampshire, what renders eighteenth-century philosophy truly 'modern' is its 'conception of alienation', namely the recognition of a new relation between

---

[15] Adam Ferguson, *An Essay on the History of Civil Society*, ed. D. Forbes (Edinburgh: Edinburgh University Press, 1966), pp. 2–3, 6.

'human beings and their non-human environment'. This was 'a period of sudden realisation that forms of life human beings have developed are beginning (or are liable) to produce modern and ugly excrescences'.[16] Already, indeed, in his much-quoted essay on the Cannibals (1578) Montaigne had realized that there was something wrong with the traditional criteria by which his fellow Europeans have commonly judged who and what is 'civilized':

I think there is nothing barbarous and savage in that nation, from what I have been told, except that each man calls barbarism whatever is not his own practice; for indeed it seems we have no other test of truth and reason than the example and pattern of the opinions and customs of the country we live in. There is always the perfect religion, the perfect government, the perfect and accomplished manners in all things . . . Those nations, then, seem to me barbarous in this sense, that they have been fashioned very little by the human mind, and are still very close to their original naturalness. The laws of nature still rule them, very little corrupted by ours.[17]

Such critical reflections were bound to undermine established conceptions about the immanent rationality of the classical-Christian heritage of Western civilization. Because although there were still many European scholars who held to the belief in the privileged historical case of Western civilization, for the majority of them the discovery of primitive societies in the New World served as a kind of 'historical demonstration' that (as Locke put it) 'In the beginning all the world was America', namely that all men were initially – and remained essentially – ignoble savages.

For European scholars in the sixteenth and seventeenth centuries, with their limited vision of what was possible in the variability of beliefs and customs, the savage cults in evidence in the New World appeared merely similar to ancient paganism, but they were still inclined to reason these similarities away by various theories of diffusion and corruption of original, that is, the old Biblical, messages. For the scholars of the Enlightenment, in contrast, the equation of what they saw among the savages and what they knew about the ancients was a 'shock of recognition': upon discovering among the savages religious beliefs and rites similar to

[16] Stuart Hampshire, 'What is Modern in Eighteenth-Century Philosophy?', *Studies in Eighteenth-Century Culture*, 2 (1971), p. 68.
[17] Michel de Montaigne, 'On Cannibals', *The Complete Works of Montaigne*, pp. 152–3.

their own they were forced, as it were, to turn inward and reflect upon the pagan origins of their own sacred lore, to reappraise whether, and to what extent, their own sublime Christian creeds were still savage and profane.[18] Thus, when Fontenelle speculated on the possible natural event which could have caused the Indians in Peru to believe their outrageous myth about a god who had intercourse with a mortal woman, then surely very few of his pious readers could fail to understand its message.[19] As Frank Manuel has observed,

Pagan religion became a living flesh-and-blood reality which was mirrored in contemporary barbarism. The development of this awareness was gradual; it required a number of generations before the two images, the literary one of the classics and the existential one of the savage or civilized heathen world, interpenetrated to such a degree that men not only reported conformities but recognized them as common human experiences.[20]

Now, the equation of Christian symbols and sacraments with pagan and savage cults had already been used by anti-Christian polemicists in antiquity. During the sixteenth and seventeenth centuries this age-old charge was revived, and much intensified, by the sectarian warfare of Protestants against Catholics. However, as one modern authority has noted, such radical attempts at showing an exact conformity between popery and the religion of the Romans, and claims that the Catholics had derived their beliefs and rites entirely from that of their heathen ancestors (as Conyers Middleton, a Cambridge don, did in his *Letter from Rome* of 1729) were bound to undermine the privileged religious position of the attackers themselves, because it 'served merely to underline the obvious – namely, the descent of contemporary religious doctrine from earlier forms of religious expression'.[21] Though such

18 As Frank Manuel has noted: 'The science of mythology broke the bounds of classical antiquity and came to be related first to the investigation of primitive religion and soon to the fundamental psychic problem of the age, the very nature of religion itself'. *The Eighteenth Century Confronts the Gods* (Cambridge, Mass.: Harvard University Press, 1958), p. 6.

19 Bernard de Fontenelle, 'Of the Origins of Fables' (1724), in *The Rise of Modern Mythology, 1680–1860*, ed. and tr. B. Feldman and R. D. Richardson (Bloomington: Indiana University Press, 1972), p. 15.

20 Manuel, *The Eighteenth Century Confronts the Gods*, p. 19.

21 Margaret T. Hodgen, *Early Anthropology in the Sixteenth and Seventeenth Centuries* (Philadelphia: University of Pennsylvania Press, 1974), p. 329.

concrete observations on the mythical origins and development of Christianity would be boldly stated in general theories of religious history only by later thinkers (D'Holbach, Hume, and Gibbon have become the most 'notorious' names) their main iconoclastic implications for traditional forms of Christian religiosity were already patently clear to Vico and his contemporaries in the Catholic stronghold of Naples.[22] Vico, for one, surely got this impression from Bayle's depiction of the transition from paganism to Christianity as an easy and natural flow of images, ideas, and rites.[23] The various schools of deism, which claimed to have discovered the initial psychic necessities underlying all the various religious theories and practices, emphatically resuscitated the ancient Lucretian-Ciceronian tradition of 'natural religion', and amplified the impression that, indeed, even the most advanced religions consisted in, or at least can be reduced to, some basic primitive beliefs.

Thus, in the wake of anthropological discoveries and comparisons, and amidst many discussions on the nature and merits of primitivism in religion and poetry (as in the famous Quarrel of the Ancients and the Moderns on the Homeric epics), Christian theologians and classical scholars were drawn into polemics on the historical origins and poetical composition of the Bible. Around the middle of the century, when Bishop Lowth's *On the Sacred Poetry of the Hebrews* appeared (1753), it was quite common to view the Scriptures as a kind of 'oriental mythology'. But, in opposition to the rationalists, the new critics sought to prove that mythology, in itself, was not false. The fact that the Bible was 'mythological' did not necessarily mean that it lacked historical authenticity and veracity. In their inquiries into the psychological and historical origins of pagan mythologies – they hoped to shed new light on the sacred origins of their own culture.[24]

It is my contention that this widespread recognition of the pagan-mythological aspects in the Christian civilization and the

---

[22] As can be seen, for example, in Pietro Giannone's *Civil History of the Kingdom of Naples* (1723), where the author construes the city's civil history according to common objective criteria and explicitly refutes Augustine's qualitative criteria for the distinction between the two *civitates*.

[23] Gianfranco Cantelli, *Vico e Bayle: Premesse per un confronto* (Naples: Guida, 1971).

[24] Christian Hartlich and Walter Sachs, *Der Ursprung des Mythosbegriffes in der modernen Bibelwissenschaft* (Tübingen: Kohr, 1952).

attempts to explain its history in utterly natural terms form the background to Vico's historical inquiries in the *New Science*. The crucial issue in his work, I would argue, is the foundation, not of ancient paganism, but rather of modern Christianity. I shall try to show how, during the many years of his immersion in the mythological lore of the ancients, Vico must have realized that the mythopoeic constitution of human reality was valid not only in the case of 'barbarian histories' but also – and perhaps especially so – in the case of 'sacred history'. Vico had, in short, to tackle the problem of the survival of essentially 'mythical' components in the Hebrew-Christian tradition. The main aim of Vico's work – an endeavour which I would call *The rehabilitation of myth* – was to fend off the rationalist attack on the myths of this tradition by elevating them to a higher level of understanding. His aim was to explain under what psychological and historical conditions these modes of religious comprehension were necessarily created, what higher metaphysical truths they served, and, ultimately, why they still persist in the collective imagination of mankind.

Vico's discovery of the mythical foundations of reality resembles, and most likely draws on, the basic world view of the humanists in the Italian Renaissance. As Eugenio Garin has noted, the lives and works of such humanists as Ficino or Alberti were permeated by the Neoplatonic sensation that the world as it appeared to them was not real, that they were only dreaming, or rather living in a dream that mankind has created for itself, its civilization. Garin quotes Alberti as saying: 'There was a time . . . when I was in the habit of basing my views on truth, my zeal on considerations of utility, my words and expressions on my innermost thoughts . . . But I have learnt now to adapt my views to the prevailing superstitions, my zeal to caprices, and to frame all my words so as to be capable of deception'. For Alberti, then, myths were all that we have, and the noble task of the man of letters in this chaotic world was to overcome the melancholy by myth-making. The Renaissance scholars did not so much believe myth, as they believed in myth: 'These myths console us and create the illusions and seductions of our daily life'.[25]

In the same vein Vico would conclude that the history of the

`25 Eugenio Garin, *Science and Civil Life in the Italian Renaissance*, tr. P. Munz (Garden City, N.Y.: Doubleday, 1978), pp. 6–7.

mondo civile does not proceed, nor can it be understood, according to strict rational logic, but according to what he terms 'poetic logic', namely the logic which its original makers, the theological poets, have used to create it:

From these first men, stupid, insensate, and horrible beasts, all the philosophers and philologians should have begun their investigations of the wisdom of the ancient gentiles . . . And they should have begun with metaphysics, which seeks its proofs not in the external world but within the modifications of the mind of him who meditates it. For since this world of nations has certainly been made by men, it is within these modifications that its principles should have been sought . . . Hence poetic wisdom, the first wisdom of the gentile world, must have begun with a metaphysics not rational and abstract like that of learned men now, but felt and imagined as that of these first men must have been, who, without power of ratiocination, were all robust sense and vigorous imagination. This metaphysics was their poetry, a faculty born with them . . . born of their ignorance of causes, for ignorance, the mother of wonder, made everything wonderful to men who were ignorant of everything. (NS/374–5)

Vico's appeal to the modern scholars of humanity to begin their investigations from the 'metaphysics' of the first men is redolent of Aristotle's well-known attempt to build his *metaphysica* on similar anthropo-historical observations. Like Aristotle, Vico perceives metaphysics according to its strict etymological meaning: it comprises any attempt by human beings to transcend their immediate physical reality – 'for the name means as much' (NS/2). And, in a series of propositions (NS/180–90), he establishes that what incites and enables man to go beyond the world of phenomenal objects is the ability to wonder about them. Here too he closely follows Aristotle, who, in a famous passage in the opening chapter of his *Metaphysics*, says that

it is owing to their wonder that men both now begin and at first began to philosophize; they wondered originally at the obvious difficulties, then advanced little by little and stated difficulties about the greater matters, e.g. about the phenomena of the moon and those of the sun and of the stars, and about the genesis of the universe. And a man who is puzzled and wonders thinks himself ignorant (whence even the lover of myth is in a sense a lover of wisdom for the myth is composed of wonders).[26]

---

[26] Aristotle, *Metaphysica* 982b 13–19, in *The Works of Aristotle*, tr. W. D. Ross (Oxford: Oxford University Press, 1928).

From Aristotle's day and through to our century this apology for mythmaking has reverberated in the works of many authors – Dante and Joyce are perhaps the most noteworthy – and Vico also developed some of its implicit meanings.[27] However, Vico went much farther than Aristotle in his effort to extend the efficacy of mythmaking beyond the very limited sphere of the 'first wonder'. For Aristotle the impact of mythical images was confined only to the initial stage of metaphysical speculation, a stage which had been duly superseded by ever more refined observations and rational theories. Vico held, in contrast, that the original poetic vision of the object and its mythical expression have survived in all its later conceptions. He did not believe, as Aristotle did, that the modern physical theories could, or should, do away with the original metaphysical visions of the ancients, but, on the contrary: that our modern critical reason and sciences must be revitalized by the topical ingenuity and the arts of the ancients. He was most emphatic in his contention that our modern 'civil world' was not only created by the poetic fictions of the first men, but still consists in them – insofar as their fictions permeate all our social practices: they persist in linguistic metaphors, religious myths, marital and burial rites, national feasts, and in all the anonymous and collective customs we live by.

The failure to literally come-to-terms with that primitive, yet highly pervasive and effective, mode of thought in human history weakened, in his view, the social theories of the Natural Law school in his time, Grotius, Selden and Pufendorf. These 'three princes of this doctrine', he maintained, failed to understand human beings in – and on – their own poetic terms; they began, as he put it, 'in the middle; that is, with the latest times of the civilized nations (and thus of men enlightened by fully developed natural reason) from which the philosophers emerged and rose to meditation of a perfect idea of justice' (NS/394). They thus failed to discover the real reasons which have always motivated human beings, even in the modern times, to sustain themselves in civil

---

27 Alfred N. Whitehead comments that 'The father of European philosophy, in one of his many moods of thought, laid down the axiom that the deeper truths must be adumbrated by myths. Surely the subsequent history of Western thought has amply justified his feeling intuition'. *Modes of Thought* (N.Y.: Free Press, 1938), p. 14. Dante's indebtedness to this Aristotelian 'axiom' has been fully exposed in Patrick Boyde, *Dante Philomythes and Philosopher* (Cambridge: Cambridge University Press, 1981).

associations: the archaic, a-rational, anonymous, and collective forces of mythical traditions, and not their own 'fully developed natural reason'. In the first edition of the *New Science* Vico explains that Grotius erred because as 'a Socinian, holding that early man was good rather than wicked', he supposed that man in the state of nature, 'solitary, weak, and lacking in all his needs' as he must have been, was nevertheless reasonable enough to react rationally to natural necessity, and thus was able to enter 'society when the tribulations of bestial solitude made him aware [of all this]'. Pufendorf, in Vico's (rather crude) view, held to similar Hobbesian views of human nature, and believed in the ability of 'early man' to overcome the difficulties and dangers of life in the state of nature solely by virtue of his rationalized utilitarian instincts. Selden's view of human nature was more historical than philosophical, but of the same kind, as he too sought to establish the primacy of some original and universal rules of morality among the gentile nations: he supposed that these descendants of Noah carried within them his Seven Commands, which, for Selden, formed the moral constitution of mankind.[28]

What these theorists and their followers offer, Vico concludes, is only 'the natural law of the philosophers (or moral theologians) [which] is that of reason', and not 'the natural law of the gentes, [which] is that of utility and force' (NS/1084). In their legal-historical treatises on the process of civilization the above-mentioned theorists gave us only their own ideal enlightened concepts of justice, and not the actual primitive images of justice which guided the gentile peoples in their long and hazardous process of civilization. The latter, Vico tells us,

> were for a long period incapable of truth and of reason, which is the fount of that inner justice by which the intellect is satisfied. This justice was practised by the Hebrews, who, illuminated by the true God, were by his divine law forbidden even to have unjust thoughts, about which no mortal lawgiver ever troubled himself . . . This same inner justice was later reasoned out by the philosophers, who did not arise until two thousand years after the nations were founded. In the meantime the nations were governed by the certainty of authority, that is, by the same criterion which is used by our metaphysical criticism; namely, the common sense of the human race, on which the consciences of all nations repose. (NS/350)

---

[28] Vico, *The First New Science*, pars. 16–18, *Selected Writings*, pp. 86–7.

In their admiration for the classical achievements in practical statecraft the modern theorists of Natural Law failed to see the historical inadequacy of the old Aristotelian-Ciceronian belief in some original principles of rationality which constitute all human societies. The search for these rational reasons for association led such political theorists as Hobbes to conceive of political 'authority' in terms which, for Vico, seemed utterly implausible. Hobbes' notion that this authority consists in some social 'covenant', an imaginary yet very real constitution of rights and duties to which all people who live in community must necessarily be rationally obliged, exemplified for Vico, quite literally, the philosophers' failure of 'not giving certainty to their reasoning by appeal to the authority of the philologians' (NS/138)! Hobbes and those followers of his who sought to explain and justify the emergence of political authority solely by appeal to the enlightened (however egotistical) reasoning of each individual failed, in Vico's view, to recognize the true savage and poetic nature of the 'authority' on which the ancient civil communities, an authority which was not at all rational but 'fortified by frightful religions and sanctioned by dreadful punishments' (NS/522). The 'three princes' of modern Natural Law failed because, like their predecessors in antiquity, they did not predicate their philosophical theories on proper philological observations of the relationship between man and community. And, Vico suggests, they failed to do so because they themselves were not, or at least did not regard themselves as, men fully rooted in their communities.

For the theorists of Natural Law since antiquity, what mattered were only individuals, not groups; in their accounts, it was always the individual who makes the community, rather than the other way round. By imagining the original state of nature to be a state of solitary 'men living together according to reason', Hobbes deduced that the individuals, inasmuch as they are all equally free and rational, are, as they have always been, the only sovereign 'authors' of their communities: 'no man is obliged by a covenant, whereof he is not author'.[29] And because society was perceived in such strictly individualistic and rationalistic terms as a voluntary association of autonomous and sovereign agents, any account of its origin and composition was methodologically confined to the

---

[29] Thomas Hobbes, *Leviathan*, ed. M. Oakeshott (N.Y.: Collier Books, 1962), p. 126.

subjective feelings, volition, and utilitarian strategies of its makers. Like their counterparts in antiquity, Hobbes, Spinoza and their followers held to 'a moral philosophy of solitaries: the Epicurean, of idlers inclosed in their own little garden; the Stoic, of contemplatives who endeavour to feel no emotion'.[30]

For Vico, in contrast, men in community are not just 'solitaries' living together radically apart from, and even against, each other, but rather individuals 'whose nature has this principal property: that of being social [*d'essere socievoli*]' (NS/2). Thus, even though he shared some of the basic assumptions of the Stoic-Epicurean philosophers and maintained, as Hobbes did, that 'the civil institutions by which men may live in human society' are born 'out of the passions of men each bent on his private advantage', he did not attribute this transformation to the calculative reason of the individual agent, but rather to what he called, rather enigmatically, the 'divine legislative mind' (NS/133) – a phrase which connotes, as I shall explain later on, that particular 'mentality' common to religious communities, where laws are sanctioned by appeal to their divine origin.

Vico's entire social theory consists in this new holistic conception of the 'reason' which constitutes society. As I have already hinted, in his notion of religious-legislative *mente* Vico consciously posited over against the narrowly rationalistic 'reason' of the individual – so magnified by the Cartesian *cogito* and by modern Epicureans like Hobbes and Stoics like Spinoza – a contrary model of the mind, based on a collective-historical 'reason' of the common people, which he termed, significantly, *senso comune*, unfortunately (even if inevitably) translated as 'common sense', but in any case such that, as Hans-Georg Gadamer has rightly seen, in Vico's usage it 'obviously does not mean only that general faculty in all men, but the sense that founds community'.[31] Vico's major achievement as a social theorist was to show that indeed it was this latter kind of reason – not a rational, but a mythopoeic one – which underlies all societies, nations, and civilizations. If, as he states in the beginning of his work, 'metaphysic should know God's providence in public moral institutions or civil customs, by which the nations have come into being and maintain themselves

---

[30] Vico, *The Autobiography*, p. 122.
[31] Hans-Georg Gadamer, *Truth and Method* (New York: Seabury Press, 1975), p. 21.

in the world' (NS/5) then its primary task must be to show how the pagans, devoid of both naturally-given *ratio* or divinely-ordained *revelatio*, were able to redeem themselves through their man-made *mythos*. And this was precisely what Vico set out to do: 'Last of all, to state the idea of the work in the briefest summary . . . [it reveals] the order in which the human minds of the gentiles have been raised from earth to heaven', namely by their gradual discovery of God (NS/2). In the process of civilization, as Vico saw it, pagan myth and Christian revelation were not so much opposed and contradictory modes of religious cognition, but simply different or, more precisely, counter-analogous means by which God disclosed Himself to men according to their different mental capacities to receive and to perceive His messages. And hence, inasmuch as the pagan myths 'raised the human minds of the gentiles from earth to heaven', and thus made them aware of the metaphysical reality, upon which alone they could sanction their civil laws and institutions, the archaic pagan myths may be said to have fulfilled the same moral and social functions in the history of the gentile nations as did the Scriptures in the history of the Judaeo-Christian nations. Or, as he put it in the *Autobiography*: 'He discovers new historical principles of philosophy, and first of all a metaphysics of the human race. That is to say, a natural theology of all nations by which each people naturally created by itself its own gods through a certain natural instinct that man has for divinity'.[32]

These critical reflections on the efficacy of 'natural theology', or 'divination', among 'all nations' were distinctly Catholic. Vico not only derived them from specifically Catholic sources – principally Augustine – but also presented and elaborated them as such. He duly saw that his main antagonists – the theorists of the Natural Law – predicated their social theories on distinctly Protestant notions of individuality, rationality, and utility. In the *Autobiography* he thus contends that 'to the glory of the Catholic religion, the principles of all gentile wisdom human and divine have been discovered in this our age and in the bosom of the true Church, and Vico had thereby procured for our Italy the advantage of not envying Protestant Holland, England or Germany their three princes of this science'.[33]

---

[32] Vico, *The Autobiography*, p. 167.   [33] Vico, *The Autobiography*, p. 173.

The above words, sincere as they are, cannot disguise the fact that Vico's Catholicism was very problematic. This is most obvious in his attempt to overcome the apparent contradiction between spontaneous mythopoeic creativity and pre-ordained (divine or natural) patterns in the history of mankind. As we shall now see, one of the most difficult tasks of his *New Science* was to prove, on logical and historical grounds, that in the construction of the civil human world human freedom and divine (or natural) necessity are not contradictory, but rather complementary.

II

Vico's dilemma can be formulated so: while committing himself to 'a truth beyond all question: that the world of civil society has certainly been made by men', he remained, at the same time, equally committed to another, seemingly contradictory truth: the Catholic belief in the fallibility of humanity and the inevitability of active divine direction throughout its life and history. In order to combine these two apparently incompatible convictions, Vico had to find new terms, which would clarify in what way the *mondo civile*, though 'certainly' made by free and creative human agents, was also, and more 'truly', created in a very determined pattern by a superior agency. Thus, towards the end of the work Vico declares that while 'it is true that men have themselves made this world of nations' it is equally true that

this world without doubt has issued from a mind [*mente*] often diverse, at times quite contrary, and always superior to the particular ends that men had proposed to themselves; which narrow ends made means to serve wider ends it has always employed to preserve the human race upon this earth. Men mean to gratify their bestial lust and abandon their offspring, and they inaugurate the chastity of marriage from which the families arise. The fathers mean to exercise without restraint their paternal power over their clients, and they subject them to the civil powers from which the cities arise . . . That which did all this was mind, for men did it with intelligence; it was not fate, for they did it by choice, not chance, for the results of their always so acting are perpetually the same. (NS/1108)

Now this and similar assertions in the *New Science* make it clear that Vico did not analyze the civil world in strictly secular terms, nor in traditional theological ones, but rather, to use the idiom recently coined by Amos Funkenstein, he practised a kind of 'secular theology'.[34] Like many philosophers at the time – Descartes, Newton, Leibniz, Bayle and others – Vico too was torn between the dictates of faith and reason. He tried to mediate between them by crossing the traditional disciplinary boundaries between theology and science, and by blending the issues and genres of these hitherto separate fields of knowledge. He did this by subjecting divine matters to secular inspection, as well as by exposing human and natural affairs to metaphysical illumination. As the passage quoted above indicates, in his work he examined scholastic terms like Divine Providence in a secular context of inquiry, using new empirical tests and proofs (rather than old theological ones) to check their efficacy and to imbue them with new relevant meaning.

More significantly still, Vico's basic attitude in his attempt to mediate between providential and human creativity, rather than set them over against each other, is characteristic of his peculiar 'mediative' mode of inquiry in all other matters which involved 'human choice'. As I have noted already, Vico in his *New Science* was largely concerned with a particular kind of problems, or 'essential tensions', arising out of a basic duality of human nature – a duality reflected by the term itself – between the 'human' and the 'natural' in man. This tension permeated the conflicts between mind and body in man, between *nomos* and *physis* in social life, between spontaneous creativity and pre-ordained divine or natural patterns of development in the history of mankind. I have also noted that in dealing with such problems of freedom vs. determinism in the human world Vico devised a unique method of mediation. He tried, as a rule, to resolve the essential tension between freedom and determinism – the two extreme *absolute* positions – by emphasizing the *relative* freedom of human creativity. As Karl Löwith has observed, what Vico 'reviews in the one thousand and one hundred and twelve paragraphs of the *New Science* is the *semi-creative* city of fallen man'.[35] As we shall see later on, he rejected the polar positions of both Calvin and Pelagius as being too extreme and exclusive, and opted instead for the middle-position of Augustine: like the latter, he would argue that

---

[34] Amos Funkenstein, *Theology and the Scientific Imagination from the Middle Ages to the Seventeenth Century* (N.J.: Princeton University Press, 1986), pp. 3–9.
[35] Karl Löwith, *Meaning in History* (Chicago: The University of Chicago Press, 1949), p. 134.

in making their civil world people have not been fully determined by divine or natural necessities, nor motivated solely by their rational volition, but rather by what they themselves have created – their traditional beliefs, customs and institutions. In the first edition of the *New Science* Vico uses the metaphor of God as the 'divine architect' and people as 'builders' of the social world, but is careful not to imbue this metaphor with too rationalistic meanings, emphasizing that God 'has sent forth the world of nations with vulgar wisdom as its rule. Vulgar wisdom is a common sense possessed by each people or nation, which regulates our social lives, in all our human activities, in such a way that they should be in accord with whatsoever everyone in the people or nations feels in common.'[36]

This 'mediative' solution is evident in the passage quoted above. Faced with the dilemma concerning the creation of the civil world – either by Divine or by natural-human will – Vico looked for a solution that would mediate between, retain and transcend both: he introduced a middle-agency between God and Man which he termed Mind (*mente*). Vico's assertion that the civil world 'without doubt has issued from a mind often diverse, at times quite contrary, and always superior to the particular ends which men had proposed to themselves' has become a major bone of contention among Vichian scholars, because it poses serious problems for both the Catholic and the secular interpretations of his work. As regards this passage, scholars have been unable to decide, as perhaps Vico himself could not, whether the Mind in question is wholly transcendent over against the minds of the individuals, or whether it is immanently inherent in them.[37] It is clear that, in using this term, Vico purports to explain the fact that people in society come to take a common and constructive course of action while keeping with their own egotistical volition. Although each member in society acts only in accordance with his or her own will, they all ultimately do things regardless of or even

---

[36] Vico, *The First Science*, par. 46, in *Selected Writings*, p. 105.
[37] Leon Pompa, *Vico: A Study of the 'New Science'* (Cambridge: Cambridge University Press, 1975), pp. 51–61, sums up the main modern interpretations of Vico's concept of 'Providence'. On the historical-theological meanings of the concept and its secularization in Vico and later authors, see Amos Funkenstein's *Theology and the Scientific Imagination* (New Jersey: Princeton University Press, 1986), pp. 202–89. For a brilliant exposition of Vico's 'mediative' solution, see Sandra Luft, 'Creative Activity and the Secularization of Providence', *Studies in Eighteenth-Century Culture*, 9 (1979), pp. 337–55.

in spite of that will, as if obeying a prior and superior will. What is not entirely clear from Vico's presentation is whether this latter kind of will is that of God, as his Catholic interpreters maintain, or whether, as his radical interpreters claim, that will is the 'general will' of the social group.

The most obvious interpretation, and certainly the one most strongly implied by Vico, is that this *mente* is synonymous with the divine providential intelligence. Vico indeed attributes to *mente* all the traditional characteristics of providence, describing it as a supernatural agency which operates in the human world according to its own will and plan, regardless of what men want and do, and 'without human discernment or counsel' (NS/342). There is no reason to doubt his firm Catholic beliefs on that matter as some commentators, in his time and ours, have done. And yet, though Vico was thoroughly committed to the transcendent-supernatural conception of providence, he was aware that this conception, if pushed to its extreme conclusions – as Calvin had done – would lead to a deterministic view of divine providence as being impervious to human volition and creativity. Vico did not doubt, of course, that in an *absolute* sense of the term God was the creator of the civil world, just as He was the creator of the world of nature. He maintained, however, that since God's mode of creativity was unique to Him – 'For God, in his purest intelligence, knows things, and, by knowing them, creates them' – the really crucial problem was to explain the *relative*, yet highly effective, way in which human beings have created their own world. Yet, as we shall now see, Vico insisted that the creation of human institutions has throughout history been closely determined by the capacity of people to receive and perceive divine institutions. The 'history of human ideas' which he proclaims is, in fact, a history of the human perceptions of the divine. Thus, in one of the most resounding, and typically obscure, orations in the *New Science*, Vico declares:

To complete the establishment of the principles which have been adopted for this Science, it remains . . . to discuss the method which it should follow. It must begin where its subject matter began. We must therefore go back with the philologians and fetch it from the stones of Deucalion and Pyrrha, from the rocks of Amphion, from the men who sprang from the furrows of Cadmus or the hard oak of Vergil. With the philosophers we must fetch it from the frogs of Epicurus, from the cicadas of Hobbes, from the simpletons of Grotius; from the men cast into this world without care or aid of God, or whom Pufendorf speaks. This is the science the philologians and philosophers have given us of the principles of humanity! Our treatment of it must take its start from the time these creatures began to think humanly. In their monstrous savagery and unbridled bestial freedom there was no means to tame the former or bridle the latter but the frightful thought of some divinity, the fear of whom is the only powerful means of reducing to duty a liberty gone wild. To discover the way in which this first human thinking arose in the gentile world, we encountered exasperating difficulties, which have cost us the research of a good twenty years. We had to descend from these human and refined natures of ours to those quite wild and savage natures, which we cannot at all imagine and can comprehend only with great effort. We must start from some notion of God such as even the most savage, wild and monstrous men do not lack. That notion we show to be this: that man, fallen into despair of all the succours of nature, desires something superior to save him. But something superior to nature is God, and this is the light God has shed on all men . . . We must therefore proceed from a vulgar metaphysics, such as we shall find the theology of the poets to have been, and seek by its aid that frightful thought of some divinity which imposed form and measure on the bestial passions of these lost men and thus transformed them into human passions. (NS/338–40)

Vico built his entire theory on the classical observation – which Machiavelli and his followers strongly reaffirmed – that 'wherever a people has grown savage in arms so that human laws have no longer any place among them, the only powerful means of reducing it is religion' (NS/177).[38] He surmised that in this case, as indeed in all others, the etymological and historical meanings of the term reveal its essence: religion, he correctly established, comes from *religere*, 'to tie', 'to bound', and that, he argued, is precisely what religion has accomplished throughout history – it has tied human beings to God and by so doing has also bound them together (NS/503). Vico inveighed against Bayle, who thought that there could be 'nations in the world without any knowledge of God', and against Polybius, who suggested that 'if there were philosophers in the world there would be no need in

---

[38] Historians of religious thought have commonly ignored Vico. The best contextual study of Vico in that tradition is still Frank Manuel, 'Vico: The "Giganti" and their Joves', in *The Eighteenth Century Confronts the Gods* (Cambridge, Mass.: Harvard University Press, 1959), pp. 149–67. See also Samuel Preus, *Explaining Religion: Criticism and Theory from Bodin to Freud* (New Haven: Yale University Press, 1987), pp. 59–83.

the world of religions' (NS/1110). Historical experience, Vico was convinced, would prove both of them wrong. His own investigations convinced him that 'if religion is lost among the peoples, they have nothing left to enable them to live in society: no shield of defence, nor means of counsel, nor basis of support, nor even a form by which they may exist in the world at all' (NS/1109). He was equally opposed to the pragmatist theorists of religion, to thinkers like Machiavelli, Hobbes, or Spinoza, who sought to explain the indispensability of religion in strictly natural-historical terms, reasoning that primitive peoples – or rather their rulers – cunningly invented divine concepts and institutions for their own utility. On the whole, though he was much impressed by the Lucretian attempt to naturalize religion, he rejected it and its modern modifications, as being inimical to the Catholic doctrine of revelation; yet, in this case, as in so many similar ones, he tried to mediate between the opposed doctrines rather than setting them over against each other. He opted for an 'occasionalist' solution, namely for a position which retained both kinds of explanation, arguing that the religious process could not have occurred without some prior act of divine intervention, without an 'occasion' which aroused in men the very idea of the divine.[39] His aim was to show that it was

divine providence [which] initiated the process by which the fierce and violent were brought from their outlaw state to humanity and by which nations were instituted among them. It did so by awakening in them a confused idea of some divinity, which they in their ignorance attributed to that to which it did not belong. Thus through the terror of this imagined divinity, they began to put themselves in some order. (NS/178).

Vico, thus, affirmed the axiom that it was indeed providential agency which set the whole religious process in motion. And yet, it is quite clear that the emphasis in this axiom, as in the entire *New Science*, is on the way in which the *human* mind has perceived the *divine* mind, not the other way round. The real problem, and the only possible task, of the historian of religion, is not to discover

---

[39] Vico's affinity to the modern occasionalist theory of 'accommodation' has been elaborated by Amos Funkenstein, 'Natural Science and Social Theory: Hobbes, Spinoza, Vico', in *Vico's Science of Humanity*, ed. G. Tagliacozzo and D. P. Verene (Baltimore: The Johns Hopkins University Press, 1976), pp. 187–212.

what God thought and did about man, but rather what man thought and did about God. Or, to put it in the more precise technical terms Vico uses, the task was not so much to demonstrate the act of *Revelation* – the action of the divine agency towards men, but rather that of *Divination* – the reaction of human beings towards God. And so, though he certainly believed in the Biblical revelation and other sacred acts in which God disclosed meanings to man, Vico was, as it were, more fascinated by the pagan acts in which human beings gave meaning to God. His aim was to show that while, on the one hand, they have themselves indeed created their civil institutions 'according to their own ideas', on the other hand, these very ideas have been inspired and formed by their growing awareness of the divine. In his work therefore Vico did not so much enquire what 'divine providence' actually did to, but rather how it had been perceived by, human beings. As we shall see later on, he limited the role of divine providence to very indirect interventions through utterly natural phenomena of thunder, lightning, and similar 'occasions' which, when

apprehended by such human sense as could have been possessed by rough, wild, and savage men who in despair of nature's succours desired something superior to nature to save them . . . permitted them to be deceived into fearing the false divinity of Jove because he could strike them with lightning. Thus, through the thick clouds of those first tempests, intermittently lit by those flashes, they made this great truth: that divine providence watches over the welfare of all mankind. So that this science becomes in this principal aspect a rational civil theology of divine providence, which began in the vulgar wisdom of the lawgivers, who founded the nations by contemplating God under the attribute of providence, and which is completed by the esoteric wisdom of philosophers, who give a rational demonstration of it in their natural theology. (NS/385)

Vico was aware that any conception of Providence which curbed the theological claims for its absolute transcendence was dangerously close to the classical theogonic theories of Xenophanes, Epicurus and above all Lucretius, whose famous description in the fifth book of *On the Nature of Things* of the human creation of the gods nevertheless exercised a strong and lasting fascination on Vico.[40] In his time these theories were being revived and further

---

[40] On Vico's youthful infatuation with Lucretius, see Fausto Nicolini, *La Giovinezza di G. B. Vico* (Bari: Laterza, 1932), pp. 120–6. On the pervasion of Lucretian themes in the *New*

expounded in expanded fashion by natural philosophers of religion like Spinoza, Fontenelle and Pierre Bayle.[41] Their attempts to elaborate the psychological and political conditions under which human beings have come to conceive of the notion of providence seemed to have fully naturalized it; and this approach was thus bound, as Vico duly feared, to deprive providence of all its supernatural meanings and sanctions. He therefore had to make clear that despite his implicit criticism of the old theological conception of providence as being too transcendent and impervious to human affairs, he certainly did not advocate such new naturalistic attempts to bring providence right down to earth. The natural philosophers of religion, he saw, failed because, confining themselves only to physical causes and laws operating in or outside man, they managed to explain only how primitive peoples must have sensed and reacted to natural reality, not how they could have perceived metaphysical reality in and through nature. Instead of reducing all religious sentiments to mere psycho-physical reactions to natural reality – as, for example in the Lucretian-Hobbesian reduction of religiosity to fear – they ought to have explained the 'metaphysical' – literally, that which leads to what lies beyond and above the merely 'physical' – urge which is so evident in these sentiments. For it was obvious to Vico that these sentiments attested to man's desire and ability to transcend earthly physical reality by living up to his own image of an alternative, heavenly ideal reality. The crucial problem was to explain, then, how these primitive peoples, immersed as they were in their own physical reality, came to conceive of metaphysical reality, how, in other words, they perceived and interpreted natural occurrences as supernatural actions. However, Vico's revealing remark about the 'natural instinct that man has for religion' implies that he shared with the deists and other proponents of natural religion the fundamental conviction that in order to understand fully the nature of *revealed* religion it is necessary, or at least useful, to understand the nature of the so-called *natural* religion.

Vico was acutely aware of what many Christian thinkers from Augustine to Descartes have intimated – that before anything

Science, see Enzo Paci, *Ingens Sylva: Saggio sulla filosofia di G. B. Vigo* (Milan: Mondadori, 1949).
41 Leo Strauss, *Spinoza's Critique of Religion*, tr. E. M. Sinclair (New York: Schocken Books, 1965), pp. 37–52.

could be revealed to them, human beings must have had an idea about that thing. And inasmuch as human beings have always perceived God in and through the world around them, all religions are in a sense religions of revelation: it was the natural world which revealed to them something of the divine and something of their own nature and destiny. In Augustine's words: 'What is now called the Christian religion, has existed among the ancients, and was not absent from the beginning of the human race, until Christ came in the flesh: from which time the true religion, which existed already, began to be called Christian'.[42] On this point as on many others, Vico followed Augustine's 'middle-way', attempting, as it were, to mediate by psychological and historical means between the natural and the revealed religions rather than setting them over against each other. In considering religion to be a general human activity that signifies a natural apprehension of God, and which as such must be analysed by the objective means of philosophy and philology, Vico shared the same principles of the proponents of natural religion; and yet, he strongly rejected their attempts to fully naturalize this activity, because this endeavour was liable to portray religion as merely a human apprehension of God, and not at all dependent upon a divine self-disclosure. His main mediative effort was to show that not only the Christian religion, but also the pagan ones, were based on an act of revelation, or what he calls (perhaps echoing Malebranche) an 'occasion' in which God revealed himself to the early peoples in a thoroughly natural way – that is, through natural objects, and by means of their natural perceptual capacities. At the same time, while elaborating this natural process in which the pagans grasped and developed their gods, he hinted at (but, for obvious reasons, never explicated) the similar natural, that is, mythopoeic, modes in which *all* human beings have always apprehended God:

And here, by the principles of this new critical art, we consider at what determinate times and on what particular occasions of human necessity or utility felt by the first men of the gentile world, they, with frightful religions which they themselves feigned and believed in, imagined first such and such gods and then such and such others. The natural theogony or generation of the gods, formed naturally in the minds of

---

[42] Augustine, *Retractiones* i.13, quoted in E. E. Evans-Pritchard, *Theories of Primitive Religion* (Oxford: Oxford University Press, 1982), p. 2.

these first men, may give us a rational chronology of the poetic history of the gods . . . [it] enables us to determine the successive epochs of the age of the gods, which correspond to certain first necessities or utilities of the human race, which everywhere had its beginnings in religion. (NS/7, 734)

'Christian theology' was the final and most sublime stage in the history of human apprehension of God, but, being human, it inevitably contained aspects from prior and inferior stages: it was, Vico says, 'a mixture' of the 'poetic theology' of the mythmakers and the 'natural theology' of the metaphysicians of antiquity with 'the loftiest revealed theology' of the Hebrew prophets and their great interpreters; in his view, 'all three [were] united in the contemplation of divine providence' in different, yet equivalent, degrees of comprehension (NS/366). The task of the historian of religion was to probe the ancient and primitive religious literature in order to explain how the abstract monotheistic conception of God evolved out of its concrete polytheistic images. As we shall now see, Vico pursued this line of inquiry in his account of the origin of religion among the pagans. He concentrated on one particular case-study, the birth of the Roman god Jupiter, to whom he consistently and significantly refers as Jove. It seems to me that Vico's choice of name in this case is not accidental: he may well have chosen the rather archaic name *Jove*, instead of the more common Jupiter, in order to accentuate, by way of its resonant association to *Jehova*, the similar theogonic aspects in the Hebrew recognition of God. And by choosing Vergil's saying *A Iove principium musae* – 'From Jove the muse began' – as the motto for the first edition of the *New Science*, Vico underlined the universal significance which man's initial poetic creation of the divine had and still has for all fallen human beings.

Vico's attempt to discover the original psychological motives for the awakening of religious cognition in the 'vulgar metaphysics' of ancient mythology is akin, in its conceptual thrust, to the attempts of modern theorists of religion to discover these motives in primitive folklore. And inasmuch as Vico conjectured that human beings must have conjured up this 'frightful thought' while experiencing extremely violent natural phenomena like the thunderstorm in the forest, his theogonic theory can be seen as an episode in the long phenomenological tradition stretching from Lucretius through Spinoza to Rudolph Otto; like the latter, Vico too tried to show how the explicit notion of God evolved out of an implicit awareness of a *mysterium tremendum*. His originality lies in his attempt to historicize this process, to find and reconstruct the actual 'occasion' of religious awakening in the post-deluvian history of the gentile nations.[43]

According to Vico, the *ferini* were the descendants of Ham and Japhet, who 'without the religion of their father Noah, which they had repudiated . . . were lost from one another by roving wild in the great forest of the earth' and 'as the result of it all were reduced, at the end of a long period, to the condition of beasts'. These people forgot the true knowledge of God, but did not lose it altogether; Vico is careful to note that they retained a certain sensual memory of it (NS/383). Their *notitia dei insita* were dormant for a long time, and only rekindled 'on certain occasions ordained by divine providence (occasions which our Science studies and discovers)' (NS/13). The most momentous occasion was that of the thunderstorm in the forest, when, 'shaken and aroused by terrible fear', they reacted as human beings always do when they are 'ignorant of the natural causes producing things, and cannot even explain them by analogy with similar things' – they 'attributed their own natures to them'. By projecting their fears and desires onto the natural phenomena revealed to them, they created, *in their own image and likeness,*

the first divine fable, the greatest they ever created: that of Jove, king and father of men and gods, in the act of hurling the lightning bolt; an image so popular, disturbing, and instructive that its creators themselves believed in it, and feared, revered, and worshipped it in frightful religions . . . and to all of the universe that came within their scope, and to all its parts, they gave the being of animate substance. This is the civil history of the expression 'All things are full of Jove' (*Iovis omnia plena*). (NS/379)

The immediate object of religious cognition at this stage is concrete nature, the true God being only a vague and veiled target which men aim at, as yet quite unaware of it; because of the limitations of their mind, which is 'naturally inclined by the senses

---

[43] The experience of 'de caelo terroribus' – 'that haunting awareness of transcendental forces peering through the cracks of the visible universe' (Philip Wheelright) – has been much discussed in the phenomenological literature on religious awakening and conversion. The classic account is Rudolph Otto, *The Idea of the Holy*, tr. J. W. Harvey (Oxford: Oxford University Press, 1950), pp. 12–24.

to see itself externally in the body' (NS/236), the *ferini* could come to recognize Him in His true metaphysical nature only in and through physical nature. For the historian of humanity this theogonic process is eminently revealing, as it records the real historical process in which these people, who 'were all robust sense and vigorous imagination', gradually came to conceive of God in less sensual and more imaginative ways, moving up, quite literally, from the strictly physical boundaries of their mind and world towards ever more metaphysical domains. The crucial moment in that process was the transition from the wholly pantheistic vision of *Jovis omnia plena*, the stage in which human beings still sensed and imagined God to be present in and identical with nature, towards the stage in which they distinguished between God and nature, ultimately realizing that God was a transcendent being beyond nature. In his theory of the emergence of religious sentiments among the pagan nations Vico thus devised a modern version of *praeparatio evangelica*, a psycho-historical rather than purely theological one, the principal aim of which was to trace the natural history of the idea of God among the nations through its changing images and attributes.

As we saw above, Vico noted that 'in that state their nature was that of men all robust bodily strength, who expressed their very violent passions by shouting and grumbling, [and therefore] they pictured the sky to themselves as a great animated body'; but, precisely because they imagined nature to be a superhuman being they surmised that it must have 'meant to tell them something by the hiss of his bolts and the clap of his thunder'. 'And thus', he concluded,

they began to exercise that natural curiosity which is the daughter of ignorance and the mother of knowledge, and which, opening the mind of man, gives birth to wonder. This characteristic still persists in the vulgar, who, when they see a comet or sundog or some other extraordinary thing in nature, and particularly in the countenance of the sky, at once turn curious and anxiously inquire what it means. (NS/377)

In that moment, Vico explains, men were no longer, or at least not only, sensually impressed by what they experienced but rather attempted to interpret it in symbolic terms; they understood natural events as divine signs:

The first men, who spoke by signs, naturally believed that lightning bolts and thunderclaps were signs made to them by Jove; whence from *nuo*, to make a sign, came *numen*, the divine will, by an idea more than sublime and worthy to express the divine majesty. They believed that Jove commanded by signs, that such signs were real words, and that nature was the language of Jove. The science of this language the gentiles universally believed to be divination, which by the Greeks was called theology, meaning the science of the language of the gods. (NS/379)

Divination, the human ability to translate the mere physical event of the 'thunderclap' into the metaphysical concept of 'God's voice', a voice which commands man through natural signs, indicates, as it were, that man has arrived at a new and higher stage of religious consciousness: its object now is not the *nuo*, the physical sign which establishes the causal relationship between God and nature, but the *numen*, the metaphysical sign which establishes the moral relationship between God and man.

Thus, inasmuch as they translated the language of the gods into human terms, and interpreted it as divine commands which they must understand and fulfil, human beings liberated themselves from the tyranny of nature: nature was now understood to be only the means, or language, by which God spoke to them. 'Thus it was fear which created gods in the world; not fear awakened in men by other men, but fear awakened in men by themselves' (NS/382). This new realization about the reciprocal relationship holding between them and God, the first truly religious cognition, found its expression in the changing 'titles' which they attributed to Jove. In the initial, utterly physical stage, in which human beings did not yet conceive the deity in reflective terms, they attributed to Jove 'the two titles, that of the best [*optimus*] in the sense of the strongest [*fortissimus*]' and 'that of the greatest [*maximus*] from his vast body, the sky itself'. Later on, however, as soon as they began to interpret and understand natural events in terms of divine signs addressed to themselves, that is as commands, laws, and duties by which they must abide or else perish, they developed the more refined religious sentiments of awe, gratitude, and hopes for salvation, and so conferred on Jove 'the title *Soter*, or saviour', and '*Stator*, stayer or establisher' (NS/379). 'Divination', the human attempt to understand the 'divine reason', thus turned out to be, for Vico, the formative impulse in 'the metaphysics of the human race', the practice 'on which all the gentile nations arose' (NS/167).

Among the pagan nations this art of divination was exercised to perfection by the *autori*, the theological poets, who alone were allowed to interpret natural events under their own auspices so as 'to make sure of their meaning' (NS/250, 342, 381). Vico acknowledges that their mystical interpretations and predictions may seem arbitrary, even manipulative, and, to the Christian observer, utterly vain: the 'divine reason', he notes, can, after all, be properly 'understood only by God', whereas 'men know of it only what has been revealed to them'. This 'divine reason' has been duly revealed to the Hebrews and then to the Christians directly 'through the prophets and through Jesus Christ to the Apostles, by whom it was declared to the Church', while the gentiles, on the other hand, could only perceive it 'through the auspices, the oracles, and other corporeal signs' which they, in their 'robust sense and vigorous imagination', interpreted as 'divine messages' (NS/948). 'It was on the natural prohibition of this practice, as something naturally denied to man, that God founded the true religion of the Hebrews, from which our Christian religion arose' (NS/365).

Yet, having thus pointed out this essential difference between the true Judaeo-Christian prophecies and the pagan auguries, Vico does not just dismiss the latter as false; he seeks instead to discover what they meant to their makers. Intent as ever on historical mediation rather than philosophical contraposition between seemingly opposed modes of thought and their different 'truths', he thus shows how this 'vulgar wisdom' of the theological poets, which consisted in forbidden and seemingly futile attempts to discover the ultimate divine reason behind all the fortuitous happenings, actually reflected the 'esoteric wisdom' of the metaphysical philosophers, because it established for the first time some permanent Law in the epiphenomenal world. He approves of Homer's words that among the Greeks such acts of divination (most notably, the Oracles of Delphi) demonstrated 'knowledge of good and evil', and, similarly, suggests that the Roman priests who conducted the rites of the *auspices* were quite deft in conveying through them important moral and social messages. It was only by such acts of divination, namely by sacrificial attempts to 'understand the auguries well so that the divine warnings and commands of Jove might be duly obeyed' (NS/10), that 'laws' could be established in any human society. Vico repeatedly evokes the etymological affinity between *Ious* (the Latin name of Jove) and *Ius*, law, in order to suggest that men became 'just in virtue of the supposed piety of observing the auspices which they believed to be divine commands of Jove' (NS/14).

Vico saw, then, that the attempts of the *divinari* to fix in the yet-unknown reality already-known patterns and events – however arbitrary and manipulative they may seem to us – were in fact necessary, and therefore beneficial, to the process of humanization among the gentile nations. By imposing a certain order and aims on the empty time these pagan soothsayers filled it with meaning, and so helped human beings to overcome the unbearable experience of *horror vacuui*. Pagan divination, then, is primarily a deeply conservative mechanism which gives man-in-the-world a measure of reliability and orientation, and as such its function is very much like that of Hebrew prophecy and, by implication, similar to the more modern systems of philosophy and science. In a sense all of these must be viewed as different yet equivalent systems of rules devised by human beings in order to control and determine their new and unbearably contingent experience. As cultural endeavours they all have a common aim which is, to use Hans Blumenberg's phrases, that of rendering the terrifying 'absolutism of reality' to the comfortable 'absolutism of humanity', namely, they all render objective reality according to the subjective 'wishes and images' of human beings.[44] As Vico put it in one of his most profound observations: the pagan art of '*divinari*, to divine, [consisted in the ability] to understand what is hidden *from* men – the future – or what is hidden *in* men – their consciousness' (NS/342). I take this rather enigmatic sentence to mean something like Coleridge's notion that 'All true insight is foresight': in Vico's formulation it would appear that the pagan *autori* in their divination, much like the Hebrew prophets in their prophecies, were so successful because, and inasmuch as, their foresights of 'what is hidden from men – the future' were, in fact, insights into 'what is hidden in men – their consciousness'. In their visions of the future the pagan soothsayers evoked and projected the deepest anxieties of the present, and thus enabled their audience to become aware of and cope with them:

---

[44] Hans Blumenberg, *Work on Myth*, tr. R. Wallace (Cambridge, Mass.: MIT Press, 1985), p. 8.

Hence new principles are given to moral philosophy, in order that the esoteric wisdom of the philosophers may conspire with the vulgar wisdom of lawmakers. By these principles all the virtues have their roots in piety and religion, by which alone the virtues are made effective in action, and by reason of which men propose to themselves as good whatever God wills. (NS/14)

By using such higher-critical (or what we would nowadays call hermeneutical) arguments to make sense of the practice 'on which all the gentile nations arose', Vico's larger and more practical aim was to undermine some contemporary views which to him seemed inimical to the Christian tradition. In this case, he was able to counter the rational-critical opinions of Spinoza, Bayle, and other modernists, who dismissed all ancient prophecies, sacred as well as pagan, as priestly acts of manipulation and control over terrified believers. His intention here was to fend off the rationalist attack on prophecy as such by elevating the act itself (regardless of its contents) onto a higher level of understanding – that of human self-creativity by poetic means:

Thus was born the first fable, the fundamental principle of the divine poetry of the gentiles or of the theological poets. Its birth was wholly ideal, as that of the best of fables must be, for, from his own ideas, the poet gives to things which lack it the whole of their being. Thus it is as masters of the art themselves assert: that it is entirely a product of the imagination, be it the art of the painter of non-pictorial ideas or of the painter of representations. This resemblance to God the creator explains why poets, like painters, are called 'divine'.[45]

Vico's concrete observations on the efficacy of divination among the pagans thus had some important philosophical implications with regard to the problem which we have raised in the beginning of our discussion – the problem of human creativity vs. divine or natural pre-determination in history. Already in the first edition of the *New Science*, while admitting that divination was 'a vain science of the future, employing certain sensible intimations, believed to be sent to man by the gods', he noted that this false science 'conceals two great principles of truth: that a divine providence must exist' and 'that men must possess free will through which, if they so desire and should they make use

---

[45] Vico, *The First New Science*, par. 257, *Selected Writings*, p. 142.

of it, they can escape that [fate] which, without such provision, should otherwise be theirs'. In that respect, it was closely related to a problem, which, as Vico relates in his *Autobiography*, had tormented him in his youth – the problem of 'the free use of the will'.[46]

III

Vico was much aware of the age-old disputes which since late antiquity had surrounded the notion of 'free will'. During the sixteenth century this notion became a focus of bitter controversy first between Christian Humanists like Erasmus and Augustinian Reformers like Luther, and then, in the wake of the Catholic Counter-Reformation, between the Jesuits and the Dominicans. Whereas the Jesuits argued that in any moral activity divine grace acts not upon but with human volition and thus allowed the individual believer a relative freedom of the will, the Dominicans held that because human volition is so poor and evil it could never, it itself, be conductive to salvation, and hence concluded that divine grace was absolutely necessary for any moral activity. During the seventeenth century this controversy was taken over, and much intensified, by other Catholic sections, like the Quietists who drew the most radical conclusions from the doctrine of the Jesuit Molinos, and called for tranquillity and silent or 'mental prayer' instead of official ceremonies, and, on the other hand, the Jansenists who drew the most extreme conclusions from the Augustinian doctrine of human corruption after the Fall in order to deny any measure of free will. In this ongoing battle the Jesuit-Quietist polemicists were commonly accused by their more disciplinarian opponents of 'Pelagianism', who in turn were accused of 'Calvinism'. These two generic terms were also used by Vico to characterize, and distance himself from, the two opposing factions which were active in Naples at the time. Vico did not openly engage in this controversy, but he was very much aware of its cardinal problems and theories, and in his own way also tried to resolve some of its essential tensions. Let us see, then, how his theory of civilization is related to this religious controversy.

---

[46] Vico, *The Autobiography*, p. 119. See also the comments in *The First New Science*, pars. 47–8.

Now, in emphasizing the poetic-inventive aspects of human reality, and arguing that the early peoples managed to overcome the natural state of being because they were 'natural poets', Vico shared the essential philosophy of man of the Renaissance and Christian Humanists. Like Dante, Ficino, Campanella, and Bruno he too viewed man as primarily a 'poet' – which, as Vico reminds us, 'is Greek for "maker"' (NS/376) – a being, namely, who, in the famous words of Pico, was unique and superior to all other beings by virtue of his creative rather than merely productive faculties. Man, in other words, was a creature that was not confined to what it was by nature, because he could always become what he wished to be by actively creating and living up to his own ideal images of himself. Vico's entire anthropological philosophy was founded on this principle of human self-creativity, although, as we shall now see, in developing his own theory of mythical creativity, he radically challenged the individualistic and rationalistic assumptions of both his predecessors and his contemporaries.

During the sixteenth and seventeenth centuries, amidst the hectic wars of religion, the Renaissance view of man became increasingly problematic. Like many Catholic Humanists in his day, Vico's most acute problem was how to uphold the Humanist ideals of freedom of will and creativity against the extreme opponents of these ideals – the various Catholic Augustinians and the more extreme Protestants who denied fallen man any capability of self-assertion, as well as against the extremist proponents of these ideals – primarily the libertines, who, in their exaltation of man, tended towards pagan, or at best Pelagian, indifference.[47] Ultimately, as he records in the *Autobiography*, Vico opted for 'the doctrine of St Augustine', which, as interpreted by the Jesuit Etienne Deschamps, steered 'midway between the two extremes of Calvin and Pelagius, and equidistant likewise from the other opinions that approach these two extremes'.[48] In his own time, he found the same old polar positions of 'fate' and 'chance' reaffirmed, respectively, by the modern exponents of 'Stoic' determinism and 'Epicurean' libertinism: 'the latter asserting that

---

[47] On the diffusion of French and Dutch Libertine theories in Naples at the time, see Enricu Nuzzo, 'Il congedo della *saggezza moderna* nella cultura napoletana tra '600 e '700: Vico e la tradizione dei *moralisti*', *Bollettino del Centro di Studi Vichiani*, 17–18 (1987–8), pp. 25-114.

[48] Vico, *The Autobiography*, p. 119.

human affairs are agitated by a blind concourse of atoms, the former that they are drawn by a deaf chain of cause and effect' (NS/342). He, however, inveighed against 'Stoic' thinkers like Spinoza who, Vico claimed, by identifying everything (including God) with Nature, and subjecting all beings to her laws, completely undermined the validity of freedom, spontaneity, and hence of 'free will', insofar as it was dependent on such notions; similarly, he opposed 'Epicurean' thinkers like Hobbes who, by reasserting the materialistic-atomistic idea that all beings, including man, were only 'bodies in motion', moving at random according to their inner will-power, or natural 'endeavour', inflated the efficacy of 'free will' beyond meaningful proportions.

As we saw above, Vico shared the anarchic 'Epicurean' view that history displays no visible congruence between the original human motives of the individuals ('each bent on his own private advantage') and their ultimate social ends ('the civil institutions by which they may live in human society') (NS/132–3, 1108). But he inferred from this fact neither that such self-defeating human actions are utterly arbitrary and irrational, nor that they are strictly utilitarian, and hence rational, as the Natural Law theorists would have it. Rather, he attempted to show that even those actions which so patently fall short of our strictly cognitive and practical standards of rationality are, in fact, quite reasonable. And they are reasonable not just because they happen to be beneficial to the common welfare of mankind, but mainly because they are continually performed 'with intelligence' and 'by choice' by each individual. They are performed, that is, with a certain immanent social 'reason', such that is not deduced by each individual from his or her own experience, but rather imparted by the collective-historical experience of the community, through its traditional customs and institutions. Vico, as he himself noted, derived this mediative solution from Augustine's views about man's original state and possible options in the world.[49]

Augustine's view of 'free will' was rooted in his fundamentally negative view of human nature in general, and of the deficiency of human reason in particular. We find the clearest explication of this position in his well-known polemics against the Christian Stoic

---

[49] On the Augustinian trends in Naples, see Fausto Nicolini, *La religiosità di G. B. Vico: Quatro saggi* (Bari: Laterza, 1949), p. 9.

Pelagius. In that controversy he sought, above all, to counter the latter's refutation of Original Sin. In order to do so he had to refute Pelagius' philosophical and anthropological theories about the value of the individual, and the efficacy of his will and rational capacities in achieving goodness without the help of divine grace. Augustine rejected this early version of individual rationalism as being too favourable to man, and therefore harmful to him. Fallen man, he argued, had to protect his hard-won humanity from the intrusions of natural forces, both from outside and from within himself. More than that, he needed a constant reminder of his sinful origins and weak constitution. The Biblical and ecclesiastical traditions provided such a reminder. They taught man all that he could or needed to know about God's actions and purposes in the world, and thereby enabled him to use his limited, yet free, will to understand and follow God's will. In that sense, and only in that sense, man could be said to have free will. Following these tragic premises Augustine then challenged the Pelagians and other positivists of the day and argued that by affirming what they perceived to be man's true nature and place in the world they loosed his metaphysical moorings and set him adrift. While his adversaries sought to liberate man from past commitments and authorities by refuting the ancient traditions as mere old fantasies, Augustine saw these as crucial for linking or even binding the Christian believer to a higher and truer reality; such traditions forced men, through continuous and repetitive rites, to reenact the dramatic events, real or imagined, which had made them what they are.

Vico, as I shall now show, while working out his theory of the social determination of 'free will' held to these basic Augustinian ideas about the mediative and constructive functions of metaphysical traditions. In his view, the Jansenist and Protestant theorists of free will, who claimed to follow Augustine's teaching on this topic, betrayed his humanistic message because they ignored this aspect in his thought. They reached their pessimistic and fatalistic conclusions because, having modelled their entire philosophical anthropology on Adam after the Fall, they came to view all human beings as essentially doomed to a life of total passivity in oblivion, and hence ruled out the possibility of any active attempt on the part of man towards the attainment of salvation. Divine Grace, in their view, was absolutely impervious to human intentions and actions. Vico rejected this view of man as incompatible with his Catholic and Humanistic views. He believed that 'man is not unjust by nature in the absolute sense, but by nature fallen and weak', that is, human beings can, and must, work towards the attainment of grace and salvation. He adopted, therefore, an alternative model figure of man, that of 'Adam before the fall, in the ideal perfection in which he must have been created by God' which is, and must be reiterated, as 'the first principle of the Christian religion'. By depicting the gradual efforts of man to perceive God through His occasional signs Vico intended his work to be a

demonstration of the Catholic principles of grace: that it operates in man when his condition is one not of negation but of privation of good works, and hence of a potentiality for them which is ineffectual; that it gives effect to this potentiality; and that it therefore cannot act without the principle of free choice, which God aids naturally by His providence. (NS/310)

This Augustinian principle of faith determined Vico's anthropo-historical view of human civilization. This becomes clear when we read, for example, his account of the birth of humanity among the gentile nations. In its main narrative and thematic contours, Vico's account of the 'Thunderstorm in the Great Forest of the Earth' is analogous to the Biblical account of the equivalent occasion in the history of the Hebrews – the Fall in the Garden of Eden. The central theme in both stories is the awakening of religious and moral sentiments in man; and both relate it to a traumatic event in which man was suddenly exposed in his human 'nakedness': just as in the Biblical story (Gen. 3.7–10) Adam became aware of his sinful behaviour and inferiority through feelings of sexual shame – *I heard the sound of thee in the garden, and I was afraid, because I was naked; and I hid myself* – so too in Vico's narration the *primi uomini* were surprised by the thunder in the act of copulation and, having thus become aware of their permissive manners, they fled from the forest into nearby caves, where for the first time 'the act of human love was performed under cover, in hiding, that is to say, in shame; and they began to feel the sense of shame which [is] the color of virtue' (NS/504). In both stories, then, the awakening of religious conception of divine magnitude is intimately related to emotions of human weakness,

albeit not just to mere 'fear', as Lucretius and his modern
followers surmised, but to 'shame': Vico points out that the
primi uomini, unlike other animals, were not just frightened by
the thunder, but rather, like Adam and Eve, they immediately
knew that they were naked in the world; and just like the Biblical
heroes who, upon that realization, *sewed fig leaves together and
made themselves aprons,* so these pagan *giganti* too 'gave up the
bestial custom of wandering through the great forest of the earth
and habituated themselves to the quite contrary custom of
remaining settled and hidden for a long period in their caves'
(NS/388). The parallels between the two stories are clear, as is the
common meaning: the gentile nations, much like the Hebrews,
could properly begin their course of civilisation only after the
traumatic expulsion from their respective states of nature, from
states of idleness in utter naturality, once 'they began to feel the
sense of shame'.

In these historical-theological investigations into the origins of
pagan religion Vico closely follows Augustine's teachings and
examples on the fallibility of human nature. This is more obvious
in the *First New Science* where he treats Biblical events more fully
and seeks to relate them more closely to events in the history of
the gentiles. It is in these passages that he reveals his debt to
Augustine, as, for example, in extending the latter's notion of
original sin to the pagan nations as well: 'In such mode, from this
sense of bestial lust, providence first tinged the face of these lost
men with the blush of shame, and certainly no nation has ever
existed which did not blush, for human matings occur in all
nations'. For Vico this common 'sense of shame' proves that the
original sin is universal, and that it 'is one of those origins [of
humanity] beyond which it is foolish curiosity to seek anything
earlier, which is the most important mark of origins'. Vico, however, makes it clear that this sense is not simply and wholly natural
to man, but rather is possible only among those who have a prior
and superior awareness of God:

At what point did men begin to feel ashamed of themselves in that state
of bestial freedom in which they were able to feel shame neither before
their sons, to whom they were by nature superior, nor before one
another, when they were both equal to one another and equally incited
by the promptings of lust? Hence, if we do not bring our inquiry to a halt
[when we arrive] at *shame felt before God* – but not the likes of naked Venus,

Hermes or Mercury or obscure Priapus – humanity could never have arisen from the men of Hobbes, Grotius and Pufendorf . . . From this first and oldest principle of all – humanity began.[50]

As these last remarks indicate, Vico's Augustinian theology of shame was set to refute the Enlightenment's ideology of fear. His conclusion that the most fundamental human emotion in religion is shame (*pudor*) and not fear (*timor*) signifies what I have defined as his 'radical humanism' in a most poignant way. Because, whereas fear is a wholly natural reactive attitude to external stimuli, and as such is common to all animals, then the emotion of shame is unique to man: it comprises a self-reactive attitude to internal demands based on moral conventions. And even though Vico still quoted approvingly the famous saying of Statius that 'Fear first created gods in the world' (*Primos in orbe deos fecit timor*) (NS/191), he reinterprets this saying as meaning that indeed 'it was fear which created gods in the world; [yet] not fear awakened in men by other men, but fear awakened in men by themselves' (NS/382) – a fear, namely, which man himself produces in himself out of the awareness of sin.[51] By advancing such anti-naturalistic theories about the foundation of religion, and all consequent human institutions, Vico has clearly superseded the simplistic fear theories of classical authorities like Lucretius, Cicero, and Sextus Empiricus and their modern interpreters and followers in the Enlightenment. In his view, humanity was born out of, and still consists in, religious sentiments of awe and obedience to divine commands; but these, in turn, arose out of, and consist in, what is most uniquely human – the capacity to choose freely whether to hold to them or not:

Upon this divine authority followed human authority in the full philosophic sense of the term; that is, the property of human nature which not even God can take from man without destroying him . . . This authority is the free use of the will, the intellect on the other hand being a passive power subject to truth. For from this first point of all human things, men began to exercise the freedom of human choice to hold in check the motions of the body, either to subdue them entirely or to give them better direction (this being the conatus proper to free agents) (NS/388)

---

[50] Vico, *The First New Science*, par. 58, *Selected Writings*, p. 111.
[51] Angela Maria Jacobelli-Isoldi, *G. B. Vico: Per una 'scienza della storia'* (Rome: Armando editore, 1985), pp. 21–42.

Thus, by combining his new psycho-historical insights into the theogonic process among the pagan nations with the standard Biblical account of Genesis, Vico was able to work out a unified theory of the historical origin and growth of conative emotions out of momentous 'occasions'. In so doing he established the primacy and vitality of foundational events – be they wholly natural ones like the thunderstorm in the forest or, as he tacitly implies, more historical ones like those which are recorded in the Scriptures – in the formation of moral emotions and traditions by which alone man can live. Like Augustine, then, Vico too believed that man 'has free choice, however weak, to make virtues of his passions' (NS/166), but since human beings were peculiarly unfitted to survive in the world on their own basic physiological and mental capacities (their intellect, even when fully developed, was only 'a passive power subject to truth') they therefore needed constant saving grace from God, in the form of 'occasions' to help them actualize their potentiality for good works, or – what produced the same effect – in strong mythical traditions which preserve and may revive such effective occasions.[52] Vico's axiomatic premise that 'To be useful to the human race, philosophy must raise and direct fallen man, not rend his nature or abandon him in his corruption' (NS/129) thereby acquires a specific Catholic meaning, and is clearly intended to counter not only the Stoic and Epicurean philosophies in their old and new guises, which merely 'rend' man's nature, but also those religious creeds, ancient and modern, which 'abandon him in his corruption'. The last sentences of the standard edition of the work reiterate its Catholic message:

To sum up, from all that we have set forth in this work, it is to be finally concluded that this Science carries inseparably with it the study of piety, and that he who is not pious cannot be truly wise. (NS/1112)

This pronouncement defined what the *New Science* is all about: it is a psychological and historical 'study of piety' – how man has

---

[52] Insofar as he related the origin of religious and social institutions to momentous *occasiones*, Vico might well be seen as the first systematic theorist of what Norman O. Brown has called 'the traumatic conception' of civilization; this Vichian intimation of Freud, which so impressed James Joyce, inspires Brown's hilarious *Closing Time* (N.Y.: Random House, 1973). See also the insightful comments of Stuart Hampshire, 'Joyce and Vico: The Middle Way', in *Vico's Science of Humanity*, p. 329.

become, and must remain, a pious being even though 'by his nature', he was doomed to be an essentially rebellious creature.

Vico admitted, as Hobbes and his fellow natural-rational and utilitarian theorists of society had also done, that what incites human beings in society is always their egotistic will – but he refused to simply equate this will with the natural instincts and rational dictates of individual self-preservation. He thought that men, while consciously obeying only their *private* motives – the imperative 'narrow ends' of self-preservation – have always been guided, quite unconsciously, by *public* motives as well, namely by more altruistic considerations, which have promoted the 'wider ends' of 'the preservation of the human race upon the earth'. His main counter-argument was that what motivates and determines the actions of human beings in social life, and what ultimately renders them 'mindful', is not merely the brutal (however enlightened) egotism, the will of self-interest (or *volontà* as he terms it), but rather a different and more socially determined kind of will, a will informed by the interests of the entire community (which he terms *umano arbitrio*) – and which alone is the proper 'human choice'.[53]

Vico's argument is that human beings who are motivated solely by their *volontà*, seeking to fulfil only what they desire, do indeed enjoy a total freedom of will. But this kind of freedom, which Vico calls 'natural liberty', is delusive and self-destructive: it is bound to create the anarchic-hedonistic society of the original state of nature, and might lead to the total disintegration of society, where people would 'live like wild beasts in a deep solitude of spirit and will, scarcely any two being able to agree since each follows his own pleasure or caprice' (NS/1106). When, on the other hand, people are motivated by *umano arbitrio*, that is when they are called upon to pursue common ideals rather than private desires, to follow rules and traditions and to fulfil duties and commitments, their freedom of will is, indeed, greatly inhibited. However, Vico contends that it is only under such limiting conditions, in what he calls 'civil liberty' (as against 'natural liberty'), that men can be truly free. In the 'bestial state' at either end of the historical cycle men, 'because of their corrupted nature, are under the tyranny of self-

---

[53] A. Robert Caponigri, 'Umanità and Civiltà: Civil Education in Vico', *Review of Politics*, 31 (1969), pp. 477–94.

love, which compels them to make private utility their chief guide. Seeking everything useful for themselves and nothing for their companions, they cannot bring their passions under control to direct them towards justice': they cannot be free because they can never fulfil nor free themselves from their ambitions. Thus, they have no real 'human choice' to be what they would like to be; they must be, rather, what they are by nature. Paradoxically, man becomes free from 'the tyranny of self-love' only by becoming a 'member of the society of the family, of the city, and finally of mankind': 'Unable to attain all the utilities he wishes, he is constrained by these institutions to seek those which are his due; and this is called just' (NS/341).

Vico's contention that man can become truly free only by practising his 'human choice', even though this choice is, in turn, determined by the social traditions of his community, may seem to be contradictory – unless, that is, we perceive the full meaning of the term *umano arbitrio*. For, as we have seen in our treatment of the 'principles of humanity', in Vico's scheme everything 'human' must, by definition, be 'arbitrary' – namely, artificial and conventional, not natural. Humanity consists for him precisely in the ongoing effort of men to uphold some arbitrary norms of behaviour over against their own natural liberty. We can thus see, that it was chiefly due to his elaboration of the philosophical and historical implications of *umano arbitrio* that Vico was able to mediate between Pelagius and Calvin; he was able to show, precisely as Augustine had done, that when people willingly adhere to the traditional beliefs and practices of their society, their actions are both free and determined. He could now argue that people in society are free inasmuch as they hold to these traditional norms and rules 'by choice'. They are aware that these customs, having been established by others – their ancestors – are utterly arbitrary, contingent and conventional, and have authority only insofar as they themselves, by their own choice, continue to hold to them. At the same time, inasmuch as human beings are always born into a social reality which dictates to them these norms and rules, their 'human choice' is also strongly determined, alas, not by any eternal and universal divine or natural laws, as ancient and modern Stoics like Calvin and Spinoza assumed, but rather by their own traditional customs and laws.

Vico's notion of socially-determined 'freedom of will' is

compatible with what the so-called 'communitarian' critics of liberalism in our time argue, namely that the self is not prior nor superior to the society in which it is 'situated'. These critics are revisionist inasmuch as they believe that we are all necessarily constrained by the 'authoritative horizons' of our social orders, and therefore cannot, and should not try to, free ourselves so imperiously from their traditional values and norms. Their revision of modern liberalism is an attempt to revive classical republicanism and its public philosophy which, in the words of a modern commentator, has always consisted in the belief that

self-fulfilment and even the working out of personal identity and a sense of orientation in the world depend upon a communal enterprise. This shared process is the civic life, and its root is involvement with others: other generations, other sorts of persons whose differences are significant because they contribute to the whole upon which our particular sense of self depends.[54]

On this account, individual freedom and self-determination are always exercised within socially given roles and relationships, and not by standing away from them. As Charles Taylor says, being free to question all our social norms and roles is a rather senseless aim, because a truly free choice should be evaluative and reflective, not impulsive, and could thus be made and become meaningful only against a 'background of shared values'. The liberal belief that freedom of choice is worth pursuing as an ideal in itself, as if for its own sake, is perverse and self-defeating because 'complete freedom would be a void in which nothing would be worth doing, nothing would deserve to count for anything. The self which has arrived at freedom by setting aside all external obstacles and impingements is characterless, and hence without defined purpose.' It is always our social tradition 'which sets goals for us, which thus imparts a shape to rationality and provides an inspiration for creativity'.[55] Thus, for example, we would not consider someone who exercises freedom of choice by making many marriage choices as more moral, nor indeed more free, than someone who keeps the original marital commitment and duties.

---

[54] William Sullivan, *Reconstructing Public Philosophy* (Berkeley: University of California Press, 1982), p. 158.
[55] Charles Taylor, *Hegel and Modern Society* (Cambridge: Cambridge University Press, 1979), pp. 157–9.

As we recall, this latter case involved the same kind of moral obligations which led Vico to establish his second 'principle of humanity', that of marriage, as an essentially civil – rather than merely social – practice. For he saw that in upholding such a 'civil institution' against our 'natural liberty' we attain a 'civil liberty', in which alone our freedom of will becomes rational and creative. For when we exercise our freedom of will within this more restrictive range of options, and according to more communal necessities and normative aspirations, it becomes literally more deliberate – it has fewer choices, but these are based on firmer – or so-called 'second order' – motivations, on what Vico would call 'public grounds of truth' (*publici motivi del vero*).[56]

Vico defined this human ability 'to hold in check the motions of the body, either to subdue them or to give them better direction' as *conatus*, and decreed that only 'this freedom of human choice [*umano arbitrio*]' is truly human, since it is unique and 'proper to free agents' only (NS/338). What Vico meant by *conatus* is more or less synonymous with 'endeavour', but I think it can be better defined by the modern term 'inhibition'. In the physiological literature of the time *conatus* was in fact used in that sense, to describe the emotional resistance to thought or action. Yet, unlike and against the major theorists of *conatus* in his time who, on the whole, sought to explain the creation of conative emotions in psycho-physical terms, Vico's aim was historical: he sought to show that our most common and seemingly natural conative emotions are, in fact, historical, that they came into being 'at certain times and in certain guises', on particular 'occasions' which occurred in the mythical ages, and yet can and must be retrieved. As we shall see, Vico's psychological analysis of 'free will' – indeed, the entire historical theory of the *New Science* – is subsumed in this new and distinctly socio-historical conception of *conatus*.

Vico may have borrowed the concept of *conatus* from ancient Stoic origins (Cicero, Galen), as well as from various contemporary sources – Descartes, Hobbes, Leibniz and other 'theorists

---

[56] Harry Frankfurt, 'Freedom of the Will and the Concept of a Person', *Journal of Philosophy*, 67 (1971), pp. 5–20. I have elaborated on Vico's communitarian concept of truth in my ' "The Public Grounds of Truth": Vico's Critical Theory', *New Vico Studies*, 6 (1988), pp. 59–84.

of mechanics'.[57] *Conatus* was originally used as a geometrical concept, signifying the potential or tensional motion of a body still inactive as, for example, the point in space which holds and extends the line. During the seventeenth century the concept acquired more dynamical connotations, as well as analogical psychological meanings, and was commonly used by moral philosophers to define the tensional counter-action, or the energetic 'endeavour' required to restrain natural desires. Hobbes fashioned this concept in order to mediate between the egotistic-materialistic and the voluntaristic capacities of man. He attempted to explain thereby the inner psychological process by which human beings manage to overcome – or literally to *de-liberate* – their impulsive 'appetites and aversions' through their ability to create and impose on them abiding conventional meanings as, for example, when they establish common nominal terms in language, or contractual obligations in society. Vico too appraised *conatus* as the ability of human beings to invent and set up conventional norms over against their natural impulses: 'This control over the motions of their bodies is certainly an effect of the freedom of human choice, and thus of free will, which is the home and seat of all the virtues' (NS/340). And yet, though his notion of *conatus* owed much to Hobbes and 'the theorists of mechanics' he thought that their general naturalistic assumptions and methods of inquiry rendered their concept of *conatus* too materialistic and deterministic. He rejected the Hobbesian attempt to explain the creation of conative emotions in man by general psycho–physical and rational terms, and sought instead to explain it by concrete socio-historical and poetic ones. *Conatus*, he argued, must be viewed as a 'virtue of the spirit' (NS/504): the ability to resist a thought or action must be attributed to the metaphysical, not the physical, capacities of man. Vico occasionally defined *conatus* as a 'metaphysical point', by which he meant to denote, quite literally, those ultimate mythical images or ideas which enabled the 'first men', and still help us, to transcend basic physical impulses.

[57] On Hobbes' and Leibniz' theories of the concept, see John W. N. Watkins, *Hobbes' System of Ideas* (London: Hutchinson, 1972), pp. 85–96; Vico's indebtedness to these and other theories is explicated in Jeffrey Barnouw, 'Vico and the Continuity of Science', *Isis*, 71 (1980), pp. 609–20.

The natural philosophers of morality have all conceived of common conative emotions such as fear, shame, and guilt in strict natural-rational and utilitarian terms, and thus reduced them, and all morality, to certain rationalized instincts which, they surmised, must naturally arise in every man as he consistently seeks to satisfy and justify the appetite for his own good under a variety of circumstances. Vico thought that this instinctual theory of *conatus*, like all other naturalistic accounts of man, was inadequate, because it implied a new kind of biological determinism. 'But to impute conatus to bodies', he argued, 'is as much as to impute to them freedom to regulate their motions, whereas all bodies are by nature necessary agents' (NS/340). He made it clear that conative emotions like, for example, the inhibition of incest, which appear to be intuitive, common to all, and therefore may be thought of as utterly natural reactions, are in fact culturally conditioned. In Vico's account, the sensitivity with regard to incest is an emotional reaction which has evolved, and still persists, midway between the instinctual attraction to, and the rational rejection of, a particular act, a conflict which is resolved in the mediative moral and religious sentiments which inhibit our consciousness. It thus owes its efficacy, like other conative emotions, to strong unconscious messages built into the mind of the individual by traditional beliefs – through linguistic phrases, religious images, mythical tales, communal rites, and similar poetic fictions which incite yet arrest our emotions.

Vico surmised that even the most common emotions and beliefs in social life, as, for example, those which permeate the three 'principles of humanity' – religion, marriage, and burial of the dead – do not evolve in each person by nature but, in fact, arise out of collective experiences of the whole social group. In what seems to be the most speculative, and nearly Freudian, aspect of his theory of *conatus*, Vico purports to show that the common sensual reactions which are naturally associated with these habitual customs – fear of God, shame of sexual promiscuity, respect for the dead, and so on – have all evolved out of, and are still experienced as, traumatic events, or, in his term, 'occasions' (*occasioni*) which, whether real or imagined, are nevertheless believed by all the members of the community to have occurred *in illo tempore*.

As we shall see in the next chapters, Vico developed his entire theory of 'historical mythology' upon this psychological-historical observation. The fact that 'men are naturally impelled to preserve the memories of the laws and institutions that bind them in their societies' and that 'all barbarian histories have fabulous beginnings' (NS/201–2) implies that even the most fabulous tales about specific 'occasions' in which particular customs and institutions 'came into being at certain times and in certain guises' must be thought of as historically significant. Such tales, to be sure, can not be taken as a proof that the events described in them had really happened. Indeed, they are likely to remain forever beyond the range of historical verification or anthropological proof. They indicate, however, what the people who have preserved them 'over long periods of time' believe to have happened. And inasmuch as such tales are used to explain and justify why certain normal practices and institutions must be upheld, we can reveal in and through them the original dramatic situations in which these habitual norms, practices, and institutions came into being; they suggest, as it were, in what ways these situations were once resolved and must in time be further resolved. Thus, insofar as the people take such pseudo-historical events as the Biblical events of the 'Fall' or the 'Deluge' or the 'Covenant' – or, as Vico would suggest, the 'Thunderstorm' – to have been the foundational moments in the history of their societies, moments which must be not only remembered but also re-enacted, such events are, in a very real historical sense, true. For Vico, the very fact that a certain archaic tale persists in our minds and cultures indicates, first of all, that the dramatic predicament and its resolution are still alive and relevant. Vico, in any case, believed that ancient and primitive myths, as well as common 'vulgar traditions', and, more generally still, all prejudices – may yield us these concrete historical truths about the coming-into-being, the *nascimento*, of all our human institutions.

Vico generally defined this network of constitutive collective-historical memories, beliefs and customs as the 'common sense' (*senso comune*) of the community:

Human choice (*L'umano arbitrio*), by its nature most uncertain, is made certain and determined by the common sense of men with respect to human needs or utilities . . . Common sense is judgment without reflection, shares by an entire class, an entire people, an entire nation, or the entire human race. (NS/141–2)

Vico's phrases in this passage are redolent of Aristotle's well-known definition of common sense as that 'which is held generally or by the most'.[58] Like Aristotle, he too sought to designate thereby those common sensibilities which distinguish and unite individuals into a social whole through commonly held beliefs and values. Given these distinctive communitarian aspects of the term *senso comune*, it seems to me it could be more accurately, if somewhat less elegantly, translated as 'collective sense'.[59] In this respect Vico's notion of *sensus communis* is akin to other eighteenth-century formulations like Montesquieu's *Esprit generale*, or Herder's *Volksgeist*: like the latter terms 'common sense' connotes the holistic aspect in social life, signifying the intersubjective and largely impersonal process of decision-making in civil association, that which enables its individual members to reach a common view, or 'judgment', with regard to the basic rules and ideals of social life. 'Common sense' is that judgment, a judgment which, in Santillana's words, 'has been built into every event with which we are involved, the many causes that brought it into being'.[60]

In his notion of 'judgment without reflection' – a phrase which literally means prejudice – Vico elucidates and sums up his main argument about the socio-historical determination of individual free will. Vico significantly presents this kind of judgment as both common and sensual, because his aim here was to explain the creation of a truly common way of social life by sensual rather than rational means, by shared memories and images or myths rather than by an *ad hoc* notional social contract. He attempted to clarify thereby the process of socialization through tradition. In this process human beings, who have realized that they are unable to regulate their affairs by their individual instincts for reason, adhere to common sense 'by choice', knowing that in sharing traditional beliefs and practices, or prejudices, they rely, in fact, on what the collective-historical experience of the group has proved to be the most beneficial 'with respect to human needs or

---

[58] Aristotle, *Ann. Pr.* 24b 11.

[59] The literature on Vico's various formulations of *senso comune* is vast. Noteworthy are those commentators who emphasize its *social* connotations over its *epistemological* ones: Leon Pompa, *Vico*, pp. 27–36; Giuseppe Giarrizzo, 'Del "senso comune" in G. B. Vico: Note vichiane', *De Homine*, 6 (1988), pp. 89–104; John D. Schaeffer, 'Vico's Rhetorical Model of the Mind: *Sensus Communis* in the *De nostri temporis studiorum ratione*', *Philosophy and Rhetoric*, 14 (1981), pp. 152–67.

[60] Giorgio Santillana, 'Vico and Descartes', *Osiris*, 9 (1950), p. 210.

utilities'. For this reason Vico depicts 'common sense' as a practical, not theoretical, knowledge of the specific 'human needs or utilities' which pertain to a certain community. Such knowledge can therefore be gleaned by the members of the community – or, for that matter, by its scientific observer – only by acquaintance with its particular linguistic and moral habits, and not through any application of universal rules and laws. Or, to use Vico's own terms, this common sense could be attained by an immediate *coscienza* rather than by abstract *scienza*. Vico's *senso comune* is quite different from, and even opposed to, the more familiar usages of this term in his times, principally those of the Natural Law theorists, who employed it to denote those prudential precepts of reasoning which are purportedly shared by and known to all human beings 'by nature'. Vico agreed, indeed, with the latter theorists that certain moral notions (like those underlying the three 'principles of humanity') are naturally known to all people, and thus constitute the *comune natura alle nazioni*; but he made it clear that since in each nation these common notions are perceived and practised differently, the task of the scientist of humanity must be to trace them in their different cultural manifestations, and not to reduce them to their common natural origins. In our own very modern terms we could say that Vico sought to overcome epistemology and concentrate on the sociology of knowledge – to move, in other words, from theories of and about the mind of the individual to practices of common sense of all people. Hence his conclusion that

the principles of this science must be rediscovered within the nature of our human mind and in the power of understanding, by elevating the metaphysics of the human mind – which has hitherto contemplated the *mind of individual man*, in order to lead it to God as eternal truth, which is the most universal *theory* in divine philosophy – to contemplate the *common sense of mankind* as a certain human mind of nations, in order to lead it to God as eternal providence, which should be the most universal *practice* in divine philosophy.[61] (emphasis added)

By emphasizing the fact that the 'human choice' of each man is 'by its nature most uncertain' and therefore must be amended by the collective-historical 'common sense of men' Vico appears to have had the same conservative sensibilities which were to evolve

---

[61] Vico, *The First New Science*, par. 40, *Selected Writings*, pp. 98–9.

into a major political ideology later on in the century, most notably in Edmund Burke's well-known apology for 'prejudices'. In his *Reflections on the Revolution in France* Burke attacked the great ideals of 'this enlightened age' – rationalism and individualism – as impractical, and therefore ruinous, illusions about human nature, typical to all revolutionary zealots who ignore the fact 'that we are generally men of untaught feelings':

We are afraid to put men to live and trade each on his private stock of reason; because we suspect that the stock in each is small, and that the individuals would do better to avail themselves of the general bank and capital of nations and ages . . . [we] think it more wise to continue the prejudice, with the reason involved, than to cast away the cost of prejudice, and to leave nothing but the naked reason; because prejudice, with its reason, has a motive to give action to that reason, and an affection which will give it permanence. Prejudice is of ready application in the emergency; it previously engaged the mind in a steady course of wisdom and virtue, and does not leave the man hesitating in the moment of decision, sceptical, puzzled, and unresolved.[62]

Burke's definition of the English Common Law as a prejudicial 'wisdom without reflection, and above it' is strikingly similar to Vico's definition of 'common sense', though it is unlikely that Burke had ever read Vico. These similarities attest, rather, to a common trend of thought among those European thinkers in the eighteenth century whom one could define as enlightened conservatives. For such thinkers as Hume, Gibbon, Herder, and most of the Scottish Moralists were radical modernists in philosophy yet conservative in politics. They were well aware of the mythical constitution of their socio-political orders, as were their opponents, the Enlightenment radical mythoclasts; but, unlike the latter, these enlightened conservatives committed themselves to protecting this traditional order. Against the rationalist attack on the myths of tradition they employed new, 'higher critical' tactics of defence – they elevated these myths to a higher level of understanding by explaining the necessary psychological and historical conditions which produced these modes of religious or political comprehension, and which still sustain them in the collective imagination of nations. Vico's religious and political

---

[62] Edmund Burke, *Reflections on the Revolution in France* in *The Works of Edmund Burke* (London: Bohn's Standard Library, 1853), II, p. 359.

sensibilities align him to that party of enlightened conservatism. In order to fully understand this aspect in his thought we must first recall how he reached this position while searching for the 'principles of humanity'.

In our treatment of that matter we have noted that Vico's ultimate rationale for the choice of these particular customs was based on the empirical observation that human beings perform these 'natural customs' with the utmost seriousness: 'And in no nation, however savage and crude, are any human actions performed with more elaborate ceremonies and more sacred solemnity than the rites of religion, marriage and burial' (NS/333). This 'philological' observation of human actions is based, however, on some more fundamental 'philosophical' insight into the deeper reasons as to why such customs are performed in that way – with 'elaborate ceremonies' and 'sacred solemnity'. Unlike Voltaire, who summed up his comparative cultural inquiries into the Manners and Mind of the nations with the conclusion that underlying them all there is a certain universal moral reason, *le bon sens*, which render them all differently but equally civil, what Vico seems to have discovered in his inquiries into 'the deplorable obscurity of the beginnings of the nations and into the innumerable variety of their customs' was the common mythopoeic element in all moral norms, laws and institutions, the fact, namely, that humanity is only tenuously held together by some essentially a-rational beliefs and practices. He would have agreed with Alfred Whitehead's observation that 'a social system is kept together by the blind forces of instinctive actions, and of instinctive emotions clustered around habits and prejudices'.[63]

In a certain sense, then, Vico's entire new science of humanity derives from his new perception of the distinctly *formal* aspects of pagan culture, that is to say, from his ability to understand the efficacy of the excessive ritualism in their cultures. For rationalist critics like Bayle or Voltaire dismissed pagan religions (and, by implication, a great deal of Judaeo-Christian lore) precisely because they appeared to consist only of ritualistic performances, which were seemingly devoid of any moral or historical content. Like these critics Vico too was appalled by the brutality of ancient

---

[63] Alfred N. Whitehead, *Symbolism: Its Meaning and Effect* (Cambridge: Cambridge University Press, 1958), pp. 68–9.

and primitive rites, and indeed was able to discern this brutality even in the classical epochs that these critics glorified – for example, in the 'golden ages' of Socratic Athens or Augustan Rome: 'For certainly Roman history will puzzle any intelligent reader who tries to find in it any evidence of Roman virtue where there was so much arrogance, or of moderation in the midst of such avarice, or of justice or mercy where so much inequality and cruelty prevailed' (NS/668). And yet, whereas Bayle saw in the rites of the pagans only irrationality and venality, a proof of their inability to reason morally ('The pagans imputed the origins of the punishments which the gods visited upon them to the neglect of some superstition and not to the impurity of their lives, and therefore they believed that they had done enough if only they re-established the rite which had been forgotten')[64] – Vico, in contrast, perceived the deeper, and more generally human, reasons that motivated men, then as now, to follow such archaic and rigid patterns of behaviour. In a similar vein he endorses Augustine's view on the 'virtue of the Romans' as being void of any true moral value, and explains its apparent efficacy in keeping Roman society intact in psychological and historical, not moral, terms, namely as a set of qualities which were natural to the patrician society of heroes who, as a rule, believe in words and live out their myths (NS/38). On the whole, then, Vico readily and repeatedly noted that indeed

it was a fanaticism of superstition which kept the first men of the gentiles, savage, proud, and most cruel as they were, in some sort of restraint by main terror of a divinity they had imagined. Reflecting upon this superstition, Plutarch poses the problem whether it was a lesser evil thus impiously to venerate the gods than not to believe in them at all. But he is not just in weighing this cruel superstition against atheism, for from the former arose the most enlightened nations while no nation in the world was ever founded on atheism. (NS/518)

Such ambivalent reflections on the culture of the pagans suggest that Erich Auerbach was, as always, right in his remark that Vico differed most radically from both the thinkers of the Enlightenment and of Romanticism precisely because he neither rejected nor succumbed to the primitivism of foreign and ancient peoples.

---

[64] Pierre Bayle, *Pensées diverses sur la comète*, quoted in Manuel, *The Eighteenth Century Confronts the Gods*, p. 31.

When Vico looked at these peoples, Auerbach has noted, he 'admired – with an admiration so overwhelming that it proved to be stronger than his horror – the terrible cruelty of their magic formalism'.[65] I would like to substantiate this perceptive observation by generalizing it: For Vico realized that *all* human cultures, and not only that of the ancient or newly-discovered pagans, were founded on the 'terrible cruelty of magic formalism'. He perceived man to be, by nature and history, a 'ceremonial animal'.[66] For he saw that the 'elaborate ceremonies' which we find in all known societies are the defensive means which human beings have devised and employ to protect themselves from the constant threat of physical stimulations, both internal and external; by imposing 'sacred solemnity' on certain 'natural customs' which have proved to be absolutely necessary to their civility, but have not yet been – and indeed may never be – fully grounded in human consciousness and society by rational persuasion, they impute to them moral authority which obscures, and transcends, their human, all-too-human, origins. The 'formal' ritual ceremonies by which modern people still pray, get married, or bury their dead are indeed archaic – but Vico, unlike their critics in the Enlightenment, regarded them indispensable for the ongoing, never really ending, process of civilization. Thus, even though the absolute necessity of any of the above mentioned customs might be challenged by modern observers, as in fact Bayle had earlier done, Vico could still claim that the very fact that people have always observed them in such ritualistic manner and have turned them, indeed, into obligatory *mythical* – rather than merely prescriptive rational-social – commands, serves as a kind of a practical-historical proof for their indispensability. By elaborating on the concept of 'common sense' as the essential teaching of all our ancient mythologies, both the sacred and the profane, Vico was able to show, *contra* the rational and historical critics of such mythologies, that these apparently irrational narratives do, in fact,

---

[65] Erich Auerbach, 'Vico and Aesthetic Historicism', *The Journal of Aesthetics and Art Criticism*, 8 (1949), p. 115. See also Gino Bedani, 'The Poetic as an Aesthetic Category in Vico's New Science', *Italian Studies*, 31 (1976), pp. 22–36.

[66] This phrase is used by Wittgenstein to account for the 'deep and sinister character' of rituals which we derive when we observe them – a sensation which arises not from external knowledge of their 'history' but rather 'from an experience in our inner selves'. *Remarks on Frazer's Golden Bough*, ed. R. Rhees, tr. A. C. Miles (Retford: The Brynmill Press, 1979), pp. 7, 16.

have a 'reason' of their own, the practical, collective, and truly historical experience of mankind which operates beyond and against our mere theoretical, personal, and short-sighted ambitions. Furthermore, in his contention that the classical myths, however fabulous they might appear to us, must nevertheless be considered as truthful in their narration of past events, because their authors encoded in them the seminal experience gained through these events, Vico was able to bridge the polarity between pagan mythology and sacred history.

What finally distinguishes the *New Science* from all other historical works of its day, then, is precisely this attempt to take the mythologies of past and primitive cultures seriously, to unlock them with a new 'master key', and thereby render them, by appeal to our shared *sensus comunis*, as 'true narrations' of the human condition:

It follows that the first science to be learned should be mythology or the interpretation of fables; for, as we shall see, all the histories of the gentiles have their beginnings in fables, which were the first histories of the gentile nations. By such a method the beginnings of the sciences as well as of the nations are to be discovered, for they sprang from the nations and from no other source. It will be shown throughout this work that they had their beginnings in the public needs or utilities of the peoples and that they were later perfected as acute individuals applied their reflection to them. This is the proper starting-point for universal history, which all the scholars say is defective in its beginnings. (NS/51)

This last appeal to the historians may help us to settle the issue which we raised at the beginning of this section: namely, how to account for Vico's seemingly contradictory claims, on the one hand, his insistence on the radical difference in nature between the Hebrew-Christian and the gentile nations and the incommensurability of their respective sacred and profane histories and, on the other, his claim to have found the universal principles of humanity and to have forged a science of the whole historical *mondo civile?* Vico's mediative solution to these queries is clear: he seeks to show how 'the world of nations, or civil world', or what we now call Western Civilisation, has evolved from both these traditions, which, beyond all their apparent differences, consist in one pervasive practical human experience – the 'common sense of mankind'. If, as Vico argues, every *mondo civile* is distinguished by its common sensibility, that is by a certain 'judgment without reflection' which, operating through traditional patterns of belief and behaviour, renders the choices of its individual members 'certain and determined', then the task of the historian who studies this *mondo civile* must be to somehow grasp this integrative sensibility, a task which, according to Vico, can best be carried out by recourse to the pre-rational, mythological heritage of men. The duty of a philologist of Western Civilization (which Vico perceived himself to be) can thus be clearly stated: it is to trace the constitution of this 'common sense' from both its sacred and profane histories which, for Vico, are equally 'true narrations' of one universal history – which is the

ideal eternal history traversed in time by the histories of all nations. Wherever, emerging from savage, fierce, and bestial times, men begin to domesticate themselves by religion, they begin, proceed, and end by those stages which are investigated here . . . There will then be fully unfolded before us, not the particular history in time of the laws and deeds of the Romans or the Greeks, but . . . the ideal history of the eternal laws which are instanced by the deeds of all nations in their rise, progress, maturity, decadence, and dissolution [and which would be so instanced] even if (as is certainly not the case) there were infinite worlds being born from time to time throughout eternity. (NS/393, 1096)

Vico's notion of 'ideal eternal history' has been much debated by interpreters of his work. Croce and like-minded Idealists have emphasized the human 'idealistic' component of this notion. Though Vico's notion that 'the order of ideas must follow the order of institutions' (NS/238) reverses their belief in the primacy of ideas and ideals in history, they take the 'ideal eternal history' to be a history of those seminal progressive ideas which motivate the entire historical process of social transformations. By relating it to other central notions of Vico's theory of historical knowledge like that which confines it to the 'modifications of our human mind', they generally interpret it as implying that we can discover the entire historical course of any society by recovering its constructive plan and patterns in the minds of its original makers and by remaking them in our own minds.[67] More empirically-minded commentators, however, tend to interpret this notion as implying, or at least analogous to, modern hypothetico-deductive method in

---

[67] This is the position attributed to Croce and Berlin by W. H. Walsh, 'The Logical Status of Vico's Ideal Eternal History", in *Vico's Science of Humanity*, p. 144.

science, where we conduct inquiries by deducing hypothetical theories from some rudimentary observations and assumptions, and then go on to correct this counter-factual – seemingly 'ideal and eternal' – model of affairs by testing predictions through factual observations and experiments. On their account, Vico's 'ideal and eternal history' is a hypothetical and predictive model of that kind – for, even on his account, no history, not even that of Rome which he otherwise believed to be exemplary in its full manifestation of political events and transformations, could ever display the precise, law-like, pattern of the 'ideal eternal history' of his *New Science*. They heavily rely on the passage quoted above which seems to affirm that this view, alas, as will be shown below, contradicts other, less positivistic, pronouncements in the *New Science*.[68] The religiously-minded interpreters may be seen to draw on these interpretations, and yet steer away from both as they refer to what could, and in some way must have been, Vico's original model for this notion – the Augustinian notion of *historia sacra*, a divinely-programmed history which exists before and above the earthly practised *historia profana* through which it merely unfolds, though its general pattern can be discerned in the scriptures and other sacred books and deeds of the makers of Christianity.[69]

I think that all three options are viable, though none is satisfactory, and in any case they must not be thought of as exclusive and necessarily incommensurable. Following my line of interpretation, I would like to suggest – in a true Vichian fashion – a mediative solution, to point to a common cohering theme which could fuse the three options into one. My argument is that what Vico offers in the notion of 'ideal eternal history' is a conscious 'myth', a modern historical one, his own, but one which, like the ancient myths he had explicated, was true for his maker – a 'true narration' of the modern historian of civilization who subsumes it in a certain universal pattern of growth and decay common to all nations. I trust that Vico himself says as much in the most revealing statement of this notion:

Our Science therefore comes *to describe* at the same time an ideal eternal history traversed in time by the history of every nation in its rise,

[68] This position is fully expounded by Leon Pompa in his *Vico*, pp. 97–111.
[69] This is the general position of F. Amerio, *Introduzione allo studio di G. B. Vico* (Turin: Società Editrice Internazionale, 1947).

development, maturity, decline, and fall. Indeed, we make bold to affirm that he who *meditates this Science narrates to himself this ideal eternal history so far as he himself makes it for himself by that proof 'it had, has, and will have to be'.* For the first indubitable principle . . . is that this world of nations has certainly been made by men, and its guise must therefore be found within the modifications of our own human mind. *And history cannot be more certain than when he who creates the things also narrates them.* (NS/349) (emphasis added)

Before attending to Vico's notion of 'ideal eternal history' I would like to reassert what I take his 'science' to be – because, clearly, it is this latter notion which determines the meaning of the 'ideal eternal history'. The point here is that for all his claims about discovering the 'eternal laws', and hence the scientific structure, of history, Vico was well aware that a positive science of history, even in its more hypothetico-deductive form, though possible, was ultimately rather vacuous – as was geometry when compared with physics. This is the ironical point he makes when he goes on to compare the 'ideal eternal history' with 'geometry' in the passage quoted above, and says that his Science has 'a reality greater by just so much as the institutions having to do with human affairs are more real than points, lines, surfaces, and figures are' (NS/349). It is true that Vico was very much aware of the applications of this hypothetico-deductive method to contemporary social and historical sciences, as in Hobbes's counter-factual construction of the 'state of nature' or the 'conjectural' accounts of anthropo-history in the Scottish Enlightenment. But the more telling fact is that he repudiated the practitioners of this method precisely for (what he considered) these methodological ('Cartesian') fallacies. Aiming to be scientific in the hard, positivistic, sense of the natural sciences, they produced works which were bound to be too schematic, mere theories with highly abstract and much too general terms, and as such lacking any relevance to human affairs, which, he knew, are always 'dominated by chance and choice, which are extremely subject to change and which are strongly influenced by simulation and dissimulation'.[70] It is unlikely that, given all his hostile attacks on the purely 'philosophical' assumptions and procedures of this method, he would have construed one himself. Vico was equally aware of the dangers in the utterly

---

[70] Vico, *On the Study Methods of Our Time*, in *Selected Writings*, p. 23

non-positivistic theories of history, the merely narrativist ones, for he established, as a rule, that all historical narratives, both those of the 'nations' which the historians use as well as their own, those of the 'scholars', were liable to all kinds of 'conceits'. Indeed, the very act of narrativization by which we ascribe a certain coherent form to chaotic reality (normally, that of a story with a well-ordered plot from beginning to end, causal connection between events, etc.) is some kind of a conceit. But Vico believed that there are narratives which are not merely told, but actually lived, and they are those 'great' narratives which constitute religious and national identities. Such narratives, which alone merit to be called 'historical myths', were, for him, both ideal and real, eternal and historical: they were the 'true narrations' in which people have always believed and lived. It is for this reason that he says in the passage quoted above that his Science 'comes to describe' – and not to determine or predict – the historical courses and recourses of the 'ideal eternal history', so that 'he who meditates this Science narrates to himself this ideal eternal history so far as he himself makes it for himself by that proof "it had, has, and will have to be"', for 'history cannot be more certain than when he who creates the things also narrates them' (NS/349).

This passage has caused considerable confusion among commentators who have variously identified its nominative subject to be either 'the historical agent' (the original poet of history) or 'the historian' (reading Vico's work). Surely what Vico meant here is the latter version, because only the present and future reader-historian could meditate this (Vico's) Science. But in a way, the ambiguity here is genuine, and Vico might have had in mind both subjects – as if meaning to say that both the original poetic maker ('who creates the things [and] also narrates them') and the modern scholar of history equally participate in the same narrative process of making history insofar as they both make and remake its constitutive narrative myth for themselves. And what this myth narrates is an ideal and eternal, not a real and empirical, account of history, a truly 'sublime history', purified, as it were, of all the accidents, distortions, and misfortunes which normally occur and obscure our vision of the basic pattern of the cyclical evolution of mankind. What we, like our ancestors, could ever discover in history is not a scientific law or model but only a narrative account of it, one which 'travers' its chaotic happenings into the coherent form of a well-ordered story of the rise, development, maturity, decline, and fall of all peoples, societies, nations, and civilizations – a fictive pattern which is not so much deduced hypothetically from scientific observations of objective natural reality as mused by poetic impressions of subjective human reality. The pagan mythological divinations, like the sacred Biblical prophecies, are the 'true narrations' which inspire this view of history, as well as Vico's Science of it – and should also inspire 'he who meditates' it insofar as he identifies and 'narrates to himself' its constitutive myths.

CHAPTER 3

The revision of mythology

And surely the myths are, as a whole, false, though there is
truth in them too.

Plato, *The Republic*, 377a

Mythologia, prima rerum historia, cur hactenus infelix?

G. B. Vico, *De universalis jure*, II, P.P., I, 9

I

The Survival of the Pagan Gods in Western Christian civilization, as
Jean Seznec has taught in the book bearing that title, is so obvious
that it needs no proof: 'Even the gods were not *restored* to life',
writes Seznec, 'for they had never disappeared from the memory
or imagination of man'.[1] The legendary figures of Prometheus,
Orpheus, and Narcissus; the heroic adventures of Jason, Odysseus
and Aeneas, and the tragic tales of Medea, Oedipus and Antigone;
these and other tales have exercised an unbroken authority over
the imagination of poets, philosophers, theologians, explorers,
and laymen in the West.[2] Although these Greek figures are clearly

---

[1] Jean Seznec, *The Survival of the Pagan Gods: The Mythical Tradition and Its Place in
Renaissance Humanism and Art* (N.J.: Princeton University Press, 1972), p. 3.

[2] The modern literature on classical mythology is immense. A good informative survey is
Yves Bonnefoy (ed.), *Mythologies*, trans. Wendy Doniger *et al.* (Chicago: The University
of Chicago Press, 1991). For anthological surveys of its multifarious receptions,
interpretations, and appropriations through the ages, see Jan de Vries, *Forschungs-
geschichte der Mythologie* (Freiburg-Munich, 1961); Karl Kerényi (ed.), *Die Eröfnung des
Zugangs zum Mythos. Ein Lesebuch*, Wege der Forschung 20 (Darmstadt: Wissenchschaft-
liche Buchgesellschaft, 1967). For studies on specific periods: antiquity – H. J. Rose, *A
Handbook of Greek Mythology, Including Its Extension to Rome* (London: Methuen & Co.,
1964); the middle ages – Otto Gruppe, *Geschichte der klassischen Mythologie und Religions-
geschichte während des Mittelalters im Abendland* (Leipzig: Teubner, 1921); the Renaissance
– Jean Seznec, as in n. 1 above; the modern period – Burton Feldman and Robert
Richardson (eds.), *The Rise of Modern Mythology, 1680–1860* (Bloomington: Indiana University Press, 1972); contemporary culture – John B. Vickery (ed.), *Myth and Literature:*

defined by and in concrete local conditions, they have not been confined to them; on the contrary, they have proven to be perfectly adaptable to changing times and tastes. To the European eye they appeared to be supra-national, seemingly devoid of any religious or ethnic identity, and over the centuries they have created a network of concrete references which, alongside the Biblical figures, established for all the European nations a complete repository of ideas and examples on which they have built much of their own cultural lores. 'Because Greek myths encode certain primary biological and social confrontations and self-perceptions in the history of man', writes George Steiner, 'they endure as an animate legacy in collective remembrance and recognition. We come home to them as to our psychic roots.'[3] It is for this reason that the attempt of the Church Fathers and their medieval successors to rout the pagan deities and their philosophical apologists was doomed to fail. As Douglas Bush has noted, even in periods when mythological motives were blotted out from European literature, they never disappeared from it: they remained there, as he puts it, in 'animated suspension', waiting to be rekindled.[4]

On this account, what is required of the historian of mythology is an explanation not of the passive survival of classical myths throughout European history, but rather of their active revival in specific periods, especially in periods when they were least expected to reappear. The century of European Enlightenment was such a period. While in earlier and later periods of revival – in the Renaissance and in Romanticism – there was a genuine and open interest in classical mythology, and attempts both to discover and to weave it into contemporary writing, from around the middle of the seventeenth century onwards we witness a conscious

Contemporary Theory and Practice (Lincoln: University of Nebraska Press, 1966). For more critical studies of modern theories, see: Geoffrey S. Kirk, *Myth. Its Meaning and Functions in Ancient and Other Cultures* (Berkeley: University of California Press, 1970); Jean-Pierre Vernant, 'The Reason of Myth', in *Myth and Society in Ancient Greece*, tr. J. Lloyd (London: Methuen, 1980), pp. 186–242; Walter Burkert, 'Griechische Mythologie une die Geistesgeschichte der Moderne', in *Les Études classiques aux XIXᵉ et XXᵉ siècles: Leur place dans l'histoire des idées* (Geneva: Fondation Hardt, 1980), pp. 159–99; Marcel Detienne, *The Creation of Mythology*, tr. M. Cook (Chicago: The University of Chicago Press, 1986); Percy S. Cohen, 'Theories of Myth', *Man,*. n.s. 6 (1969), pp. 337–53.

[3] George Steiner, *Antigones* (Oxford: Oxford University Press, 1984), p. 301.

[4] Douglas Bush, *Mythology and the Renaissance Tradition in English Poetry* (N.Y.: W. W. Norton, 1963), p. 293.

attempt to suppress and get rid of it. As Thomas Sprat declared in his *History of the Royal Society* (1667):

But from the time in which the Real Philosophy has appear'd, there is scarce any whisper remaining of such Horrors [of mythology] . . . the course of things goes quietly along, in its own true channel of Natural Causes and Effects. For this we are beholden to Experiments; which though they have not yet completed the Discovery of the True World, yet they have vanquished those wild inhabitants of the False World, that us'd to astonish the minds of Men . . . The Wit of the Fables and Religions of the Ancient World is well-nigh consumed . . . They have already served the Poets long enough; and it is now high time to dismiss them.[5]

This hostile attitude prevailed in practically all the critical studies of classical mythology at the time. Yet, the fact is that it was precisely during this same period – and out of the same sentiments – that the discussion about myth was emphatically revived in numerous scholarly and artistic works. As a survey of contemporary literature would show, from around 1680 and throughout the eighteenth century the idea of myth became a topic of lively interest in the works of philosophers, theologians, and historians.[6] The fables of antiquity, which have always 'been there' as decorative figures in the salons and drawing rooms of the upper classes, suddenly became problematic: for the ideologists of the Enlightenment, sure and proud in their rational civility and superiority over all the uneducated 'others' – be they the primitive natives in the New World or in their own society – sensed that the classical figures and tales were improper and even dangerous to their moral and aesthetic standards of civility.[7] And it was primarily due to their efforts to make sense of their own vulgar and irrational heritage that, for the first time since the middle of the sixteenth century, European scholars were once again beginning to show real interest in the popular culture and religion of the ancient world. The many popular essays on mythology, distributed throughout the continent in every language, bear witness to that sudden rise in interest. These essays set new critical standards of research and comparative interpretation in that age-old genre,

---

[5] Thomas Sprat, *The History of the Royal Society*, ed. J. I. Cope and H. W. Jones (London: Routledge and Kegan Paul, 1959), pp. 339, 341.

[6] Jean Starobinski, 'Le mythe au XVIIIᵉ siècle', *Critique*, 33 (1977), p. 977.

[7] Geoffrey Hartman, 'False Themes and Gentle Minds', *Philological Quarterly*, 62 (1968), pp. 55–68.

and, most significantly, they introduced new meanings into the term 'mythology' itself: though known and discussed by scholars in the West since antiquity, it was not until around the turn of the eighteenth century that scholars began to use 'mythology' in its more proper, but less common, meaning of a 'science of myth'. This new conception of the old term heralded a new awareness with regard to the more universal meaning of myth, and its wider range of application. For while earlier writers on mythology used the term only denotatively, namely to designate a particular set of ancient narratives – primarily the Greek and Roman myths – the new writers, in contrast, used it connotatively, to signify a wider range of narrative practices, as, for example, the folklore of the Amerindians, or the 'vulgar' beliefs of the lower classes. And they used the term myth in a new discursive mode, not just to describe or interpret these narratives, but rather to explain them.[8]

For the great Italian mythographers of the sixteenth century – Giraldi, Cartari, and Conti are the most notable – mythology was primarily a literary amusement, or, at best, a repository of icons and emblems which, if properly interpreted, could be used for moral didactic purposes. Even such a rational critic of 'follies' like Erasmus advocated the employment of these archaic tales in order to make moral precepts compelling and memorable. In his *De Copia* (1512) and *Parabolae sive Similia* (1514) he offers fables and mythological examples as devices for scholars, lawyers, and other rhetoricians.[9] Interested as they were only in the immediate relevance of what the ancients wrote to their own readers, they fudged all the mental and literary differences between their own times and archaic primitive times. In their massive encyclopaedic collections they thus treated classical myths as objects of ornamental, rather than historical, value. Their interpretative efforts were limited mainly to collecting all the available sources and to summarizing the artistic and philosophical interpretations of past commentators, the most influential of whom was Boccaccio, whose *Genealogia deorum gentilium* (1351–60) preserved, and

---

[8] James Engell, 'The Modern Revival of Myth: Its Eighteenth-Century Origins', in *Allegory, Myth, and Symbol*, ed. M. Bloomfield (Cambridge, Mass.: Harvard University Press, 1981), pp. 245–61.

[9] Seznec, *The Survival of the Pagan Gods*, pp. 257–78.

enriched, the late classical and medieval explanations of myth in the Stoic allegorical tradition.

Now, the allegorical interpretation of myths enjoyed a long and unbroken tradition from antiquity to the Renaissance and beyond.[10] The belief in some arcane wisdom contained in the ancient myths has always inspired mystics and philosophers to look for, and eventually to demonstrate, their own truths in its figures and tales. This belief was shared, or at least used, by sceptical Stoics in antiquity and by pious Christians in the Middle Ages to justify their mythological inquiries. And it proved equally convenient for the writers of the Renaissance, enabling them to reason away all the absurdities and obscenities from what was, after all, the most foundational tradition of the entire classical culture. Note, for example, Montaigne. Though he was very critical of the interpretive methods of the allegorists, and doubted whether Homer could really have 'meant to say all they make him say, and that he lent himself to so many and such different interpretations that the theologians, legislators, captains, philosophers, all sorts of people who treat of sciences, however differently and contradictorily, lean on him and refer to him', he also shared their more fundamental belief that the ancient myths did contain some arcane wisdom: 'Most of Aesop's Fables have many meanings and interpretations. Those who take them allegorically choose some aspect that squares with the fable, but for the most part this is only the first and superficial aspect; there are others more living, more essential and internal, to which they have not known how to penetrate.'[11] Indeed, so pervasive was that belief, that even a rationalist critic of antiquity like Descartes succumbed to its temptation. In his *Rules for the Guidance of our Native Powers* (1628) he expressed his conviction 'that certain primary seeds of truth implanted by nature in our human minds . . . had such vitality in that rude and unsophisticated ancient world' that they could still be useful to the moderns. In Descartes's view, such scientific truths are to be found, for example, in the mathematical works of Pappus and Diophantus, but, he adds, these writers 'by a certain baleful craftiness kept the secrets of this

---

[10] Don C. Allen, *Mysteriously Meant: The Rediscovery of Pagan Symbolism and Allegorical Interpretation in the Renaissance* (Baltimore: The Johns Hopkins University Press, 1970).
[11] Michel de Montaigne, *The Complete Works*, pp. 442–3, 298.

knowledge to themselves'. They did so in order to protect their own reputation as great inventors, but also to keep these truths from being abused by either the ambitious rulers or the ignorant masses.[12]

This last argument was habitually used, and subverted, by religious officials in order to denounce, and yet preserve, the mythological lore of the pagans. In that way, as Seznec has noted, even though 'in principle, the Church condemned the use of allegory, she encouraged it in fact'.[13] And he goes on to show how from the late sixteenth century onward, the most important pagan decorations were executed for cardinals who thus appear to have 'encouraged not only by their counsel, but by actual commissions, the abuses which it would rather have been their duty to check'. Other Catholic humanists, and above all the Jesuit missionaries, found it 'both legitimate and easy to juggle with mythology in a symbolic sense, in order to make it reveal the truths of the Scripture'.[14] In their attempt to justify this religious policy these Church officials readily reiterated the claim that ancient myths had been created by cunning priests who sought to disguise in their forms dangerous religious or philosophical truths from the ignorant masses, because in so doing they could depict them as not essentially contrary to the sacred tales: seen in this light the ancient myths appeared to be not malicious distortions but only unfortunate corruptions of sacred Biblical truths. According to this theory, pagan mythology was an historical result of, and theological proof for, the process of decay which befell mankind once it had lost touch with the rational and moral precepts of the true religion. Yet, inasmuch as the adherents of this theory (Cardinal Bossuet, it seems, was its last great representative in the late seventeenth century) conceived the ancient myths to be no more than a pagan fabulation of sacred Biblical truths, simply a literary creation devoid of any truths of its own, they lagged behind the philosophical practitioners of the allegorical method, who, at least, were ingenious enough to believe that the classical myths contained some unique and authentic truths of the pagans, their innermost visions of natural and social reality.

---

[12] René Descartes, *Descartes' Philosophical Writings*, pp. 17–18.
[13] Seznec, *The Survival of the Pagan Gods*, p. 275.
[14] Seznec, *The Survival of the Pagan Gods*, p. 265.

Bacon's well-known *On the Wisdom of the Ancients* (1609) was the most notable – and last – achievement of this long and illustrious tradition.[15] This work was well-known and influential among scholars of myth in the seventeenth century and, as I shall make clear in greater detail later on, it proved to be particularly significant for Vico. Bacon believed in an Adamic age of wisdom and bliss, an age in which men still lived in and knew nature intimately. He regarded the Greek myths as 'neither being the invention nor belonging to the [later] age of the poets themselves, but as sacred relics and light airs breathing out of [those] better times, that were caught from the traditions of more ancient nations and so received into the flutes and trumpets of the Greeks'.[16] In his view, the fanciful figures and tales of classical myths were allegories that disguised, whether consciously or not (Bacon could not make up his mind), some authentic primordial visions of reality. And yet, for all his genuine insights about the pre-rational origin of mythical truths, Bacon did not really advance the science of myth, because, inasmuch as he believed that the truth of myth lay beyond the myth itself which was only a later artificial ornamentation of that truth, and as such no more than an 'aromatic or enigmatic method' invented by priests and poets for the 'infoldment' of clear and truthful visions, his conception of myth was still very much rooted in the rather sterile tradition of allegorism. And even though his allegorical expositions of various myths were – as Vico would say – more 'learned and ingenious' than those of his predecessors, they were not more 'true' with regard to myth itself. Seeking to find a science in the Greek myths, rather than make a science out of them, he did not regard the term mythology itself as problematic or worthy of investigation; he did not seem aware of what ought to be the primary and most crucial issue in any theory of myth – namely, the fact that myth has a logic of its own, a logic which could explain not only classical myth, and not only myth itself, but other human phenomena as well.

As I have mentioned above, it was only around the turn of the eighteenth century that the term 'mythology' broke the age-old bounds of classical antiquity and came to be related to other, more

---

[15] Francis Bacon, *On the Wisdom of the Ancients*, in *The Philosophical Works of Francis Bacon*, VI, pp. 689–764.
[16] Bacon, *On the Wisdom of the Ancients*, p. 696 .

immediate and relevant phenomena. And, as I shall now suggest, these changes in the meanings of the term reflect a significant change in the relationship of the European scholars to their classical heritage. The myths of antiquity, well-known and long familiar, could become objects of scientific knowledge only after they had been defamiliarized to an audience which had always regarded them as natural. Because, as long as the Europeans were still too intimately close and loyal to these tales, they could not gain the necessary critical distance to examine them objectively; paradoxically, it was only when they became more alienated from the classical myths that they could come to understand them better. And this is where theorists of myth in the early Enlightenment, thinkers like Fontenelle, Leclerc, Banierre, or Warburton, differed most radically from their predecessors and followers alike: unlike the mythographers of the Renaissance or the philosophers of myth in Romanticism, they did not admire the classical myths, nor did they, for that matter, reject them, as other, more pious or rationalistic generations, did. They developed, rather, a new, somewhat ambivalent attitude towards classical mythology: as Frank Manuel so neatly phrases it in the title of his classic work on the subject, they 'confronted' this mythology.

Inasmuch as the men of the Enlightenment regarded themselves (to use Peter Gay's term) as 'modern pagans',[17] they rejoiced in classical mythology, and relished this richest lore of pre- and anti-Christian ideas and figures; they readily used them to subvert the sacred religious and national traditions of their own cultures. At the same time, however, as champions of modern gentility, they were appalled by the apparent rudeness of these tales. Their commitment to the culture of 'paganism' was ideological rather than notional or emotional. As Fontenelle put it, while the ancients 'glutted themselves on these fables because they believed them . . . we indulge ourselves in them with just as much pleasure but without believing in them'.[19] Even when they treated classical myths seriously, and it must be added that they hardly if ever did so, they remained, on the whole, rational,

---

[17] Peter Gay, *The Enlightenment: An Interpretation*, vol. 1: *The Rise of Modern Paganism* (London: Weidenfeld and Nicolson, 1970).
[18] Bernard de Fontenelle, 'Of the Origin of Fables', in *The Rise of Modern Mythology 1680–1860*, p. 18.

objective and detached. Where previous generations of interpreters saw sublime mysteries, they saw only rude and childish fantasies, which could be explained by commonsense psychology. As Hans Blumenberg has observed: 'Nothing surprised the promoters of the Enlightenment more, and left them standing more incredulously before the failure of what they thought were their ultimate exertions, than the survival of the contemptible old stories – the continuation of work on myth'.[19] The promoters of the Enlightenment have thus continued to work on myth, as they still do, trying to clarify by means of their scientific terms why and how myth still worked on them.

The Enlightenment's attempt at a scientification of myth was inspired and informed by the geographic and ethnographic discoveries of the previous century. As such, mythology presents a typical case of what Michel de Certeau has aptly defined as heterology – the 'science of the other'.[20] According to de Certeau, heterology comprises all the various 'scientific' means by which the European writers in the sixteenth and seventeenth centuries sought to make sense of what they initially perceived as utterly senseless in the behaviour of the Amerindians and all the other 'others'. These attempts at making sense of the other through science attest to the linguistic inability of these writers to understand the others and to explain them 'in their terms'; instead, they defined the others in their own terms, according to their own values and norms. The European observers were aware of these hermeneutical fallacies, and sought to overcome them in various ways, either by referring to their own authority as truthful reporters (de Certeau notes that they commonly used subjective, even sensual, experiences like 'I felt', 'I saw', 'I heard' and so on to ascertain 'the real that is lost in language'),[21] or, as has become increasingly more fashionable, they looked for some 'common language' with the others beyond their respective natural

---

19 Blumenberg, *Work on Myth*, p. 274.
20 Michel de Certeau, *Heterology: Discourse on the Other*, tr. B. Massumi (Minneapolis: University of Minnesota Press, 1986). On Vico's 'heterological' insights – like the 'conceits' of nations and scholars; the historicity of cultures and sciences; or the truthfulness of 'vulgar traditions' – and their significance for modern anthropology, see Michael Herzfeld, *Anthropology Through the Looking-Glass: Critical Anthropology in the Margins of Europe* (Cambridge: Cambridge University Press, 1987), esp. pp. 23–5, 78–81.
21 Michel de Certeau, ' "Of Cannibals": The Savage "I" ', in *Heterology*, p. 69.

languages – a language of images and gestures, of social practices, religious rites, seasonal ceremonies, and the like. Their own classical and national mythologies proved particularly useful for this comparative enterprise.

The literature of travelogues, missionary relations and commercial reports mapped a new mythological world, a strange – but very real – world of icons and rites; and because these myths of the new world were so meaningful and alive they infused new meaning and life into the myths of the old world, turning its giants, cave-men, bards, and warriors from mere literary images into real human beings. At the same time, the exposure of the true nature of ancient paganism and its depiction as a savage cult similar to those of the newly-found peoples created a mental distance between the characters of classical mythology and their modern interpreters and consumers, who could not use them any longer as mere legendary figures for easy amusement and instruction. For the new theorists of myth classical mythology was no longer a form of ancient literature, but rather a form of primitive life. Note, for example, the words with which Joseph Lafitau, a Jesuit missionary to New France in the early eighteenth century, introduces his work on the manners of the savage Amerindians:

I have sought in these practices and in these customs for traces of the most remote antiquity: I have read with care those of the most ancient authors who have treated of the manners, laws, and usages of the peoples with whom they had some acquaintance; I have compared these manners with one another; and I must say that if the ancient authors gave me some light to support various happy conjectures concerning the Savages, the customs of the Savages gave me some light to understand more easily and to explain several things which are in ancient Authors.[22]

As he observed the Indian institutions of vestal virgins, practices of abstinence, or initiation rites Lafitau recalled similar examples from ancient literature, which made the strange beliefs and rites of the savages seem more commonplace. He duly concluded that these – and all other – forms of mythmaking develop from the same generative conditions. And as de Certeau has noted, for Lafitau, the primitive Amerindians appeared to be both authentic

[22] Joseph Lafitau, *Moeurs des savages Amériquains comparées aux moeurs des premiers temps* . . . (Paris: Saugrain et Hochereau, 1724), pp. 1–5.

and similar to the biblical patriarchs of Western Civilization so as to 'have the force of "authorities"'.[23]

Yet, for all his genuine observations, Lafitau was not yet ready, or willing, to see the full philosophical implications from his comparative investigations, namely that such generative conditions must also be those of his own enlightened culture. Other, more radical thinkers like Fontenelle, Bayle, Montesquieu, Swift or Hume drew precisely these conclusions. For them, the various forms of mythology manifested the working of a pre-rational mentality common to all human beings, one that pertained not only to the primitive or ancient cultures, but also to their own. In so doing they introduced a slight, yet significant change in the comparative studies of myth: because the mythographers of the sixteenth and seventeenth centuries were still unaware of, or unready to acknowledge, the mythical nature of their own religious beliefs and rites, they commonly looked for similarities and conformities only between the contemporary primitive and the ancient pagan myths; the new scholars of mythology, in contrast, openly admitted that their culture was still largely mythical and, seeking to portray it as such, they willingly compared the savage myths to their own traditional beliefs and rites.

In any case, the contribution of the Enlightenment theorists of myth to the science of mythology was significant – to say the least. In the philosophical and historical treatises of Fontenelle and Bayle myth was used, for the first time, as a technical category of explanation, a device by which they sought to decipher human experience and history, to discover in and through its various manifestations in different cultures the psychic unity of mankind. Whereas Bacon was still looking for a science *in* ancient mythology the new scholars were intent in making a science *of* it. As Fontenelle put it in the conclusion of his essay *On the Origins of the Fables*:

So let us not look for anything in the fables except the history of the errors of the human mind. It is less capable of error when it knows to what extent it is subject to error. For it is not a science to cause one's head to be filled with all the extravagances of the Phoenicians and the Greeks, but it is a science to know what led the Phoenicians and the Greeks into

---

[23] Michel de Certeau, 'Writing vs. Time: History and Anthropology in the Works of Lafitau', *Yale French Studies*, 59 (1980), p. 42.

these extravagances. All men are so much alike that there is no people whose folly shouldn't make us tremble.[24]

It is, perhaps, quite significant that the works of both Lafitau and Fontenelle were published in the same year – 1724, the year in which Vico completed his *New Science*. A brief comparison between the three will clarify where, and in what way, Vico's new science of myth differed most radically from that of his contemporaries.

We have noticed that both Lafitau and Fontenelle, however different their methods and aims in the study of myth, shared the same deep notion of what myth was all about: they both sought to identify the 'mythical' with what was savage and ancient, to define it as the 'archaic' which is not yet civil and modern, and thereby to exclude it as such from their own cultural systems. It was, in the final analysis, this identification of the *mythical* with the irrational, rather than with the merely a-rational or pre-rational, and the subsequent attempts of theologians, philosophers and historians to reason it away from their systems of belief and knowledge, rather than integrate it into them, which hampered their attempts to make sense, let alone science, of myth. Ernst Cassirer has thus rightly argued that the Enlightenment failed to understand the 'specific nature of the mythical consciousness' not because it lacked philological and anthropological data about archaic culture, but because the persistent and pervasive force of this consciousness in the modern age offended their most cherished convictions and ideals about the hegemony of reason.[25] What they could not understand, or accept, was that their philosophical path-setters in antiquity had actually taken these tales seriously, and fervently so: 'How, indeed, was it possible' – asks Gibbon – 'that a philosopher should accept, as divine truths, the idle tales of the poets, and the incoherent traditions of antiquity, or, that he should adore, as gods, those imperfect beings whom he must have despised, as men!'[26] How, indeed, could 'the thin texture of the Pagan mythology' have been maintained in that ancient age of reason, or in any age of reason for that matter? That was the

---

[24] De Fontenelle, *Of the Origins of Fables*, p. 18.
[25] Ernst Cassirer, *The Philosophy of Symbolic Forms*, tr. R. Mannheim (New Haven: Yale University Press, 1953), II: *Mythical Thought*, p. 3.
[26] Edward Gibbon, *The Decline and Fall of the Roman Empire* (N.Y.: The Modern Library, n.d.), I, p. 27.

crucial question to which Gibbon, and in one way or another all the thinkers of the Enlightenment, sought an answer.

Gibbon's own answer merits specific consideration because more than any other thinker in his age (or, indeed, at any time) he was really able not only to know, but also to feel what mythical life in antiquity must have been like. Commenting on Roman society in the mid fourth century he says that in the age of Julian the gods were still alive, as, in a sense, they have still been for him:

Our familiar knowledge of their names and characters, their forms and attributes, seems to bestow on these airy beings a real and substantial existence . . . every circumstance contributed to prolong and fortify the illusion: the magnificent temples of Greece and Asia; the works of those artists which had expressed, in painting and in sculptures, the divine conceptions of the poet; the pomp of festivals and sacrifices; the success-ful art of divination; the popular traditions of oracles and prodigies; and the ancient practise of two thousand years.[27]

His critical evaluation of the later interpretations of that living reality is scathing: 'As the traditions of Pagan mythology were variously related, the sacred interpreters were at liberty to select the most convenient circumstances; and as they translated an arbitrary cypher, they could extract from any fable any sense which was adapted to their favourite system of religion and philosophy'.[28] And yet, when he turns to the myths themselves he discards them as utterly 'superstitious', which, in his (Humean) jargon means primitive beliefs arising out of, and basically confined to, merely sensual-imaginary impressions of natural reality. Such facile and anarchic impressions do not contain any real or true insights into human reality worthy of historical interest because, for Gibbon, all the religious sentiments of the Polytheists were just too various, loose, uncertain to make any sense of them. Armed with such clear cut conventions of what was 'real' in the world, and what was 'rational' in our perception of it, Gibbon was absolutely certain that mythology was not, and could not be, 'true' in any sense of the word. For the philosophical historian all myths were not real pictures of reality but rather mere primitive and dispensable images, or, to use Gibbon's favourite term, a sheer 'folly' of the human mind. Gibbon was thus unable, or unwilling, to admit that the philosophers of antiquity might

---

[27] Gibbon, *Decline and Fall*, I, p. 759.   [28] Gibbon, *Decline and Fall*, I, p. 761.

have genuinely believed in those irrational traditions. He concluded that there must have been some deeper reason, a
pragmatic or cunning reason, which he identifies with 'authority'
– or, as we would call it, reason of state – which compelled those
men, who otherwise 'asserted the independent dignity of reason',
to resign 'their actions to the commands of law and custom':
'Viewing, with a smile of pity and indulgence, the various errors of
the vulgar, they diligently practised the ceremonies of their
fathers, devoutly frequented the temples of the gods; and some-
times condescending to act a part on the theatre of superstition,
they concealed the sentiments of an atheist under the sacerdotal
robes'.[29] In their ironic treatment of mythology those ancient
reasoners simply recognized what Plato had already seen, and
what a modern reasoner like Spinoza would reiterate in some
famous lines in the *Theologico-Political Treatise* – that 'in despotic
statecraft, the supreme and essential mystery is to hoodwink the
subjects, and to mask the fear, which keeps them down, with the
specious garb of religion, so that men may fight as bravely for
slavery as for safety'.[30] Such views appealed to the thinkers of the
Enlightenment, most of whom supported the absolutist regimes of
the time; on such grounds they were willing to understand, and
ready to forgive, the persistence of myth in ancient and in their
own high cultures. As Peter Gay has noted, for the thinkers of the
Enlightenment 'myth could be sympathetically understood only
after it had been fully conquered, but in the course of its conquest
it had to be faced as the enemy'.[31]

Such was the 'climate of opinions' among theorists of myth in
the century of the Enlightenment. And it is in the context of these
intricate, yet utterly negative, modes of thinking about mythology
that I propose to reassess Vico's positive redefinition of myth as
vera narratio, a 'true story'. This redefinition, I shall argue, was
unique in the history of mythology, because in it Vico treated myth
in a thoroughly positive manner, regarding it as a unique mode of
expression, complete with its own forms, history, and even logic.
In the same year in which Lafitau and Fontenelle depicted myth
as erroneous and false, Vico declares that

[29] Gibbon, *Decline and Fall*, I, p. 27.
[30] Spinoza, *Theological Political Treatise*, in *The Works of Spinoza*, tr. R. H. M. Elwes (N.Y.: Dover Publications, 1951), I, p. 5.
[31] Gay, *The Enlightenment: An Interpretation*, I, p. 37.

The definition of μνθος is 'true narration' but it has continued to mean 'fable', which everybody has hitherto taken to mean 'false narration'', while the definition of δογος is 'true speech', though it is commonly taken to mean 'origin' or 'history of words'. Hence the etymologies which we have inherited are highly unsatisfactory for understanding the true histories of the origins signified by words. In the following meditation we shall therefore reveal new principles of mythology and etymology, showing that fables and true speech meant the same thing and that they constituted the vocabulary of the first nations.[32]

I shall elaborate on Vico's definition of myth later on, but here I would like to spell out what I take to be its main message: By depicting *mythos* and *logos* as different, yet compatible, modes of discourse Vico not only challenged those philosophical theories that deemed the *mythical* mode of thought to be false simply because it was more archaic than the *logical* one, but he attacked also the historical theories based on this conception of myth, those which viewed human history in general as a process of progression from *mythos* to *logos*, as a process of enlightenment which, to paraphrase Kant's famous dictum, consisted in the rational emancipation of humanity from its 'self-imposed bondage' to myth.

Vico refused most emphatically to view *mythos* and *logos* as essentially opposed to each other, and regarded the two instead as complementary; for him they constituted two different yet equivalent modes of thought by which human beings have sought to make sense of reality, the one by imaginary tales projected onto reality and the other by empirical theories derived from it. Vico agreed, of course, that the latter way was much more successful in explaining and controlling reality, but, unlike the more enthusiastic champions of the Enlightenment in his time, he did not think that this fact alone made myth obsolete. He denied that humankind, however disenchanted with the world it has or might ever become, could live without the metaphysical significance that myth introduces into the world. Much as he believed in general cultural progress through transformation of 'divine' and 'heroic' images into ever more refined 'human' concepts, Vico was still convinced that we are the inheritors of former modes of thought and behaviour. The past survives and infiltrates the present time

---

[32] Vico, *The First New Science*, par. 249, *Selected Writings*, p. 139.

in all the spheres of cultural creativity, and above all in languages:
'The poetic speech which our poetic logic has helped us to understand continued for a long time into the historical period, much
as great and rapid rivers continue far into the sea, keeping sweet
the waters borne on by the force of their flow' (NS/412). The
realization that such mythical idioms infiltrate all the norms and
forms of modernity prompted Vico to make this truth clear to an
age which naïvely believed it had overcome its mythical
inhibitions. By discovering the 'true original meaning' of myth,
i.e., what myth meant for its makers, he hoped to clarify how its
archaic, concrete, and poetic images evolved into our modern,
abstract, and rational ideas. He believed that

as much as the poets had first sensed in the way of vulgar wisdom, the
philosophers later understood in the way of esoteric wisdom; so that the
former may be said to have been the sense and the latter the intellect of
the human race. What Aristotle said of the individual man is therefore
true of the race in general: *Nihil est in intellectu quin prius fuerit in sensu.*
That is, the human mind does not understand anything of which it has
had no previous impression. (NS/363)

These 'organicist' notions about the mythopoeic origins and
growth of knowledge were largely ignored, or rejected, by the
enlightened 'philosophers', who thereby failed to realize the
historicity of their own knowledge.[33] Vico, on the other hand,
fused them into his major methodological postulate: that
'doctrine must start from the point where the matters of which
they treat first began to take shape' (*Le dottrine debbono cominicare
da quando cominiciano le materie che trattano*) (NS/314). He duly saw
that in order to know our social-historical world we must perceive
its inner 'poetic logic'; by which he meant that we must trace the
transformation of poetic and concrete images of reality into our
rational abstract concepts, and not merely impose the latter on
reality as if they were absolute and eternal, as 'the philosophers'
did. Philosophy, therefore, if it is to be a true science, must, like all
other *dottrine*, become a history of its own subject-matter: it must
start from the point where the matter of which it treats – the *logos*
– first began to take shape, which means that it must retrace its
evolution in and through and out of *mythos*. The primary task of

[33] This is a main theme in Alasdair MacIntyre, *Whose Justice? Which Rationality?* (London:
Duckworth, 1988).

philosophy, then, is to reconstruct a true *mythology*, a task which must begin where the term itself began. Mythology, Vico reasoned, when taken in its original etymological sense and historical perspectives, means a primeval history with logos, or a history of primeval logos. Both of these – the poetic logic which permeates ancient historical narratives, as well as the mythical origins and poetic development of logical thinking – must be regained if we are to understand the mental modes, the *modificazioni*, which actually constituted our *mondo civile*.

Vico's reinterpretation of mythology proceeded in stages. The main problem with these archaic tales was precisely that though 'originating among the first savage and crude men' they had been 'later perfected as acute individuals applied their reflection to them'. This fallacy, which Vico calls 'the conceit of the scholars . . . who will have it that what they know is as old as the world' (NS/127) has, in his view, hampered all the major theories of mythology 'from Plato and Aristotle down to Patrizzi, Scaliger, and Castelverto' (NS/384). They all assumed that the *sapienza riposta* of their own *tempi illuminati, colti e magnifichi* could have been known to men who lived in times which must have been *piccole, rozze, oscurissime*.

For the wisdom of the ancients was the vulgar wisdom of the lawgivers who founded the human race, not the esoteric wisdom of great and rare philosophers. Whence it will be found . . . that all the mystic meanings of lofty philosophers attributed by the learned to the Greek fables and the Egyptian hieroglyphics are as impertinent as the historical meanings they both must have had are natural. (NS/384)

Significantly, among the 'great and rare philosophers' whom he criticizes, Vico singles out Plato and Bacon, two of his 'favourite authors'. Much as he admired their philosophical works, Vico felt that as interpreters of the ancient myths they both erred because they did not set the myths in any coherent historical framework which would delimit the range of their possible meanings, and as a result they came to attribute to them inflated meanings, either too negative (as in Plato's *Republic*) or too positive (as in Bacon's *On the Wisdom of the Ancients*), but in any case meanings which could not possibly have been those conceived by their original makers:

In this connection we inquire into the reasons why the philosophers later had such a desire to recover the wisdom of the ancients, as well as into the occasions the fables provided them for bestirring themselves to meditate lofty things in philosophy, and into the opportunities they had for reading their own hidden wisdom into the fables. (NS/37)

From the outset, then, Vico's theory of myth assumed wider critical and ideological dimensions: it was designed to lay down a new foundation for the cultural history of Western civilization, based on a new perception of mythology as 'true narration'. And since Vico himself developed his theory of myth out of and against those of 'his authors', Plato and Bacon, I shall elaborate his theory by juxtaposing it with theirs.

II

Ever since Plato decreed, that for the sake of moral and social integrity in the state, 'we must begin . . . by a censorship over our myth-makers', the debate about the legitimacy of mythical beliefs in rational and civil society has never been laid safely to rest.[34] The problem with myth, as Plato duly recognized, is that though 'the myths are, as a whole, false, there is truth in them too': a 'truth', presumably, pertaining to humankind's deepest need for common meaning, order and purpose in life, and one which has been created and woven by many generations into those traditional tales which still persist in our minds and cultures.[35] Plato was aware that these tales, which have been told since the beginning of time and have been taken up, passed on and transmitted through the ages, formed the most effective system of communicating educational and political messages in the Greek city. He duly sought to utilize them for his own purposes.[36] Whereas in the *Republic* his treatment of myth is negative, and is

---

[34] The best philosophical and historical account of this debate is still Ernst Cassirer, *The Myth of the State* (New Haven: Yale University Press, 1946).

[35] Plato, *The Republic* 377–8, tr. P. Shorey, Loeb Classical Library (Cambridge, Mass.: Harvard University Press, 1942). For similar pronouncements on the verity of myths, see *Phaedo* 61b, *Phaedrus* 259c–d, *Laws* 682a.

[36] On the dialectics of credulous and critical criteria of truth in Greek culture, and the evolvement of a unique 'modality of belief' which enabled Plato and other critics of mythology to uphold and even recreate the classical myths, see Paul Veyne, *Did the Greeks Believe in Their Myths?*, tr. P. Wissing (Chicago: The University of Chicago Press, 1988), p. 113.

concerned mainly with the most scandalous episodes in the ancient mythology, his attitude in the *Laws* appears to have become more tolerant and even positive with regard to myth. For he was, in fact, seeking to create a new mythology in the city, the contents of which was to be his Laws. As the lawgiver of the *Republic* Plato's dilemma was not so much to eliminate myth from its constitution, but to control it. He rightly saw that the efficacy of myth, that particular ancient and popular tale which everyone has heard and remembers, lies in its being a non-discursive kind of knowledge, such that is obtained through information common to all, replete with opinions which were based simply on 'what they say' (for this is the exact meaning of mythology), that it was, in short, distinctly and thoroughly traditional. And as he realized that the ideal *Republic*, like all other cities, could not do without -(and indeed needed) such archaic foundations, he ruled that in it the *mythos* should be disciplined by *logos*, by critical philosophy, by a written law. Ultimately, then, it was his predilection for philosophical or other 'disciplined' myths that made Plato so hostile to the ancient Homeric myths. In his view, the Homeric myths were ruinous to the city because they disguised the origin of its moral law, rooting it in fabulous, mostly immoral, deeds of gods and heroes. Even the most heroic tales, he thought, were liable to cause moral and political disintegration (*anomie*), since they attributed the laws to super-human agents, and thus acquitted the citizens of their authorial responsibility to them. And since Plato's main ambition in the *Republic* was to re-establish the *nomos* of the state on new philosophical premises, the ancient mythological ones had to be discredited. Thus, even though in his pragmatic politics of mythology Plato appears to tolerate myth, in the final analysis, his basic view of myth in itself remains negative throughout: 'there is from long ago' – and always will be – 'a quarrel between philosophy and poetry'.[37]

Plato's charges still reverberate in the vast literature on myth. Echoing A. N. Whitehead's famous remark, it might be said that the history of mythology is nothing but a series of footnotes to Plato. His paedeic strictures on mythmaking have inspired all

---

[37] Plato, *The Republic* 607b. This and other ambivalent statements on myth are discussed by Ludwig Edelstein, 'The Function of Myth in Plato's Philosophy', *The Journal of the History of Ideas*, 10 (1949), pp. 463–81.

successive attempts to purge cultural systems such as religion, philosophy, science and history of their archaic myths. In one way or
another, all the theorists of myth have always attempted to answer
the essential dilemma posed by Plato – how could the Greeks, the
founders of rationality, continue to believe in savage and absurd
tales, to attribute to their gods such horrific crimes as incest,
adultery, cannibalism, patricide and a myriad of other indecent
acts?

Vico shared and reiterated many of Plato's views about the
latent immorality of the ancient myths:

For Orpheus then founds the humanity of Greece on the examples of
an adulterous Jove, a Juno who is the mortal enemy of the virtues of
the Herculeses, a chaste Diana who solicits the sleeping Endymions at
night, an Apollo who gives oracular responses and pursues to the point
of death modest maiden Daphnes, a Mars who, as if it were not enough
for the gods to commit adultery on earth, carries it even into the sea with
Venus . . . Such examples, powerful divine examples as they are (though
such fables may contain all the recondite wisdom desired by Plato and in
our time by Bacon of Verulam in his *Wisdom of the Ancients*), if taken at
face value would corrupt the most civilized peoples and would incite
them to become as bestial as the very beasts of Orpheus. (NS/80)

The important point to note, however, is that this would be the
case only *if* these tales were *taken at face value*, that is if their
interpreters ignored the specific historical conditions in which
they originated and wherein alone their 'true historical meaning'
– that which their original creators could have conceived – can be
found. Vico believed that

these treacherous reefs of mythology will be avoided by the principles of
this Science, which will show that such fables in their beginning were all
true and severe and worthy of the founders of the nations, and only later
(when the long passage of years had obscured their meanings, and
customs had changed from austere to dissolute, and because men to
console their consciences wanted to sin with the authority of the gods)
came to have the obscene meanings with which they have come down to
us . . . Because religion was important to the men of Greece, and they
feared to have the gods opposed to their desires as they were to their
customs, they attributed their customs to the gods and gave improper,
ugly, and obscene meanings to the fables. (NS/81, 221)

In Vico's view this original habit of identifying the myth with
everything which men conceived to be negative – became the

pattern of all subsequent interpretations of mythology in Western civilization. The problem of morality was not in the poetic license of myth, but rather in the rational discipline of his interpreters. It is important to set Vico's theory of myth in the context of these distinctly 'negative' understandings of myth because, as Marcel Detienne has recently argued, the modern theories of myth which emerged in the Enlightenment and flourished in the positivistic schools of the nineteenth century, those which, on the whole, identified, and subsequently dismissed, the mythical epochs and aspects of our modern culture as residual elements of primitive irrationality in it, have derived their main conceptual and tactical arguments from the anti-mythological tradition in ancient Greece: 'The moral judgments of the nineteenth century', he writes, 'are sanctioned by the righteous severity of the ancient philosophers'.[38] According to Detienne, this tradition, which originated with Xenophanes (c. 530 BC) and culminated with Thucydides and Plato a century later, opposed the mythical stories because they were stories of a particular kind: they were traditional, not critical, stories. As stories which have been told since the beginning of time and always taken up again, they thrived on spontaneous oral-popular modes of creativity, and were thus conceived to be subversive to the stories told by the critical authors – which were controlled by the intellectual elite and passed on in writing. The struggle between the 'two cultures' in ancient Greece ultimately led to the literal subordination of the *mythical* to the *logical*, to what Detienne has called 'the invention of mytho-logy', by which he means the formation of a philosophical discourse about – and against – poetic myth, an attempt, namely, to impose scientific criteria onto what was, and must always remain, a non-scientific endeavour. Detienne further notes that the modern concept of myth that we have inherited from this critical tradition has acquired its negative meaning and connotations in a peculiar way, not just because myth itself was considered to be negative, but rather because it is a concept which has always been defined negatively, that is in reference to what is not myth: the mythical has been commonly opposed to what is religiously true (myth is false), philosophically rational (myth is irrational),

---

[38] Marcel Detienne, *The Creation of Mythology* tr. M. Cook (Chicago: The University of Chicago Press, 1986), p. 82.

historically real (myth is fictitious), and so on. As Detienne has put it:

A true mytho-logic begins with the others. Thus, exclusionary procedures multiply in the discourse of the science of myths, borne on a vocabulary of scandal that indicts all figures of otherness. Mythology is on the side of the primitive, the inferior races, the peoples of nature, the languages of origins, childhood, savagery, madness – always the *other*, as the excluded figure. At the same time, with each of these partitions mythology shifts, changes form and content: it becomes the incredible which religion lays before itself; the irrational that reason grants itself; the savage as the inverse of the civilized; it is what is absent, what is over and done with; it is ancient madness.[39]

Plato, who first used the term 'mythology' in that critical sense, is thus regarded by Detienne to have been its most lethal critic. At the same time, however, inasmuch as Plato did not merely criticize ancient mythical poetry, but sought to understand why it exercised such a strong fascination – not only on the vulgar masses, but on himself as well – he might as well be regarded as its most creative critic. Plato ultimately came to the conclusion that the secret of myth lay in its capacity to evoke, in order to 'satisfy and please', emotions that have 'never been properly educated by reason or even habit'. Thus, for example, 'in regard to the emotions of sex and anger, and all the appetites and pains and pleasures of the soul which we say accompany all our actions', this poetry 'waters and fosters these feelings when what we ought to do is to dry them up, and it establishes them as our rulers when they ought to be ruled'.[40] Ancient mythology thus failed the ultimate test of poetry in classical culture – that of *sublimation*. What this notion means has been succinctly defined by a modern scholar: 'that man can, in feeling and in speech, transcend the human'.[41] Socrates in his final discussion with Glaucon in *The Republic* makes it clear that Homeric poetry, because it consists only in realistic imitation of natural passions, fails to lift the soul and its faculties above matter.

For Vico, and for the eighteenth century at large, this moral test was still the most common criterion by which to evaluate

---

[39] Marcel Detienne, 'Rethinking Mythology', in *Between Belief and Transgression*, ed. M. Izard and P. Smith (Chicago: The University of Chicago Press, 1982), p. 47.

[40] Plato, *The Republic* 606b–d.

[41] Thomas Weiskel, *The Romantic Sublime* (New Haven: Yale University Press, 1976). p. 1.

myth.[42] In what follows I shall argue that Vico conceived his theory of myth – and effected its rehabilitation – partly in response to this Platonic depiction of myth as essentially immoral poetry. He did it by revising the classical theory of 'the sublime' which, as formulated by pseudo-Longinus, was immensely influential in his time. While the many other adherents of this theory in his time followed the Platonic tradition and judged the morality of ancient mythology in absolute aesthetic terms, Vico, in contrast, judged it in historical terms, seeking to understand the 'sublimative' role of myth in the process of civilization:

The first men of the gentile nations, children of the nascent mankind, created things according to their own ideas. But this creation was infinitely different from that of God. For God, in his purest intelligence, knows things, and, by knowing them, creates them; but they, in their robust ignorance, did it by virtue of a wholly corporeal imagination. And because it was quite corporeal, they did it with marvellous sublimity; a sublimity [*sublimatà*] such and so great that it excessively perturbed the very persons who by imagining did the creating, for which they were called 'poets', which is Greek for 'creators'. Now this is the threefold labor of great poetry: (1) to invent sublime fables suited to the popular understanding; (2) to perturb to excess, with a view to the end proposed; (3) to teach the vulgar to act virtuously, as the poets have taught themselves. (NS/376)

The key term in this passage is *sublimità*. Technically, Vico uses the term in its common Longinian connotations, and in his judgment of ancient mythology he often invokes its well-known subjective and formal criteria for 'great poetry' – 'the power of forming great conceptions', 'vehement and inspired passion', 'figurative language', 'noble action', and 'elevated composition'.[43] All these elements are duly identified in numerous philological commentaries on Homer, whom Vico repeatedly hails, contra Plato, as 'the most sublime poet' (NS/376, 387, 445, 448, 720–87, 807, 809, 825, and passim). What enabled Vico to tout Homer as a sublime poet was, therefore, not so much a new conception of 'sublimity', but a new definition of 'poetry', such that was, as Erich

[42] T. B. Wood, *The Word 'Sublime' and Its Context 1650–1760* (The Hague: Martinus Nijhoff, 1972).
[43] On Vico's appropriation of Longinus' notions, see Gustavo Costa, 'Vico and Ancient Rhetoric', in *Classical Influences on Western Thought, 1650–1870*, ed. R. R. Bolgar (Cambridge: Cambridge University Press, 1978), pp. 247–61.

Auerbach has noted, radically opposed not only to the classical-Renaissance notion of 'poetry' as an expression of refined ideas through figurative characters, but was also radically different from that of the later Romantics, with whom Vico is usually compared. As Auerbach put it: whereas the Romantics looked upon poetry 'as undisciplined, unpolitical, and alien to all constitutive order, Vico regarded it as politically constructive, an element in the plan of providence, leading, by way of mythical conceptions . . . to a constituted order and the establishment of society'.[44]

Like Plato, then, Vico too perceived the political significance of mythical poetry, but he rejected Plato's conclusion that because of its brutal tales it was liable to cause moral and social anarchy, unless these tales were censored and refashioned according to philosophical ideas. Vico thought, instead, that it was only by means of such brutal images and tales that political messages could get through. He contended that the myths in themselves were 'true narrations' of the communal *sensus comunis*, namely tales which encoded some essential practical lessons of social life, and that they retained their original messages even when later interpreters gave them 'improper, ugly, and obscene meanings'. Above all, the poetic sublimity of these tales remained intact and effective only as long as they expressed, and touched, raw feelings. This view is reiterated, for example, in Vico's interpretation of the mythical figures of Tityus and Prometheus, whose common depiction as 'chained to a high rock with their hearts being devoured by an eagle' was one of those scenes which so horrified Socrates. For Vico, instead, this tale had a significant political lesson – it taught men to respect divine authority: 'Their being rendered immobile by fear was expressed by the Latins in the heroic phrase *terrore defixi*, and the artists depict them chained hand and foot with such links upon the mountains. Of these links was formed the great chain which Longinus admires as the sublimest of all Homeric fables' (NS/387).

Plato's failure to understand this subliminal nature of myth was symptomatic of a more basic failure: he did not understand the essentially 'poetic' make-up of the human mind and of history, and did not realize that men were beings 'who by imagining did the creating'. And, as Vico relates in the *Autobiography*, it was only

---

44 Erich Auerbach, 'Vico and Aesthetic Historicism', p. 116.

when he himself had apprehended this truth, and thereby grasped the reasons for Plato's failure, that he was able to perceive his own methodological failure in his earlier work on the *Universal Law* of civil association common to all mankind. In that work, he says, he failed because 'he tried therein to descend from the mind of Plato and other enlightened philosophers into the dull and simple minds of the founders of the gentile peoples, whereas he should have taken the opposite course'.[45] Hence, his 'great effort' in the *New Science* 'to descend from these human and refined natures of ours to these quite wild and savage natures' of the *primi uomini*. His aim was to explain, historically, how these 'first men' who were not yet able to reason (as modern man does) by 'intelligible class concepts of things', but only through the concrete and particular things themselves, managed nevertheless to create in those mythical figures of gods and heroes the moral terms and conditions by which alone they could live and must be understood.

Vico's ultimate goal was to establish, in opposition to Plato, that indeed it was not philosophy but 'poetry [that] founded gentile humanity' (NS/214), so that 'all the arts of the necessary, the useful, the convenient, and even in large part those of human pleasure, were invented in the poetic centuries before the philosophers came; for the arts are nothing but imitations of nature, and in a certain way 'real' poems 'made not of words but of things' (NS/217). Had Plato realized the way in which 'real' poetic images develop into abstract philosophical concepts, Vico seems to suggest, he would not have depicted the relationship between poetry and philosophy as that of 'an age-old quarrel': he would have seen, as Vico did, that poetry and philosophy, *mythos* and *logos*, *topica* and *critica*, are not essentially opposed, but historically complemetary, and equally valid. What Plato and other rational critics of mythology since antiquity have failed to see is that its figures and schemata are not irrational but, rather, form an alternative mode of rationalism, which stems from, and may reorientate the mind toward, a different perception of reality, one that is based not on conscious methodo-logical discourse on reality by means of abstract concepts and theories, but on unconscious mytho-logical figuration of reality by means of concrete

---

[45] Vico, *The Autobiography*, p. 194.

images and narrations.[46] And here again we can perceive Vico's position as deeply and totally anti-Cartesian: for he saw that Descartes' *Discourse on Method* was as much about itself, i.e. about Discourse, as it was about Method. Descartes conceived scientific method as consisting in the discursive signification of things, whereby they are processed into clear and distinct concepts in the mind; Vico, in contrast, forged a new scientific method which consisted in the figural signification of things, whereby they are represented in their iconical transformations in history.

In Vico's view, the first modern thinker who was able to perceive this deeper truth about myth was the third of 'his authors' – Francis Bacon. His work *On the Wisdom of the Ancients* was, as its title suggests, an attempt to understand mythology on its own terms, to see it as a coherent system of tales with its own authentic 'wisdom' rather than as a collection of deceptive and fanciful tales. And even though Vico eventually came to criticize Bacon's method as being 'more ingenious and learned than true' he was much impressed by his attempt to recover this knowledge entirely in and through mythological sources. Bacon's work, he says, marked him 'the sign of the source' whence he was to draw the main discoveries and conclusions for his *New Science*.[47]

Bacon's notion that real knowledge required a recognition of the true forms of things beyond the false images imposed on them by the human mind prompted him to present his great reform of knowledge in reflexive terms, as a new 'great instauration' of aboriginal knowledge.[48] Its end, he says, is 'a restitution and reinvesting (in great part) of man to sovereignty and power (for whensoever he shall be able to call the creatures by their true names he shall again command them) which he had in the first state of creation'.[49] Much as he detested the ideal and all forms of primitivism, and constantly hailed the vast advantages of the moderns over the ancients, Bacon was still fascinated by the innocence of the ancients, as it displayed an uninhibited relationship to the

---

[46] On the problem and history of the mythical vs. logical modes of narration in historiography, see the brilliant essay of Lionel Gossman, 'History and Literature: Literary Form and Historical Understanding', in *Between History and Literature* (Cambridge, Mass.: Harvard University Press, 1990), pp. 227–56.

[47] Vico, *The Autobiography*, p. 153.

[48] Francis Bacon, *Novum Organum*, in *The Philosophical Works of Francis Bacon*, ed. J. Spedding, R. L. Ellis, and D. D. Heath (London: Longman, 1858–74) IV, pp. 33, 51, 110.

[49] Bacon, *The Advancement of Learning*, in *The Philosophical Works*, III, p. 222.

things-in-themselves, and he sought to retrieve it for modern man. His attempt to regain the 'wisdom of the ancients' from pagan mythology was based on the conviction that 'between the hidden depths of antiquity and the days of tradition and evidence that followed there is drawn a veil, as it were, of fables, which come in and occupy the middle region that separates what has perished from what survives'.[50] And although he was ready to admit that his 'reverence for the primitive times' may have carried him too far, he was still willing to believe that

beneath no small number of these fables of the ancient poets there lay from the very beginning a mystery and allegory . . . in some of these fables, as well as in the very frame and texture of the story as in the propriety of the names . . . I find a conformity and connexion with the thing signified, so close and so evident, that one cannot help believing such signification to have been designed and meditated from the first, and purposely shadowed out.[51]

Bacon, of course, well knew that the poetic wisdom of the ancients was incomplete and much inferior to modern science. Nevertheless, he believed that it could still serve as a corrective lesson with regard to our excessively verbal and theoretical reasoning: 'Parabolical poesy is typical history, by which ideas which are objects of the intellect are represented in forms that are objects of the sense'.[52] Bacon makes clear that the mythopoeic, and even more so the pre-Socratic, approaches to nature were superior to the later philosophical ones: all the more so because their case was still one in which 'reality ruled the mind', whereas later, in Plato's case, 'ideas ruled reality', and finally, in Aristotle's case, 'words ruled ideas'.[53] With the latter original knowledge was completely discarded and lost, as immediate and concrete observation of things was replaced by abstract and merely linguistic musings about them. From then on, Bacon concludes, all attempts to approach natural phenomena directly were hampered by words and theories, or the 'Idols of the Market-place . . . which have crept into the understanding through the alliances of words and names. For men believe that their reason governs words; but it is also true

[50] Bacon, *On the Wisdom of the Ancients*, in *The Philosophical Works*, vi, p. 695.
[51] Bacon, *On the Wisdom of the Ancients*, in *The Philosophical Works*, vi, p. 696.
[52] Bacon, *De Principiis*, in *The Philosophical Works*, iii, p. 86.
[53] Bacon, *Novum Organum*, in *The Philosophical Works*, iv, p. 58.

that words react on the understanding; and this is it that has rendered philosophy and the sciences sophistical and inactive.'[54]

We can see, then, that for Bacon, as for other Protestant thinkers, real knowledge of things consisted in grasping their original forms ('the form of a thing is the very thing itself'), by which he meant the concrete natural properties of things which lie beyond the abstract conceptions which humans have of them. He duly resolved to go back to the things as nature had made them originally regardless of what they had become in history, to recognize them as they had been known to the Ancients in 'the hidden depths of antiquity' before 'the days of tradition and evidence which followed' corrupted them. 'Tradition', as he understood it, began when nature was no longer observed by individuals according to their own personal observation and reason, but was instead processed for easy consumption through the invention of 'confused and ill-defined names . . . hastily and irregularly derived from realities' which thus created all kinds of 'fictions which owe their origin to false and idle theories'.[55]

Bacon, then, was acutely aware of the historicity of knowledge, and hence of its traditionality. Inasmuch as he analysed the dynamics of its socio-linguistic composition and historical development he may well be considered the founder of the modern science of tradition.[56] A central aim of his reform of knowledge was to repair the process of tradition by devising more secure methods of control over the transmission of knowledge in society. And yet, for all his ingenuity in recognizing the nature and problems of traditional knowledge, his efforts to reform it were hampered by his ideal of knowledge, by his epistemological puritanism, which led him to believe that we could get back the things as they truly are in themselves – in their absolutely pure and original form – regardless of what they have become for us, simply by reaching them, as Gadamer once put it, 'behind the back of language'. Bacon expresses this desire in a neat fable:

It seems to me that men look down and study nature as from some remote and lofty tower. Nature presents to their gaze a certain picture of

[54] Bacon, *Novum Organum*, in *The Philosophical Works*, IV, p. 61.
[55] Bacon, *Novum Organum*, in *The Philosophical Works*, IV, p. 61.
[56] On the wider implications of Bacon's theory, see my 'Science, Tradition, and the Science of Tradition', in *Science in Context*, 3 (1989), pp. 143–73.

herself, or a cloudy semblance of a picture, in which all the minute differences of things on which the practise and prosperity of men rest, are blurred by distance. So men toil and strive, straining the eyes of the mind, fixing their gaze in prolonged meditation, or shifting it about to get things into better focus. Finally they construct the arts of disputation, like ingenious perspective glasses, in order to seize and master the subtle differences of nature. A ridiculous kind of ingenuity, is it not, and mis-directed energy for a man to climb his tower, arrange his lenses and screw up his eyes to get a closer view, when he might avoid all that laborious contrivance and tedious industry and achieve his end by a way not only easy but far superior in its benefits and utility, namely by getting down from his tower and coming closer to things?[57]

It was this (very Protestant) belief that 'True philosophy echoes most faithfully the voice of the world itself, and is written as it were from the world's own dictation' – a belief, in short, in the possi-bility of attaining knowledge that was absolutely pure and original, utterly concrete and natural and not at all verbal and historical – which, a century later, alerted Giambattista Vico to what was wrong in Bacon's conception of knowledge and in his attempt to recover it from the ancient myths. Bacon, he saw, failed to com-prehend the myths because, like Plato, he did not consider them from the proper psychological and historical perspectives – those of their makers. And these myth-makers, as Vico reminds us time and again, were not innocent observers but impulsive 'poets' of nature (NS/214, 375–6), men who were 'ignorant of the natural causes producing things', and could not 'even explain them by analogy with similar things', and therefore tended to 'attribute their own nature to them' (NS/180). His crucial discovery here, as Hayden White has brilliantly shown, was that 'the relationship between language and the world of things is not simply reflexive. Primitive linguistic representations of the world of things are not simply reversed images of the world given in sense perception, as they would be if they were only a product of thought reflecting the world of things in a language restricted to metaphors based on the identification of the external world with internal emotional states.'[58] Rather, Vico saw that mythopoeic consciousness with

---

[57] Francis Bacon, *The Refutation of Philosophy*, in B. Farrington, *The Philosophy of Francis Bason* (Liverpool: Liverpool University Press, 1964), p. 129.
[58] Hayden White, 'The Tropics of History: The Deep Structure of the *New Science*', in *Vico's Science of Humanity*, p. 72.

active and creative, not passive and merely perceptive, in its attitude to the world. The primitive myths, 'born entirely of poverty of language and need of expression' (NS/456), were thus primarily expressive, and not really designative, descriptions of reality. They could never give us a prior and more accurate cognitive representation of the world, as Bacon naively hoped, because they were initially and continually created as linguistic significations of it. Vico terms this process 'poetic logic':

That which is metaphysics insofar as it contemplates things in all the forms of their being, is logic insofar as it considers things in all the forms by which they may be signified. Accordingly, as poetry has been considered by us above as a poetic metaphysics in which the theological poets imagined bodies to be for the most part divine substances, so now that same poetry is considered as poetic logic, by which it signifies them. (NS/400)

The crucial assertion in this passage is that the external literary forms of mythology are identical with its internal philosophic logic: these forms determine what its authors could know and say about the world. This is where Vico differs most drastically from Bacon. For Bacon the linguistic figurations of ancient myths appeared to be just superfluous artistic illustrations of or philosophical reflections on an original, more authentic cognition of reality. It was this authentic, or more primitive and therefore clearer view of the 'forms of things' in their immediate concreteness, exactly as they appeared to the Adam before the post-Babelonian languages distorted them almost beyond recognition, which he hoped to retrieve. For Vico, on the other hand, the philological medium of myth – its 'vivid representations, images, similes, comparisons, metaphors, circumlocutions, phrases explaining things by their natural properties, etc.' – was its philosophical message. Such figures of speech, he thought, do not disguise the timeless structure of objective natural reality, as Bacon believed, but rather disclose the history of subjective human reality; in other words, they show us what were the actual linguistic means by which humankind established itself and its world over against the natural world.

Both Plato and Bacon, Vico realized, failed to discover the truth of myth because they looked for it through and behind its figurative language, not in the language itself. For Vico, in contrast, all myths were creations in and of this language, and not only in the obvious and trivial sense that humankind has used language to convey its immediate impressions of natural reality, but in the stronger semiotic sense that it could not have perceived nature, or anything, in any other way but in terms of its own human, all-too-human, language, that is to say, by naming its objects:

Thus the first language in the first mute times of the nations must have begun with signs, whether gestures of physical objects, which had natural relations to the ideas . . . For that first language, spoken by the theological poets, was not a language in accord with the nature of the things it dealt with (as must have been the sacred language invented by Adam, to whom God granted divine onomathesia, the giving of names to things according to the nature of each), but was a fantastic speech making use of physical substances endowed with life and most of them imagined to be divine. (NS/401)

According to Vico, our human knowledge, society, and culture have all evolved from these onomathetic powers of primitive men, since in the act of naming they not merely supplied names to already-known things, but made them known. Language was born of the *necessità di spiegarsi*, and yet it was not just exclamatory, but essentially hypostatic and iconical, seeking to distinguish the object of feeling from other objects, to emphasize its specific attributes, and establish it as a permanent topic of reference in the changing flux of experiential phenomena. The archaic myths, inasmuch as they record the earliest onomathetic attempts of primitive man to make sense of natural reality by naming and narrating its objects in man's own human terms, generally exemplify what was, and still is, the most enduring feature of myth-making in the process of civilization: the ability of man to go by means of human speech beyond the ordinary and merely given aspects of the phenomenal world, beyond what Vico (following Hobbes) calls its 'natural significations', so as to grasp and express its underlying meaning for him:

Curiosity – that inborn property of man, daughter of ignorance and mother of knowledge – when wonder wakens our minds, has the habit, wherever it sees some extraordinary phenomenon of nature, a comet for example, a sundog, or a midday star, of asking straightway *what it means*. (NS/189) (emphasis added)

These critical reflections on the failure of his favourite authors to understand the linguistic performances of myth clarified for

Vico the corrective task of his own work: to show how this language, precisely because it 'was not a language in accord with the nature of the things it dealt with . . . but was a fantastic speech making use of physical substances endowed with life and most of them imagined to be divine', enabled humankind to develop and expand its conceptual horizons beyond the 'natural significations' of reality (NS/401ff.). His most fundamental observation was that this process of signification developed from, and according to, the 'poetic tropes' in which primitive man characterized the world of things. Vico took the four major manners of speech – metaphor, metonymy, synecdoche, and irony – to be the four basic generic modes of thought by which human beings gradually came to identify and classify the natural objects in the world. Whereas other theorists of language considered these tropes to be 'ingenious inventions of writers', Vico presents them as the 'necessary modes of expression of all the first poetic nations', the basic semantic strategies which made possible, and which represent to us, the entire 'development of the human mind' (NS/409).

Primitive people first related to the world by means of metaphorical identification of things *in their image, after their likeness*, calling, for example 'head for top or beginnings; the brow and shoulders of a hill' and so forth (NS/405). They then learned to identify things in and for themselves, as distinct from themselves, and from each other – at first metonymically – by reducing the complexity of general phenomena to one particular aspect, as, most notably, in the creation of specific deities and other 'poetic characters . . . to which, as to certain models or ideal portraits' they sought 'to reduce all the particular species which resembled them' (NS/209), and then synecdochically – by comprising various particular aspects under one generally descriptive term, as when they invented 'the word "man" itself [which] is abstract, comprehending as in a philosophic genus the body and all its parts, the mind and all its faculties, the spirit and all its dispositions' (NS/407). It was only in the last, and rather late, stage in that process that human beings became aware of what they were doing in and by language:

Irony certainly could not have begun until the period of reflection, because it is fashioned of falsehood by dint of a reflection which wears the mask of truth. Here emerges a great principle of human institutions, confirming the origin of poetry disclosed in this work: that since the first men of the gentile world had the simplicity of children, who are truthful by nature, the first fables could not feign anything false; they must therefore have been, as they have been defined above, true narrations. (NS/408)

Vico's contention that primitive mythology, however fabulous it may appear to us, must nevertheless be considered as truthful in its narration of reality, relies on these linguistic premises. This poetry is truthful inasmuch as it deposits in its semantic expressions some authentic impressions of reality, such that existed before, and still exist outside, those later rational or logical conceptualizations of reality, which are always liable to verbal falsification. Vico's attempt 'to descend from these human and refined natures of ours to those quite wild and savage natures, which we cannot at all imagine and comprehend only with great effort' was motivated by such linguistic considerations: living in the age of ironic prose he sought to revive thereby the semantic potential of metaphoric poetry. 'The Vico road goes round and round to meet where terms begin', wrote James Joyce, and thus delineated the main route of Vico's inquiries in the *New Science*.[59] Vico's aim, as Joyce well saw, was to reconstruct from the evidence of language the entire process of signification:

The etymologies of the native languages . . . tell us the histories of the institutions signified by the words, beginning with their original and proper meanings and pursuing the natural progress of their metaphors according to the order of ideas, on which the history of languages must proceed. (NS/354)

Like other historians in the eighteenth century, Vico too believed in the heuristic value of etymology, in its capacity to be (as Herder would put it) 'the torch that lights a dark path for us, thus sparing us the pains of remembering the turns and windings'.[60] Taking the 'definition of etymology' to be 'true speech, *veriloquium*' Vico was following the classical (Stoic) definition of etymology as an explication of phonetic changes in words, by means of which the original truth (*to etymon* or *to alethes*)

---

[59] James Joyce, *Finnegans Wake* (N.Y.: Viking, 1939), p. 452.
[60] On the origins and functions of Vico's theory of etymology, see Andrea Battistini, 'Vico e l'etimologia mitopoitica', *Lingua e Stile*, 9 (1974), pp. 31–66.

of a word is made evident.[61] His many attempts to reconstruct in that way the history of institutions – as, for example, that of Law, *lex*, which he derives from the act of collection, first of the acorns of Oak, *illex*, and ultimately of readable letters, *legere* (NS/240) – are surely *more learned and ingenious than true*. And yet, as the example above suggests, the Vichian etymologies are not just impressionistic exercises aiming to explain the present verbal form of a word or place name, as, in his view, were the merely grammatical etymologies of Scaliger or Sanchez; rather, his etymologies were historical, or even, as we would nowadays say, pre-historical: by tracing modern abstract terms back to their 'sylvan or rustic origins' Vico sought to uncover the actual conditions and occasions in which human beings in the past confronted seminal natural and social phenomena. In his explication of words, 'beginning with their original and proper meanings and pursuing the natural progress of their metaphors according to the order of ideas' (NS/354), Vico thus not only aimed to find the original form of the word, and thereby its ultimate 'true' meaning, but also sought to comprehend, through its changing forms, all its equally true meanings – for different people at different times and places.

Thus, reflecting in his *Autobiography* on the genesis of his own mythological inquiries, Vico recalls how around 1707, upon reading Bacon's work *On the Wisdom of the Ancients* he 'was incited to look for its principles farther back than in the fables of the poets. He was moved to do this by the example of Plato who in *Cratylus* had sought to track them down within the origins of Greek language'.[62] At that stage Vico still believed, like Bacon, that the ancient mythmakers were philosophers (*Nam poeta delectando docet, quae severe philosophus*). In 1710 he modelled his *On the Most Ancient Wisdom of the Italians* on these works. Like Plato who, in his view, attempted to discover the 'ancient wisdom of the Greeks' through etymology, so too Vico sought to discover the ancient wisdom of the Italians through etymological explications of key Latin words. And, as he noted, at that stage he was still committed to the

---

[61] On Vico's employment of these classical notions, see Mario Papini, *Arbor Humanae Linguae. L'etimologico di G. B. Vico come chiave ermeneutica della storia del mondo* (Bologna: Capelli, 1984).
[62] Vico, *The Autobiography*, p. 148.

principles and methods of the Baconian philosophy. His work opens with the Baconian observation that 'the origins of a great number of words were so scholarly that they seem to have arisen not from common popular usage, but from some inner learning', and proceeds to derive many modern theories from these ancient sources. Vico's method and discoveries were harshly and justly criticized by some Venetian reviewers in the *Giornale de' Letterati*, who urged the author to look for the ancient wisdom of the Italians not just in their words, but in their practices, to find out, as it were, not just what words were used by the Italians, but what these words had actually meant to them. The original meanings of words, they argued, could not be found, as Vico erroneously thought, purely by the formal means of grammatical philology, by tracing their verbal forms and transformations in dictionaries; rather these meanings could only be gleaned by the new means of historical philology, as developed and practised by Valla and his followers, which sought to elicit the meaning of words from their authentic documents, to understand texts in their context of usage. Vico, the Venetian critics suggested, ought to have looked for the true meaning of the key-words he was investigating in the vestiges of Etruscan laws and rites and in Roman Law and religion.

Vico initially rejected their suggestion, arguing, in the common Baconian fashion, that the Etruscans purposely enshrouded their clear ideas in fanciful figures of speech. Gradually, however, as he became increasingly disenchanted with the crude and naïve empiricism of Bacon, and equally critical of the lofty word-idealism of Plato, he came to see that his critics were right, and that if 'the matchless wisdom of the ancients, so ardently sought after from Plato to Bacon's *On the Wisdom of the Ancients*' (NS/384) was to be recovered from their myths, as indeed he thought it should, then it must not be sought in their notional words alone, as in Plato's *Cratylus*, nor beyond them in the pure visions or minds of their singular great poets, as in Bacon's work, but rather in the natural and social conditions, mental range and linguistic potentialities which prevailed in those 'obscure and fabulous times' in which these fables came-into-being, or, as Vico would phrase it in the *New Science*, in the popular *sensus communis* of the people who used them, and wherein alone their 'true historical meaning' could be found.

It was, Vico writes in the *Autobiography*, both his 'dissatisfaction with [the merely] grammatical etymologies' and, on the other hand, his 'slight satisfaction with Bacon's book attempting to trace the wisdom of the ancients in the fables of the poets' which indicated to him the 'source' whence he 'in his latest works, was to recover principles of poetry different from those which the Greeks and Latins and the others since them have hitherto accepted'.[63] This 'source' was the classical mythological lore, and what enabled Vico to reinterpret it – his new 'principles of poetry' – was, as we have already noted, a radical redefinition of the concept of 'poetry' itself: he perceived poetry in socio-political, not in merely aesthetic, terms. This redefinition of poetry set him on a new track in his historical investigations. He now saw that the ancient mythologies were the natural 'vulgar' language of the common people in antiquity, not the sublime language of its singular wise men. This discovery, which Vico would sum-up in his identification of Homer with the entire Greek people, enabled him to establish 'the only principle of mythology according to which the fables bore historical evidence as to the first Greek commonwealths, and by their aid he explains all the fabulous history of the heroic commonwealths':[64] What Vico discovered, in other words, was the common-sensual origins and functions of mythology, its *ratio civilis*, the fact that its tales were primarily concerned with the common necessities and utilities of civil life.

As we shall see, in his mythological inquiries in the *New Science*, Vico still indulged in etymological explanations of words, but this etymology was, however, new, both in its orientation and subject matter. It was based on the conviction that it was indeed possible, and even necessary, to extract the meaning of social practices from the key-terms associated with them, alas not from the esoteric and high-minded concepts, but from the ordinary and most popular idioms, from its commonplaces, as these, Vico assumed, contain and may reveal the commonsense beliefs which sustained them:

The vulgar tongues should be the most weighty witnesses concerning those ancient customs of the peoples that were in use at the time the languages were formed. A language of an ancient nation, which has maintained itself as the dominant tongue until it was fully developed,

[63] Vico, *The Autobiography*, p. 153.　　[64] Vico, *The Autobiography*, p. 153.

should be a great witness to the customs of the early days of the world. (NS/151–2)

Thus, over the twenty years which separate his *On the Most Ancient Wisdom of the Italians* and the mature *New Science*, Vico not only retained his belief in language as the best repository of 'ancient wisdom', but also reiterated his commitment to etymology as the best method for unravelling it. What seems to have changed, however, is his conception of 'language' itself, which has acquired a fuller and more profound meaning and a wider connotative range, becoming roughly what we would now call a semiotic system of communication; it now comprised not just words, but all other symbolic means – mute gestures, physical objects, images, hieroglyphics – by which human beings have commonly expressed their impressions and formed their conceptions of reality. Or, to put it differently, Vico realized that if we wish to grasp how the *primi uomini* saw the world – what we need to know is not only what words they used but rather what concepts they possessed:

Thus, in their hopeless ignorance of the way in which languages and letters began, scholars have failed to understand how the first nations thought in poetic characters, spoke in fables, and wrote in hieroglyphs. Yet these should have been the principles, which must by their nature be most certain, of philosophy in its study of human ideas and of philology in its study of human words. (NS/429)

The question of the 'origin of language' was indeed one of the most heavily contested topics throughout the seventeenth and eighteenth centuries. As Jòhn Wilkins declared: 'There is scarce any subject that hath been more thoroughly scanned and debated amongst learned men than the Original of Languages and Letters'.[65] Practically all the major thinkers before and during the Enlightenment offered hypotheses about the origination and diffusion of languages among the nations. As a rule, they all shared the classical-humanistic conviction that of all the accomplishments of human beings the creation of language was the most important because without it they could not have emerged from their solitary existence in the state of nature. And because they all identified human society with the institution of

---

[65] John Wilkins, *An Essay Towards a Real Character, and a Philosophical Language* (London, 1688), p. 2.

language, the question of its origins – whether they were divine, natural, or conventional – assumed much greater significance: it was a debate on the very nature of humankind, and on the means by which it has made society. Indeed, so dominant were these latter philosophical questions on language and its relation to man and the world, that such theorists as Hobbes, Locke, Condillac, Herder, and many lesser-known thinkers who discussed the specific problem of its origins did so without much interest in, and hardly any reference to, the concrete philological evidence. As a modern authority on the topic has put it: 'the question of the origin of languages did not aim at historical and factual expla-nation of states of language in the past. It was as hypothetical as the state of nature in political philosophy, and like the latter, its aim was to understand man in the present.'[66] Vico's quest for the origins of language differed from that of his contemporaries not so much in its philosophical beliefs and aims, but in its philo-logical methods. It was as much concerned with general meditations on the linguistic competence of man, as with concrete inquiries into the particular socio-historical conditions in which it manifested itself.[67]

In the early eighteenth century the two main doctrines of the origin of language were still those which have been debated since antiquity: (a) the Biblical theory (with its Platonic intimations) which saw language as a creation of divine or some other mystical authority, a body of rules, words, and meanings that has been naturally given first to Adam and then to all human beings; and (b) the conventional theory (with its Aristotelian elaborations) which saw language as a creation of human reason, the rules, words, and meanings of which have been maintained by customary agreement among people. There were, of course, many variations on each of these doctrines, as well as different combi-nations of them, but, in principle, whoever approached the topic used these two polar positions as co-ordinates for further movements. This, at any rate, was the starting-point of Vico's investigations, but, as we have come to expect, his attempt in

---

[66] Hans Aarsleff, 'The Tradition of Condillac: The Problem of the Origin of Language in the Eighteenth Century', in *From Locke to Saussure: Essays on the Study of Language and Intellectual History* (London: Altone, 1982), p. 163.

[67] Nancy Struever, 'Vico, Valla, and the Logic of Humanist Inquiry', in *Vico's Science of Humanity*, pp. 182–3.

this case (as in so many others), was to mediate between the two extreme options. And, as we shall see, this attempt aligned him to the classical 'mediative' theory of the Epicureans, otherwise his adversaries, who attributed the creation of language not to reason (either divine or human), but to sensation and emotion.

Vico accepted, as a principle of faith, the historical verity of the description in Genesis 2:19, according to which the Lord brought the animals to Adam 'to see what he could call them; and whatsoever Adam called every living creature, that was the name thereof'. He did not see, however, any further historical significance to this story, since, according to the same story, that 'purity of the sacred antediluvian language' was lost in the confusion of tongues in Babel (NS/401, 62). From this theory Vico retained, however, the notion of the physical (or 'bodily') origins of words, the assumption, namely, that like Adam, who named the creatures according to their natural characteristics, all human beings have always named things mimetically, according to what they perceived to be their natural matter. Vico's contention that 'the first language in the first mute times of the nations must have begun with signs, either gestures or physical objects, which had natural relations to the ideas [to be expressed]' (NS/401), so that 'it was by common natural necessity that all the first nations spoke in hieroglyphs' (NS/435) betrays his debt to Plato's idealistic belief in the possibility of linguistic signs which are non-verbal, non-arbitrary, non-conventional but simply natural, reflecting reality in some direct way. This Cratylian view was shared by many philosophers in the seventeenth century. Vico must have known its ancient and modern philosophical formulations in the works of Plato, Dante, Bacon and various mystics, to which he added his own philological examples. In this way, for example, he interpreted Herodotus's story about the Scythian king Idanthyrsus who declared war on Darius the Great by sending him five natural objects, or, as Vico defines them, 'real words' – a frog, a mouse, a bird, a ploughshare, and a bow – the meanings of which Darius is said to have understood intuitively (NS/435).

Now, the assumption that there are objects which have this immediate and permanent relation to human ideas, that there are such natural signs which are meaningful in themselves, seemingly independent of human convention, is one which Vico did not seriously entertain. As we saw above, he criticized Plato and Bacon for having spun such delusions about the language of nature. He also objected to the many modern attempts to discover or construe a *mathesis universalis* which would be perfectly designative of reality. If Vico, nevertheless, elaborated a theory which was so close to the latter, he did so, I think, mainly for polemical reasons. He aligned himself to the Adamic-Cratylian theory because it implied some natural semantic connection between *res* and *verba*, and thus undermined, in his view, the basic claim of the conventional theory about the utterly artificial origin of all words:

The philologians have all accepted with an excess of good faith the view that in the vulgar languages meanings were fixed by convention. On the contrary, because of their natural origins, they must have had natural significations . . . encountering great numbers of words which give confused and indistinct ideas of things, and not knowing their origins, which had made them at first clear and distinct, have given peace to their ignorance by setting up the universal maxim that articulate human words have arbitrary significations. And they have dragged in Aristotle, Galen, and other philosophers, and armed them against Plato and Iamblicus. (NS/444)

The mistake of these philologians, like that of the political theorists of 'social contract', was that they construed their theories of intersubjective agreement on implausible anthropo-historical premises. Because they themselves were 'reasoning from the principles of Aristotle', Vico sniffs, they imputed to the early men Aristotle's own reason, 'as if the peoples that invented the languages must first have gone to school to him!' (NS/455). Yet, while he opposed the overtly rationalistic aspects in this theory, Vico accepted its more fundamental claim – that what must be explained in the study of language is not how words originated in some natural necessity but how their meanings remained in convention. And this claim proved, in his view, to be the undoing of the Epicurean-Lucretian theory of the sensual-emotional origins of language, a theory with which, oddly enough, Vico has often, albeit erroneously, been associated.

As I have hinted above, Vico was attracted to that theory because it implicitly countered both the Biblical and the Aristotelian extreme options, and claimed, instead, that words had been formed by both natural and human factors:

But the various sounds of the tongue nature drove them to utter, and convenience moulded the names for things . . . Therefore to suppose that someone then distributed names amongst things, and that from his men learnt their first words, is folly. For why should he have been able to mark all things with titles and to utter the various sounds of the tongue, and at the same time others not be thought able to have done it? Besides, if others had not also used these terms in their discourse, whence was that foreknowledge of usefulness implanted in him? . . . Lastly, what is so wonderful in this business, if the human race, having active voices and tongues, could distinguish things by varying sounds to suit varying feelings? Seeing that dumb animals, seeing that even wild beasts of all kinds are accustomed to utter sounds different and varying when they are in fear or pain . . . [68]

And yet, for all its immense persuasiveness Vico found this reversion of words to aboriginal exclamations insufficient as a theory of language. The Lucretian account did not – and could not – advance beyond this primal stage of the origination of language. What Lucretius did not explain was how the utterly natural 'sounds' (*soni*) of solitary human beings became the articulate 'voices' (*voces*) of human beings in the conversation. Much as he was impressed by Lucretius' attempt to refute the conventional theory by tracing the origin of the spoken word onomatopoeically to the sensuous character of the object it represents, he saw that this 'well-ordered deduction' of human words from purely sensual impressions and emotions was tenable only on extreme naturalistic premises, such that Vico had already rejected in the establishment of his 'principles of humanity'.[69]

For Vico, then, Lucretius' a-social theory of language was ultimately wrong because it was too closely based on Epicurus's a-social theory of human nature. The latter, he says in the *Autobiography*, 'built on his mechanical physics a metaphysics entirely sensualistic like that of John Locke, and a hedonistic morality suitable for men who are to live in solitude, as indeed Epicurus enjoined upon all his disciples'.[70] Against Epicurus and his linguistic 'philosophy of solitaries' Vico pits an alternative authority – Cicero and his linguistic philosophy of civilians. In his

[68] Lucretius, *On The Nature of Things*, Bk. v, 1028–90, tr. C. Bailey (Oxford: Oxford University Press, 1947).

[69] Antonino Pagliaro, 'Le origini del linguaggio secondo Vico', in *Campanella e Vico* (Padua: Cedam, 1969), pp. 269–88.

[70] Vico, *The Autobiography*, p. 126.

inaugural *Orationes,* Vico commonly referred to the latter's well-known notions on the civil functions of language, and shared his belief that whatever human beings have achieved in the long process of humanization they did so by virtue of their rhetorical capacities: 'What other power [than eloquence] could have been strong enough either to gather scattered humanity into one place, or to lead it out of its brutish existence in the wilderness up to our present condition as men and as citizens, or, after the establishment of social communities, to give shape to laws, tribunals, and civic rights?'[71] Following on this and similar classical examples, Vico's quest for the origins of language took a decisively social turn. While he agreed with Lucretius that many verbal forms in our language originated in sensual emotions, he saw that language itself developed as a primarily communicative, and not merely designative or expressive, activity, a medium through which men exchanged human ideas, not just animalistic feelings. He postulated that since 'ideas and language accelerated at the same rate' (NS/234); and because 'the order of ideas must follow the order of [human] institutions, [which is as follows]: first, the forests, after that the huts, then the villages, next the cities, and finally the academies' (NS/238–9); then 'this sequence of human institutions sets the pattern for the histories of words in the various native languages' (NS/240). For Vico, who was particularly interested in the history of Roman Law, how its terms were codified, interpreted and applied in different social-historical settings, the discovery of these performative and pragmatic aspects of language was crucial, because it enabled him to articulate the internal connection between social life and the language that is embedded in it. In order to understand Roman society, it was not enough to know the terms of its official language, nor even their theoretical meanings, but also their pragmatic – what Vico calls 'vulgar' – meanings and practices, what, for example, terms like 'people', 'kingdom', and 'liberty' really meant for the Roman plebs, and how these meanings differed both from those of the Roman patricians, as well as from ours (NS/105). In order to understand 'language', then, we must relate it to the common 'ideas' and 'institutions' which prevail in society. Vico saw that

71 Cicero, *De Oratore,* 1.8.33, tr. E. W. Sutton, Loeb Classical Library (Cambridge, Mass.: Harvard University Press, 1959).

'language' is not simply a code for transmitting information ('ideas') between individual agents in society, but is rather the web of interpersonal relations – or 'institutions' – that binds them together into a community where they can feel and act together. The language they use to make claims, promises, or oaths wouldn't make sense, could not be applied seriously, without social practices in which these speech acts can be carried out and sanctioned.[72]

More generally, Vico states that in harmony with the three ages of man – the divine, the heroic, and the human –

> three kinds of language were spoken which compose the vocabulary of this Science: (1) That of the time of the families when gentile men were newly received into humanity. This . . . was a mute language of signs and physical objects having natural relations to the ideas they wished to express. (2) That spoken by means of heroic emblems, or similitudes, comparisons, images, metaphors, and natural descriptions, which make up the great body of the heroic language which was spoken at the time the heroes reigned. (3) Human language using words agreed upon by the people, a language of which they are absolute lords, and which is proper to the popular commonwealths and monarchical states. (NS/32)

As this scheme makes clear, Vico mediates between all the other theories of the origin of language by fitting them into a generic theory of linguistic growth and development. While the language of concrete objects spoken in the first age contains naturalistic elements from the Adamic and the Epicurean theories, the language of abstract concepts spoken in the third age is roughly what conventionalists from Aristotle to Locke have attributed to men in the primal stage. The crucial phase in this scheme, and in the history of mankind, is the mediative stage – the language of plastic images spoken in the second age. And it was to this language, the *mythopoesis*, that Vico devoted his utmost attention. All the more so, because he considered this language, rather than the primordial 'mute language', to have been the first truly human language – it was human in the sense that it was a language that had emerged from its submersion in natural things, and its signs had become increasingly less imitative and designative, and

---

[72] On the primarily civic and historical aims of Vico's linguistic inquiries, see Tullio de Mauro, 'Giambattista Vico: From Rhetoric to Linguistic Historicism', in *Vico: International Symposium*, pp. 279–95.

ever more freely creative and expressive. The appearance of verisimilitudes, comparisons, metaphors, and images attests to the fact that in that stage the sensuous similarities of the *primi uomini* began to give way to nonsensuous similarities, that their mimetic relation to the immediate physical environment was becoming more detached and humanized. It is for this reason, as Hayden White rightly saw, that for Vico 'the theory of metaphorical transformation serves as the model for a theory of the autotransformation of human consciousness in history'.[73]

The metaphorical mode of speech consists in the transference (*metapherein*) of conceptual identity via linguistic meaning from one object to another by highlighting their natural or conventional similarities (e.g., 'man is a lone wolf', 'the eye of the storm', 'take responsibility', 'strike a deal', 'pay homage', etc.). Bearing in mind the classical Ciceronian observation that 'there are more things in the world than words', Vico duly concludes that 'the sources of all poetic locutions are two; poverty of language and the necessity of making oneself understood' (NS/34). His important suggestion here is that the early men were driven to the creation of metaphors because they had already had greater knowledge of the world, or at least knew that there was more to know about it, than their vocabulary allowed them to express. Vico relates how during their development through the three ages, they tried to make sense of reality first by feeling, then by perceiving 'with a troubled and agitated spirit', and then by reflection 'with a clear mind' (NS/218). Accordingly, 'poets were the sense and philosophers the intellect of human wisdom' (NS/779). Poetic sentences, he says, 'were formed by feelings of passion and emotion, whereas philosophic sentences are formed by reflection and reasoning. The more the latter rise toward universals, the closer they approach the truth; the more the former descend to particulars, the more certain they become' (NS/219). Now, the contrast between 'truth' and 'certainty' here seems to run counter to what Vico says elsewhere, namely that certain poetic images of virtues, most notably those of gods and heroes, are 'true', indeed even 'more true' than verbal and theoretical abstractions of them: Godfrey, thus, stands for 'military leadership' (NS/205), Hermes Trismegistus for 'civil wisdom' (NS/209), and so on. In this way,

---

[73] Hayden White, 'The Tropics of History: The Deep Structure of the *New Science*', p. 72.

Vico says, 'the first men, the children, as it were, of the human race, not being able to form intelligible class concepts of things' created their 'imaginative class concepts or universals, to which, as to certain models or ideal portraits, to reduce all the particular species which resembled them' (NS/209). The contrast between the 'imaginative universal' and the 'intelligible universal' is crucial not only to Vico's conception of metaphor, and more generally to his theory of myth, but, as Verene has rightly pointed out, to the *New Science* as a whole, as indeed Vico himself states: the discovery of the formation and operation of 'poetic characters' in language is 'the master-key of this Science' (NS/34).

According to Verene, the 'imaginative universal' is more than a linguistic invention – it is primarily and essentially a mode of perception and representation of reality whereby the 'poetic mind' imposes order on the flux of particular experiential phenomena by *imagining* some general unity and identity in them. It is able, as it were, to single out a concrete particular as exemplary, to fix it as a primary, ideal and normative case in that flux to which all other concrete particulars which seem related by phenomenal association must be referred, compared and subordinated. This activity of concept-formation in the 'primitive poetic mind' differs from the concept-formation in the 'reflective rational mind' which operates by scanning the diverse particulars in search of pre-established or presumed similarities between them, seeking, as it were, to classify them under the appropriate theoretical concept which had already been abstracted from them. So, according to Verene, metaphor, at least in its original usage, is not a conscious transference of abstract identity from one thing to another, but is the 'primal perception of identity' itself, the pre-linguistic mode in which the mind gathers a number of particulars into their normative and ideal unity: 'Metaphor is that by which identity is originally achieved in perception. It is the form perception most immediately takes. Metaphor is the first of the tropes and the first of the operations of mind in the act of knowing.'[74]

---

[74] Donald P. Verene, *Vico's Science of Imagination* (Ithaca: Cornell University Press, 1981), pp. 79–80. Friedrich Nietzsche defined metaphor in similar terms: it serves as 'a representative image standing concretely before man in lieu of a concept' (*The Birth of Tragedy out of the Spirit of Music*, tr. F. Goffing (N.Y.: Doubleday & Co., 1956), p. 55).

Verene's interpretation is important, and is certainly correct at least with regard to the earliest phase of pre-linguistic cognition among the *primi uomini*. But, for Vico, the efficacy of metaphor is not confined to this stage only, not even primarily – he seems to be more interested in, and fascinated by, the prospects of metaphoric continuities and revivals in articulate minds and fully developed literary societies (NS/412, 446, 581). As Cantelli has remarked: 'Allegory and metaphor are not bold ends in themselves; they are, rather, the means which, through continual transposition of images, permit man's mind to adjust to the definite multiplicity of meanings in a living world'.[75] And in these later times metaphorical sentences function as the semantic means by which man creates new meanings out of already known words and things. Thus, for example, when the early people wished to designate a new and more abstract concept for which they had not as yet found a word in their language they would reach towards the concept by means of available concrete terms:

Take for example the poetic phrase 'the blood boils in my heart', based on a property natural, eternal, and common to all mankind. They took the blood, the boiling, and the heart, and made of them a single word, as it were a genus, called in Greek *stomachos*, in Latin *ira*, and in Italian *collera* [which denote anger]. (NS/460)

Now, as this example shows, Vico's interest in the efficacy of metaphorical expression in the *New Science* is more anthropological and historical than rhetorical. And this concern, one could say, marks the more general thematic shift in the *New Science* at large – from rhetorical to historical problems. Vico's general theory of metaphor is largely derived from the common rhetorical teaching which, as formulated by Aristotle, held that 'to know how to invent fine metaphors means to know how to grasp the resemblances that objects bear to one another'.[76] Indeed, in his early writings on rhetorics Vico repeated this teaching almost verbatim, saying that 'the capacity to perceive the analogies existing between matters lying far apart and, apparently, most dissimilar . . . constitutes the source and principle of all ingenious, acute, and brilliant forms of expression'.[77] Nevertheless, in his *New*

[75] Gianfranco Cantelli, 'Myth and Language in Vico', in *Vico's Science of Humanity*, p. 62.
[76] Aristotle, *Poetics* 1459a.
[77] Vico, *On the Study methods of Our Time*, p. 24.

Science he came to perceive the fuller and more fundamental implications of the metaphorical competence in man: He now realized that metaphors are not just ornamental but rather primarily cognitive inventions, and as such they enabled the early peoples – as they indeed might help modern man too – not just to speak better, but to know more. This realization of the cognitive value of the metaphorical mode of seeing enabled Vico to counter the Enlightenment history of human ideas at its root: because, while Bacon and his followers in the Enlightenment regarded the advancement of learning as a gradual process in which human beings learn to see the things as they really are, Vico, in contrast, saw that this process owed as much to the human capacity to see the things *not* as they are, but rather as other things.

In Vico's view, the fact that the metaphorical representations of things do not abide by the scientific criteria of 'true knowledge' does not mean that they are wrong or harmful with regard to our knowledge of the world. The cognitive value of metaphors lies precisely in their non- or pre-scientific mode of perception, in the fact that as intuitive-synthetic combinations of sensual impressions they are not subject to the laws of analytical reason, which operates, as a rule, against such spontaneous perceptions of things. What we get in and through metaphorical representations of reality, instead, are worlds which are uninhibited by pre-established empirical relations and laws. Such representations become valuable to our knowledge of the natural world even though, and precisely because, they do not judge what and how things really are in themselves, but rather disrupt and go beyond their obvious 'natural significations' in order to invent new combinations or 'symbolic significations' of them. In this way they enable man to combine impressions which do not belong together in experience into something which does not exist in natural reality, thereby creating a new reality – the symbolic reality of the civil world. Seen in this light, the metaphorical expressions must not be viewed as primitive distortions of the world, but rather as creative representations of it, which, in Vico's view, are essential to the development of human consciousness. As he puts it in his anti-Cartesian tract on education, these linguistic inventions of similarities are crucial to scientific discoveries, because the juxtaposition of two seemingly incongruous images in figural representation might yield us a new perceptual vision of their relation in natural reality. The Cartesian method, on the other hand,

moves forward by a constant and gradual series of small steps. Consequently, it is apt to smother the student's specifically philosophic faculty, i.e., his capacity to perceive analogies existing between matters far apart and, apparently, most dissimilar. It is this capacity which constitutes the source and principle of all ingenious, acute, and brilliant forms of expression. It should be emphasized that tenuity, subtlety, delicacy of thought, is not identical with acuity of ideas. That which is tenuous, delicately refined, may be represented by a single line, 'acute' by two. Metaphor, the greatest and brightest ornament of forceful, distinguished speech, undoubtedly plays the first role in acute, figurative expressions.[78]

Vico thus relates the creation of metaphors to the imaginative faculty in man, to his ability to observe artificial similarities and to create counter-natural relations between things, to what Paul Ricoeur calls the 'capacity of "seeing as"'.[79] Vico relates this ability to the rhetorical 'wordplay', or 'wit" (*acutezza*), and more generally to the creative imagination, or ingenuity that 'penetrates and binds together in a common relationship . . . things that appear to the workaday man uncommonly fragmentary and disparate'.[80] The operative logic in this kind of concrete reasoning is *topical* rather than *critical*, which Aristotle defines as the way of reasoning 'from opinions that are generally accepted' (*Topics* 100a18, 101b13), as is the common practice in public matters like legal cases where we first consult precedents and all the relevant premises for a given problem. The *topoi* are the various common-places where this public knowledge is located, be they linguistic phrases and proverbs, memorial days and monuments, common practices and laws, and so on. By appealing to these collective sources of knowledge we get to know forgotten or even new things by re-cognition, as if by scanning and combining their concrete characters, those

---

[78] Vico, *On the Study Methods of Our Time*, p. 24. For a forceful modern defence of such metaphorical disruptions of common world-pictures (on the ground that they thereby enable us to constitute alternative 'imaginative symbolic worlds that have relations with natural reality other than those of predictive interest') see Mary B. Hesse, 'The Cognitive Claims of Metaphor', in *Metaphor and Religion*, ed. J. P. van Noppen (Brussels: van Noppen, 1984), II, pp. 27–45.

[79] Paul Ricoeur, *The Rule of Metaphor: Multi-Disciplinary Studies of the Creation of Meaning in Language*, tr. R. Czerny, M. McLaughlin, J. Costello (Toronto: University of Toronto Press, 1977).

[80] Vico, *On the Study Methods of Our Time*, p. 24.

which are already known, as it were, from previous or first encounters with them we actively re-member them into a whole. 'Imagination [*la fantasia*]', Vico says, 'is nothing but the springing up again of reminiscences, and ingenuity or invention is nothing but the working over of what is remembered' (NS/699). In this way, 'by noting the commonplaces that must all be run over in order to know all there is in a thing that one desires to know well, that is, completely' the primitive mind achieves 'acquaintance with things which must come before judgment of them' (NS/497–8).

For Vico, this ability 'to hew out topics' marks 'the primary operation of our mind'. For him this is a statement not only of historical fact, but of value: Vico sought to revive the 'art of topics' with all its intuitive and recollective modes of knowledge because he believed that in the modern era, which is totally dominated by the 'art of criticism', where men have become excessively 'ironic' in their manipulation of language, this more primitive and vivid knowledge of things in their concrete particularity 'has the function of making minds inventive, as criticism has that of making them exact'. His way and aim in advocating concrete-'topical' over against abstract-'critical' reasoning is akin to modern attempts at the rehabilitation of 'primitive thought'. Much of what he says in favour of thinking-in-and-through-objects has been reiterated, for example, by the anthropologist Claude Lévi-Strauss, who has defined *la pensée sauvage* as a 'science of the concrete'. Lévi-Strauss salutes the conceptual achievements of the savage mind, a mind which, though still unable to integrate abstract propositions into a formal theory, nevertheless manages, as does the *bricoleur*, to construe a whole world out of the concrete items which are immediately available.[81] In a similar fashion Vico celebrates the achievements of 'topical' thought: 'Providence gave good guidance to human affairs when it aroused human minds first to topics rather than to criticism, for . . . in those first times all things necessary to human life had to be invented, and invention is the property of genius' (NS/498). And for both thinkers what ultimately distinguishes man from all other creatures, and unites all humankind in one common mentality, is primarily that

---

[81] Claude Lévi-Strauss, *The Savage Mind* (Chicago: The University of Chicago Press, 1966), ch. 1.

imaginative capacity – to invent innumerable new things out of the old limited impressions. How does man invent? And what is the role of metaphor in that activity? This is the cardinal question for Vico; and his answer is spelled-out in the first of the *elementi* that comprise his work: that 'Because of the indefinite nature of the human mind, whenever it is lost in ignorance man makes himself the measure of all things' (NS/120).' Having established this psychological fact as the very first axiom in his science of man, Vico then attempted to apply it to the whole civil world and thereby explain how all human concepts and institutions in history have evolved from such subjective and poetic attempts to confer human meaning on reality.

According to Vico, of all the metaphorical modes of speech 'the most luminous and therefore the most necessary and frequent' one is that in which man imputes 'sense and passion' to 'insensate things'. It was by this kind of metaphorical projection that 'the first poets attributed to bodies the being of animate substances, with capacities measured by their own, namely sense and passion, and in this way made fables of them' (NS/404). Examples abound: 'the eyes of needles and of potatoes; mouth for any opening; the lip of a cup or pitcher; the teeth of a rake, a saw, a comb' and so on (NS/405). And, he adds, 'in general [this kind of] metaphor makes up the great body of the language among all nations' (NS/444). Now, this recognition of the essentially anthropomorphic nature of many of our linguistic and other cultural creations was not new in itself; indeed, the argument-from-anthropomorphism has been used by rational critics of religion from Xenophanes to Spinoza, as well as by modern critics of culture like Nietzsche, Freud, the post-structuralists and other Romantics, to denounce (or celebrate) the utterly fictive nature of religious and cultural authorities. Vico was well aware of the old art of criticism as practised by his predecessors, and, as I shall make clear later on, he conceived his 'new art of criticism' (*nuova arte critica*) as a direct response to their charges.

The difference between all the 'old' critics and Vico is best exemplified in the latter's attempt to emphasize the constructive, not the subversive, aspects of anthropomorphism. For Vico regarded this common fallacy of the human mind as the indispensable source of all human creativity. Note, for example, his seemingly Xenophanic account of the birth of the gods out of sensual-passionate impulses:

> But the theological poets, unable to make use of the understanding, did the opposite and more sublime thing: they attributed sense and passions to bodies, and to bodies as vast as sky, sea, and earth. Later, as these vast imaginations shrank and the power of abstraction grew, the personifications were reduced to diminutive signs. (NS/402)

The crucial term here is, of course, *sublime*, a term which in Vico's vocabulary signifies, as we have seen, the ability of man to redeem himself by means of human speech from his submersion in nature. Whereas Bacon and like-minded scholars looked for clear scientific observations behind the metaphorical language of myth, Vico, in contrast, maintained that it was only due to their creative imitation of nature *in language* – in what he terms their 'poetic physics', 'poetic astronomy', 'poetic cosmography', 'poetic chronology', or 'poetic geography' – that the first peoples were able to initiate the scientific process of the disenchantment of nature. In these brilliant, though typically speculative, interpretations of various figures and tales (NS/687ff.) Vico purports to show how 'in the fables the nations have in a rough way and in the language of the human senses described the beginnings of this world of sciences, which the specialized studies of scholars have since clarified for us by reasoning and generalization' (NS/779). Vico starts off with the basic observation that because the primitives 'spoke in [natural] signs, they naturally believed that lightning bolts and thunderclaps were signs made to them by Jove ... that such signs were real words, and that nature was the language of Jove' (NS/379), and then exemplifies how by attempting to translate the language of nature into their own human language, the primitives came to distinguish between the various natural objects, and between those and themselves. What Vico seems to have discovered is the constructive function of thinking in anthropomorphic similes, the way in which the human mind developed and came to realize itself in and through the mirror of objects:

> So that, as rational metaphysics teaches that man becomes all things by understanding them (*homo intelligendo fit omnia*), this imaginative metaphysics shows that man becomes all things by not understanding them (*homo non intelligendo fit omnia*); and perhaps the latter proposition is truer than the former, for when man understands he extends his mind

and takes in things, but when he does not understand he makes the things out of himself and becomes them by transforming himself into them. (NS/405)

The man who elucidates animate behaviour out of inanimate objects performs a peculiar act of unconscious self-recognition: by reading into the object the very qualities which it in turn re-presents to him, he becomes aware of these – his own – qualities. The 'fallacy' of anthropomorphism, then, turns out to be crucial and beneficial to man once we realize its constructive functions in the psychological-historical process which Bruno Snell has called 'the discovery of mind'; it shows us, in Snell's words, how 'human behaviour is made clear only through reference to something else which is in turn explained by analogy with human behaviour'.[82] And this is precisely what the theo-logical poets did in the metaphorical 'personification' of nature, where, by turning objects like the sky and the sea into distinct 'characters', they wrenched them out of the primordial state of undifferentiated matter, and thereby distinguished them from – and for – themselves.

The mythical figures of gods and heroes owe their inception to the same metaphorical notion of personification. According to Vico, the early peoples developed their entire conceptual world in this way. He is careful to point out, however, that the first deities (like Jove) were not yet thought out, but were merely 'felt and imagined' by those who made 'of all nature a vast animate body which feels passions and effects' (NS/375-7) as they perceived themselves to be. It was only in later stages that the pantheon of mythology, or the proper *language*, developed as human beings began to extend the designative and expressive spheres of their metaphorical language by the usage of metonymy and synecdoche. As long as they only reacted emotionally to phenom-ena they needed and used only those immediate concrete metaphors which were vehicles for primitive feelings such as fear or anger; accordingly, their vocabulary was limited to particular sensible objects and their linguistic performances to the logic of similarities. Eventually, however, they became secure enough in the world that they began to perceive and look for general

---

[82] Bruno Snell, *The Discovery of the Mind*, tr. T. G. Rosenmeyer (Cambridge, Mass.: Harvard University Press, 1953), pp. 199–200.

regularities in it, which would give their life a greater measure of reliability and orientation. They then needed a more effective vocabulary and expanded linguistic capabilities to capture the phenomena – they needed, in short, fewer words for more impressions. According to Vico, the plethora of mythical figures were invented then, as human beings sought to express in these personal idioms those general and abstract conceptions, for which they had not yet found any linguistic term.

Vico generally defines the mythical discourse which developed at that stage *diversiloquium*, which means expressions that 'signify the diverse species or the diverse individuals comprised under these genera. So that they must have a univocal signification connoting a quality common to all their species and individuals' (NS/403). He regards this discovery as *la chiave maestra di questa Scienza*:

We find that the principle of these origins both of languages and letters lies in the fact that the first gentile peoples, by a demonstrated necessity of nature, were poets who spoke in poetic characters. This discovery, which is the master key of this Science, has cost us the persistent research of almost all our literary life, because with our civilized natures we cannot at all imagine and can understand only by great toil the poetic nature of these first men. The [poetic] characters of which we speak were certain imaginative genera (images for the most part of animate substances, of gods or heroes, formed by their imagination) to which they reduced all the species or all the particulars appertaining to each genus. (NS/34)

It is for this reason, Vico says, that 'the mythologies, as their name indicates, must have been the proper languages of [such] fables', namely they were the primarily narrative attempts of primitive peoples, who were not yet able 'to form intelligible class concepts of things', to create instead by means of their deities and heroes 'imaginative class concepts or universals, to which, as to certain models or ideal portraits' they reduced 'all the particular species which resembled them' (NS/209). For these peoples, the ideal figure of the hero exemplifies a real predicate or a part in common, a certain virtue or vice which they strove to recognize in themselves. Thus, for example, the Greek people in the Homeric era created the figure of Achilles, to whom 'they attached all the properties of heroic valor, and all the feelings and customs arising from these natural properties, such as those of quick temper, punctiliousness, wrathfulness, implacability, violence, the arrogation of all right to might' and so on, while to Ulysses 'they attached all the feelings and customs of heroic wisdom; that is, those of wariness, patience, dissimulation, duplicity, deceit', and similar attributes which reflect 'the propriety of speech and indifference of action' (NS/809).

Vico considered the discovery of these 'poetic characters' to be 'the master-key of this Science', because it was this discovery of the way in which the ancient peoples formed their conceptions by means of concrete metaphors which enabled him, contrary to what he himself had assessed, to imagine and to understand (even if 'only by great toil') 'the poetic nature of these first men'. He found out that inasmuch as the ancients adopted these concrete personifications as moral and social concepts, i.e., inasmuch as they actually thought in and through their divine and heroic figures and did not just use them to illustrate or obscure more rational abstract concepts, they could well be said to have lived, and not just believed in, the myth. The ancients, Vico saw, did not merely imitate these figures, but identified themselves – and all other human phenomena – in them. And it was this insight which enabled him to arrive at his most momentous discovery in the study of 'historical mythology' – that Greek mythology was created not by Homer, the singular great poet, but rather by the common Greek people, who created Homer as well – as their 'poetic character'.

III

In the first half of the eighteenth century, the science of mythology was still largely confined to the philological investigation of the Homeric epics.[83] Only later in the century did archaeological and anthropological discoveries enable such scholars as Lowth, Michaelis, Blair, Heyne, or Herder to shed new light on the more general conditions and rules which produce that kind of literature in other, indeed in all, nations. But, as we have noticed, until

---

[83] On the wide context of Homeric studies in the eighteenth century, see Kristi Simonsuuri, *Homer's Original Genius: Eighteenth-Century Notions of the Early Greek Epic* (Cambridge: Cambridge University Press, 1979). For a comprehensive account of Vico's sources and knowledge, see Fausto Nicolini, 'Sugli studi omerici di G. B. Vico', in *Atti della academia nazionale dei Lincei*, 5 (1954), pp. 469–519.

around 1750 even such keen observers of non-European cultures
as Joseph Lafitau, attempting to make sense of the mythical tales
and practices they had recorded among the savages, needed to
compare them with the Homeric scenes and figures. In the
eighteenth century 'any change in the view of Homer, the ultimate recorded cornerstone of the mythic tradition, implied the
most serious change for all mythology, past and present'.[84] Vico's
so-called 'Discovery of the True Homer', summed-up in his notion
that 'Homer was an idea or a heroic character of Grecian men
insofar as they told their histories in song' (NS/873), could have
caused such a major change had it been made known to wider and
higher circles of scholars. When Friedrich August Wolf published
his *Prolegomena ad Homerum* in 1795, in which he established a
similar theory (on independent and much superior scholarship),
Vico's thesis was still virtually unknown. In fact, Vico himself
reached his momentous conclusions only in the latest stages of his
work and life. In the frontispiece which he devised for the second
edition of the *New Science* Vico thus saw fit to place 'the statue of
Homer on a cracked base' to signify thereby not only the false
theories of his predecessors, but his own early ruminations in
which, he says, he only 'sensed' but did not 'understand' the true
Homer (NS/6); he was even willing to admit that 'all these things
reasoned out by us or related by others concerning Homer and
his poems, [occurred] without our having intentionally aimed at
any such result – indeed, it had not even entered into our
reflections when readers of the first edition of this *New Science* . . .
men of acute minds and excelling in scholarship and learning,
suspected that the Homer believed in up to now was not real'
(NS/873). In order to fully apprehend Vico's new and seemingly
'true' Homer we must first find out what was that old and 'not
real' Homer that Vico, and other scholars, had previously
'believed in'.

Now, the question concerning the true character of Homer –
was he a sublime or primitive poet? – was the subject-matter of the
most serious literary-historical debate in that period – the so-called
Quarrel of the Ancients and the Moderns. The intellectual origins
of this debate might be traced back to the classical discussions in
Plato's dialogues and elsewhere about the poetic and moral

---

[84] B. Feldman and R. Richardson, *The Rise of Modern Mythology 1680–1860*, p. 9.

merits of Homer's work, and, more directly, to the rise of the
so-called 'aesthetic historicism' in the Italian Renaissance. As
Hans Baron has shown, already in the fourteenth century there
were many Humanists who protested against the uncritical
admiration and imitation of classical antiquity in the arts and in all
other spheres of life; by using the new critical-historical methods
of philology these scholars were able to relate the seemingly timeless works of art and literature to historical reality in antiquity, and
thereby to show how their ideas and images reflect only local, and
rather primitive, forms of life.[85] These critical observations are
echoed in Montaigne's sceptical queries, whether

it is possible that Homer meant to say all they make him say, and that
he lent himself to so many and such different interpretations that the
theologians, legislators, captains, philosophers, all sorts of people who
treat of sciences, however differently and contradictorily, lean on him:
the general master for all offices, works, and artisans, the general
counsellor for all enterprises? Whoever has needed oracles and predictions has found in him enough for his purpose. It is a marvel what
wonderful correspondences a learned man . . . draws out of him in
support of our religion . . . And what he finds in favour of ours, many of
old had found in favour of theirs.[86]

These queries were revived and much intensified in the late
seventeenth century and the first decades of the eighteenth
century, when the debate between the rationalist Moderns and the
traditionalist Ancients now concerned not only the Homeric
poetry but the legitimacy, and even very possibility, of poetry in
this new age of prose. And for both parties 'Homer' represented
poetry in its most expressive form: primal, forceful, totally alive.[87]
They differed, however, in their evaluation of the poetic and
moral virtues of this poetry. For the new Ancients – men like
Boileau, Madame Dacier, or Blackmore – Homer was the ultimate
creative genius: in his poetic speeches, descriptions, images, and
similes they found not only sublime beauty but also much ancient
wisdom, and even enough modern Reason to justify his reputation

85 Hans Baron, 'The Quarelle of the Ancients and the Moderns as a Problem for the
   Renaissance Scholarship', *The Journal of the History of Ideas* 20 (1959), pp. 3-22.
86 Michel de Montaigne, *The Complete Works*, tr. D. P. Frame (London: Hamish Hamilton,
   1957), pp. 442-3.
87 Paul Hazard, *The European Mind 1680–1715*, tr. J. Lewis May (Harmondsworth: Penguin
   University Books, 1973), pp. 381–404.

(in Plutarch's famous words) as the 'Plato of the poets'. For the Moderns, on the other hand, Homer's poetic achievement was of an altogether different kind: for Perrault, Bayle, Leclerc, or Pope found in his style and versification only roughness of feeling and thought, a testimony to the forceful, yet utterly primitive, nature of his 'original genius'. The Quarrel thus created a paradoxical situation: the Ancients admired Homer but did not really understand him; the Moderns despised Homer, but understood him much better. For as they sought to refute the 'ideal Homer' of the Ancients they exposed the sensual, cruel, and irrational facets of the poet – and thus got closer to the 'real Homer'; but the closer they got to him the more disenchanted they became with him, and so got farther away from him. Vico's 'discovery of the true Homer' was, as usual, a mediative effort: he saw that both parties erred in judging Homer according to their own modern standards – be they the poetic standards of the Ancients or the moral standards of the Moderns – and thus disjoined the unity of the poetic and the moral in Homer's epics. Whereas the Ancients exalted their own 'sublime' emotions in Homer's poetry, and the Moderns attacked them, justly, by showing how 'primitive' they really were, Vico sought to counter both by arguing that, upon his own 'principles of mythology', Homer's 'primitive' and 'sublime' emotions were not incompatible, but rather necessary. He could thus claim that Homer was 'the most sublime poet' precisely because he was also the 'most primitive' (NS/823–8). This argument countered both the claims of Ancients and the Moderns for Homer – because, on Vico's terms, Homer was neither an ancient nor a modern poet in their terms, but simply a 'natural poet', one that could be understood as such according to the new definition of 'poetry' offered in the *New Science*.

The interpretation of Homer's work was difficult because he lived in a pre-literary period, on which no other testimonies exist. Furthermore, 'since there has come down to us no writer more ancient than Homer . . . and since [all other] writers came long after him', the critical-historical methods of the philologians could not be applied to him. Vico thus notes that 'we were obliged to apply our metaphysical criticism, treating him as a founder of a nation, as he has been held to be of Greece, and to discover the truth, both as to his age and as to his fatherland, from Homer himself' (NS/788). The task of this metaphysical criticism was 'the explanation of the ideas the earliest nations naturally formed' (NS/905), and the way to find them was by appealing to 'the common sense of the human race' (NS/348). As I have already suggested, for Vico this meant an attempt at discerning in the obscure social practices of the primitive and ancient peoples those primal and universal 'civil institutions' like religion, marriage, and burial of the dead, practices, namely, which however differently they might be found to have been performed in those far places and times, would still be understandable to us insofar as we still preserve them (or, rather, as Vico would have it, they preserve us), a fact which implies that their original 'human ideas' are still shared by us. This 'metaphysical' attempt at some 'common grounds of truth' is a necessary first move in a hermeneutical motion which must bring the modern reader to some kind of affinity with the far and alien culture of Homer, to form what is nowadays called 'the fusion of horizons'. Yet, as the above passage makes clear, Vico sets this 'metaphysical' motion of identification with the 'human ideas' of the past under the constraints of rational 'criticism' of such ideas, knowing that while Homer may have had such human ideas like justice, honour, or shame – their meanings were quite different from ours. In order to find the precise meanings of those 'human ideas' Vico further limits the motions of this still rather loose 'metaphysical criticism' within the more definitive range of 'historical criticism', by which he means roughly what modern historians of ideas have taught us: that ideas become clearly and distinctly meaningful only 'in context', where the range of their possible meanings is narrower, more concrete, literally defined. The cardinal mistake of Homer's interpreters throughout the ages was that they ignored this limiting context, that they did not confine the meanings of his words to the linguistic, mental, and social conditions which prevailed in Greece during its Heroic Age. Hence Vico's conclusion that in order to discover the 'true Homer' we must not impute to him our own 'truths', nor any other 'truths' which other scholars claim to have discovered about him, but rather must 'discover the truth, both as to his age and as to his fatherland, from Homer himself'. On these strict rules of interpretation Vico set out to discover the 'true Homer'.

According to Vico, Homer appeared at a crucial moment in the history of Greek civilization, when its Heroic communities were beginning to disintegrate. Though the Greek people at the time still believed in, and lived by, the rough and cruel norms of Achilles, they were striving already towards more genteel ideals of the sages and the philosophers. The completion of Greek mythology in the Homeric age signifies that people at that stage were already thinking about myth, not just thinking through myth, when, to use Vico's own terms, they could already reflect on *la barbarie del senso* of previous generations, but this reflection did not yet turn into *la barbarie della riflessione* of later generations. According to Vico, all the great mythologies were created at such interim periods in the history of barbarism, which he terms, suggestively, as those of 'expiring barbarism' (*spirante barbarie*), that is to say at times when the peoples reached the point in which they needed to express their barbarous emotions, and thus to relieve themselves from such emotions – or literally sublimate them – by transferring them from life to art. Homer, he notes, belonged to such a late, not a 'living' but merely 'artistic' age in the history of mythology: 'First came the age of the theological poets, who were themselves heroes and sang true and austere fables; second, that of the heroic poets, who altered and corrupted the fables; and third, the Homeric age, which received them in their altered and corrupted form' (NS/905). The poetry in that last phase is more sublime than in the earlier phases, because its consumers have become more reflective, and therefore equally more barbarous, in their manners (NS/814). At such times all they can do to uplift themselves is to recall the heroic figures and their deeds, and so to realize how vulgar they have become, how, as real human beings, they have forsaken and lost their ideals. This, Vico argues, has always been the task of the mythmakers: to preserve in their 'poetic characters' the eternal ideals of society from oblivion in the vulgarity of mundane reality. Vico applies these criteria not only to Homer, but to all other mythographers, who must have all lived in such post-heroic and not-yet-human periods: 'Just so, in the returned barbarism of Italy, at the end of which came Dante, the Tuscan Homer', who 'though learned in the loftiest esoteric knowledge, filled the scenes of his *Comedy* with real persons and portrayed real events in the lives of the dead', that is to say, he consciously appealed to his audience's taste by writing his works in the vernacular language of concrete images and examples (NS/786, 817).

In his final public lecture, *On the Heroic Mind*, Vico clarified these notions most poignantly: The 'Hero' he says,

is defined by philosophers as one who seeks ever the sublime. Sublimity is, according to the same philosophers, the following of the utmost greatness and worth: first, above nature, God himself; next, within nature, this whole frame of marvels spread out before us, in which nothing exceeds man in greatness and nothing is of more worth than man's well-being, to which single goal each and every single hero presses on, in singleness of heart.

The hero exemplifies through his deeds this common human desire, and thereby 'generates for himself an immortal name'. Vico then appeals to his listeners:

But, by heaven, for a delight inexpressible, since most proper to man's nature with its strongest bent toward unity, read the poets! Observe their cast of characters, people from all walks of life, in the ethical, the domestic, the political realm, sharply delineated according to the pure ideal type, and by that very fact most real. Compared with these ideal types, men in everyday life will seem rather to be the unreal characters, for where men are not consistent their lives do not cohere. So consider, with a certain godlike mind, human nature as portrayed in the fables of great poets: even in wickedness it is most beautiful, because always self-consistent, always true to itself, harmonious in all its parts, just as the aberrant prodigies and malignant plagues of nature are perceived by Almighty God as good and beautiful in the eternal order of His Providence.[88]

It is for this reason that Vico finds Homer, with his incomparable plethora of heroes, however ugly and cruel they might seem to us, 'the father and prince of all sublime poets' (NS/823). 'The frightfulness of Homeric battles and deaths gives to the *Iliad* all its marvelousness' (NS/827). Such 'cruel and fearful descriptions of battles and deaths' and 'sentences filled with sublime passions' (NS/894–5) could not have sprung from 'a calm, cultivated, and gentile philosopher' (NS/828). Homer was 'unrivalled in creating poetic characters, the greatest of which are so discordant with this civil human nature of ours, yet perfectly decorous in relation to the punctilious heroic nature' (NS/783). The most exemplary character to that age is Achilles, the hero 'who referred every right

---

[88] Giambattista Vico, 'On the Heroic Mind', tr. E. Sewell and A. G. Sirignano, in *Vico and Contemporary Thought*, II, pp. 230, 236.

to the tip of his spear!' (NS/923). Of this type 'Homer sings to the Greek peoples as an example of heroic virtue, and to whom he gives the fixed epithet "blameless"!' (NS/667). Clearly, then, Homer's poetry did not contain the refined timeless *bon sens* that his neo-classicist interpreters – such men as Bouhours or Boileau – sought in him, but only the vulgar historical *sensus comunis* of his age. Scaliger's indignation 'at finding almost all Homer's comparisons to be drawn from beasts and other savage things' is typical to that misunderstanding: this great scholar did not realize that Homer could not have expressed his ideas but in such common sensual terms, 'which were necessary to Homer in order to make himself better understood by the wild and savage vulgar'. Vico thus concludes that

to attain such success in them – for his comparisons are incomparable – is certainly not characteristic of a mind chastened and civilized by any sort of philosophy. Nor could the truculent and savage style in which he describes so many, such varied, and such bloody battles, so many and such extravagantly cruel kinds of butchery as make up all the sublimity of the *Iliad* in particular, have originated in a mind touched and humanized by any philosophy . . . The complete absence of philosophy which we have shown in Homer, and our discoveries concerning his age and his fatherland and his age, arouse in us a strong suspicion that he may perhaps have been quite simply a man of the people. (NS/785, 806)

This total identification of the individual poet with the heroic and vulgar traditions of his people render the Homeric work its characteristic style of 'impersonal poetry', as if its process of composition was thoroughly objective, anonymous, and collective. Vico notes this, and by adding some dubious etymological explanations, he reasons that Homer was not really the original author but only the 'binder or compiler of fables' (NS/852). This conclusion as to the impersonal identity of Homer is further supported by the facts that 'the fatherland of Homer is not known' (NS/861), that 'almost all the cities of Greece laid claim to him' (NS/862), and that 'not even his age is known' (NS/864), as well as by the many titles that the Greek peoples gave to Homer – 'the father of Greek polity or civility' (NS/899), 'the father of all other poets' (NS/900), and 'the source of all Greek philosophies' (NS/901). These observations finally led Vico to the radical conclusion that Homer was not a real person, but only 'an idea or a heroic character of Grecian men insofar as they told their histories in song' (NS/873), which is equivalent to saying that 'the Greek peoples were themselves Homer . . . our Homer truly lived on the lips and in the memories of the peoples of Greece throughout the whole period from the Trojan War down to the time of Numa, a span of 460 years' (NS/875–6).

Vico's general theory about the collective creation of the Homeric epics is still considered plausible by modern scholars. And even though very few of them would go with Vico so far as to deny the very existence of the individual poet Homer, they are ready, on the whole, to accept his more moderate claim and deny the individuality of the Homeric poetry. Vico's assertion that Homer was only the 'binder or compiler of fables' is compatible with Moses Finley's conclusion, that 'the pre-eminence of a Homer lies in the scale on which he worked and in the freshness with which he selected and manipulated what he inherited, in the little variations and inventions he introduced in the stitching . . . [of] certain essentials from what older bards had passed to him'.[89] Similarly, Milman Parry draws from his field research of the oral folklore of the bards in the Balkan area the conclusion that every mythology is 'the creation of a long line or even of an entire people'. Like Vico he too regards Homer as a rather late myth-maker, already a writer who summed up 'the best thought of many poets'. Parry generally reasons that such a

traditional literary artist, sensing the force of the traditional material whence his art was derived, but no longer comprehending it, no longer finding acceptable the methods of the traditional, sought to compensate for this lack by intricacies of construction created for their own sake . . . Enamored of the meretricious virtues of art, we may fail to understand the real meaning of a traditional poem. That meaning cannot be brought to light by elaborate schematization, unless that schematization be based on the elements of oral tradition, on the still dynamic multi-form patterns in the depths of primitive myths.[90]

---

[89] Moses Finley, *The World of Odysseus* (N.Y.: The Viking Press, 1954), p. 28.
[90] Milman Parry, *The Making of Heroic Verse* (Oxford: Oxford University Press, 1970), pp. 220–1. In his review-essay on some contemporary works on Dante (1728), commonly known as 'The Discovery of the True Dante', Vico calls Dante 'the Tuscan Homer' and characterizes him, rather oddly, as an essentially naïve, and even primitive, poet: 'What was most peculiar to Dante's sublimity resulted from his having been born with the gift of genius in the era of Italy's expiring barbarism'. Quoted from Irma Brandeis' translation in her anthology *Discussions of the Divine Comedy* (Boston: Heath, 1961), p. 11. For critical comments on this and other literary theories of Vico, see Mario Fubini, 'Il mito

Following up these important observations, I think that Vico's achievement in the 'discovery of the true Homer' was of that kind: he did not fail to understand the meaning of a traditional poem. Whereas other interpreters of Homer's heroic poetry in his time were generally more enlightened than he was, and certainly superior to him in their scholarship, he was perhaps more attentive and responsive to the deep dynamic patterns of primitive myths which inspired the makers of this poetry, and – Vico could only hope – must inspire their modern interpreters. As for Vico's own interpretations of Homeric deities – they are very idiosyncratic: Juno, for instance, stands for marriage (NS/511); Diana is associated with the first human need (water) but then undergoes a series of fabulous transformations and comes to symbolize chastity (NS/528); Mars represents war (NS/565–6), Apollo, divination (NS/528), Vulcan, Saturn, and Vesta, the various field works (NS/564), and so on. These are far-fetched, often erroneous, interpretations, and the best one can say about them is what Vico said with regard to Bacon's interpretations – they are more learned and ingenious than true. Vico's achievement, it must be conceded, was not as an interpreter of ancient mythology, but rather as its theorist.

The discovery that Homer and his heroes were created by the entire Greek people as their ideal 'poetic characters', so superior in its philological insights to the merely philosophical theories of both Plato and Bacon, enabled Vico to advance not only beyond their a-historical theories of myth, but also beyond the most fashionable historical theory of myth in his time – that of the neo-Euhemerists. For the classical Euhemeric theory held that the mythical figures were real historical men, most of them social and political leaders, who had been deified by the popular imagination. But, as Frank Manuel has shown, in the eighteenth century very few mythographers committed themselves to this simplistic explanation.[91] Nevertheless, the strong anti-metaphysical attitude of ancient Euhemerism towards the myths appealed to such writers as Leclerc, Banier, Fréret, or Newton in his more leisurely mood, who generally conceived of classical civilization in scientific

---

della poesia primitiva e la critica dantesca di G. B. Vico', in *Stile e umanità di Giambattista Vico* (Bari: Laterza, 1946), pp. 173–205.
[91] Frank Manuel, *The Eighteenth Century Confronts the Gods*, pp. 103–4.

and material terms. In any case, the contention of the modern Euhemerists that the life of people in antiquity – at any rate, genuine and significant life – was thoroughly mythical, that is to say that it consisted in attempts at a reconstitution of the ideal myth in flesh and blood, bears an apparent resemblance to Vico's theory, and thus led some modern commentators to dub him too as an Euhemerist of sorts, even though Vico himself never associated himself with this school. In his work he does not refer at all to Euhemerus, and only fleetingly to his popularizer Pausanias. Although Vico, in some well-known passages of his *Autobiography*, expresses his admiration for Leclerc's historical work on ancient mythology, he does so, it seems, only in return for the latter's praise of his own work in that field.[92] Wherein, then, lies the difference between Vico's 'historical mythology' and Euhemerism?

Vico too believed that ancient mythology represented actual historical phenomena. But he differed from both the old and the new Euhemerists in his concrete identification of these phenomena. Whereas the Euhemerists sought to find behind these tales real historical persons or events which had actually happened, Vico instead argued that these tales represent only collective images of reality. 'The fables', he says, 'were true and trustworthy histories of the customs of the most ancient peoples'. They are 'histories', indeed, yet not of any specific events in the past, but rather of the shared experience gained through them. Already in his first oration he suggested that 'those who were raised to heaven among the gods are but the intelligence which each of us possesses'.[93] Thus, unlike and even against the Euhemerists, Vico claims that what we find in the ancient myths is not general glorification of concrete persons in history, but precisely the opposite – a concrete personification of some general feelings and ideas. Vico goes so far as to argue that even well-known historical figures like Romulus, Numa, or Solon were not real persons but only 'poetic characters', that is para-historical personifications of the political aspirations of the masses in Athens and Rome (NS/412ff.).

Such real or imagined personages served as concrete metaphors, or 'poetic characters', for a wider range of conceptions.

---

[92] Vico, *The Autobiography*, pp. 158–9, 164–5. [93] Vico, *The Autobiography*, p. 140.

Vico does not rule out the possibility that some of these 'poetic characters' may have been 'particular men in history', but this, he insists, is irrelevant to the process in which they have been transformed into general ideal types: inasmuch as the mythical heroes exemplified human qualities – they were, for their ancient makers and believers, more real than living human beings, in whom these qualities were only partially fulfilled. The fact that the ancients expressed their experience and knowledge in the personal idiom of this or that hero implies that they were still at a stage in which they could not distinguish man from his particular role-performance, nor could they distinguish their own personalities and actions from those of that man. For people in this stage ideal mythical figures must have been more real than actual persons, including themselves, a fact which, as Vico notes, can be confirmed by 'the custom the vulgar have when creating fables of men famous for this or that, and placed in these or those circumstances, of making the fable fit the character and condition':

These fables are ideal truths suited to the merit of those of whom the vulgar tell them; and such falseness to fact as they contain consists simply in failure to give their subjects their due. So that, if we consider the matter well, poetic truth is metaphysical truth, and physical truth which is not in conformity with it should be considered false. Thence springs this important consideration in poetic theory: the true war chief, for example, is the Godfrey that Torquato Tasso imagines; and all the chiefs who do not conform throughout to Godfrey are not true chiefs of war. (NS/205)

This observation contained for Vico a general truth about human life, which exceeded the concrete anthropo-historical conditions in which it was made – in short, a truth about the nature of truth in human life. Believing that 'the nature of institutions is nothing but their coming into being at certain times and in certain guises' (NS/147) and that 'the order of ideas must follow the order of institutions' (NS/238) Vico came to the conclusion that truth-claims in human affairs are unique and necessary to those who hold them, that they reflect their particular mental 'modifications', namely, the life-assertions which arise out of the necessities and utilities of their social condition. And if, as Vico seems to suggest, all truth-claims concerning human affairs are inevitably 'modified' in that way, then they must be understood as necessarily partial and essentially incommensurable. Hence, any philosophical attempt to judge and compare them on purely conceptual grounds, according to the seemingly absolute and timeless norms of the one who judges, is futile. What was needed, instead, was a philological attempt to judge and compare different truth-claims on historical grounds, to understand them not as absolute but only as relative perspectives of truth, merely moments in, and not the end of, the process of the 'history of human ideas'. Such truths are all various historical yet equally valid life-assertions. The task of the philologist, and truly 'new scientist', of ideas, was to clarify the historical grounds of truth-claims, and thereby to show that they are not so much opposed, let alone superior, to each other, but only different from each other.

What Vico realized, then, was that truths are analogical, not tautological, and that a cognition of what is real and what is fictional in the world is not objective and self-evident in itself but depends on the prevailing criteria of belief. Hence, the world in which the ancient Greeks lived was not, and could not be, fictional for them, because they did not perceive the difference between fiction and reality as we do. They simply lived according to norms of credulity which were primarily moral and not scientific, and were therefore much more inclusive, and far less critical, than the modern ones – about what was real in the human world. For them, the mythical tales about heroes who performed impossible actions like flying, descending to hell, or turning into gods were, for that reason, not unreal, but even more real: they described human actions which were not actual or possible for men in this world, but which, in themselves, were credible. Such descriptions extended, as it were, the range of possible human actions beyond the limit of natural reality, but not beyond that of human reality. They kept them within the limits of what Vico calls 'credible impossibility [*l'impossibile credibile*]' – which, he adds, is the 'origin' and 'the proper material' of all worthy poetry (NS/383). The problem of myth in the modern era is that its original credible impossibilities have become – for us – incredible:

The fables in their origin were true and severe narrations, whence *mythos*, fable, was defined as *vera narratio*. But because they were originally for the most part gross, they gradually lost their original meanings, were then altered, subsequently became improbable, after that obscure, then scandalous, and finally incredible. (NS/814)

Vico knew that he was living in a post-mythical age, and that his task in making sense of myth was much more complicated than that of the ancient writers, or even Dante, who still lived in an age which was largely myth-oriented. If, nevertheless, he did try to find the 'original meaning' of the ancient myths it was because he sensed that the corruption of these 'severe and true' meanings was a sign of much more wide-spread deterioration: it signified the general loss of religious innocence, awe and obedience. 'Because religion was important to them, the men of Greece, lest the gods should oppose their desires as well as their customs, imputed these customs to the gods, and gave improper, ugly, and obscene meanings to the fables' (NS/221). Vico's attempt to retain the 'true meanings', or 'truths', of ancient myth for people in the modern age, people who have become, in his view, critical and utterly incredulous (NS/1106), was destined to expose them to the truths of innocent credulity. And the way to discover these plain truths was philological – one had to glean them from the literary form in which they have been expressed, that is to say, as *narrative* truths. Such truths are not easily understood by us because they are conveyed in actions, and not in ideas; their moral messages are not spelled out in creeds, but are re-enacted in the dramatic happenings of rituals and other ceremonial occasions.

In defining myth as *vera narratio*, Vico did not mean to argue that myth was a true statement about the nature of physical or historical reality, as the philosophers would have it. By reiterating the fact that myth 'was not a language in accord with the nature of the things it dealt with . . . but was a fantastic speech making use of physical substances endowed with life' he admitted that myth in itself is indeed a lie or a false story – because it represents untruthfully natural or historical realities; and yet, he could nonetheless maintain that it is a true story – insofar as it expresses truthfully archaic and profound realities concerning the needs and aims of men. What the new scientist of myth must do, then, is to explain the moral and generally human messages of all myths, even of those which seem to deal only with nature. Ultimately, these tales were primarily concerned with the common necessities and utilities of civil life, and their 'original meaning' resides in their *ratio civilis*. The scholar of myth must therefore translate their natural idioms into historical ones: 'These divine or heroic characters were true fables or myths, and their allegories are

found to contain meanings not analogical but univocal, not philosophical but historical, of the peoples of Greece and of those
times' (NS/34).Vico was the first theorist who saw that in mythology we do not have history-as-it-really-was, but rather, as Bernard
Knox has put it, a

history in which the original core of genuine memory, if indeed that ever
existed, had been transformed by the selective emphasis of the oral
tradition. Over many generations of oral transmission, stories change on
the lips of tellers to reflect new preoccupations, new attitudes. And in
such a process only what remains meaningful and relevant will survive.
The oral tradition, myth, 'what they say', emphasizes and preserves only
what is memorable.[94]

To sum up: in defining myth as *vera narratio* Vico implies that
the *truth* of myth consists not in its modes of cognition or representation of reality but rather in its mode of *narration* of it. Vico,
it seems, was the first student of myth who saw this crucial aspect –
that in a non-literate and highly traditional society the narrative
modes in which myths operate are particularly effective in transmitting its *ratio civilis* among its members and also between
generations. What makes mythical discourse so effective is the fact
that it is not an abstract treatise on social institutions, but a concrete story which relates them to dramatic persons and actions:

Since barbarians lack reflection, which when ill used, is the mother of
falsehood, the first heroic Latin poets sang true stories; that is, the
Roman wars. And in the returned barbarian times, in virtue of this nature
of barbarism, the Latin poets like Gunther, William of Apulia, and
others again sang nothing but history, and the romancers of the same
period thought they were writing true histories . . . And in virtue of this
same barbarism, which for lack of reflection does not know how to feign
(whence it is naturally truthful, open, faithful, generous, and magnani-
mous), even Dante, though learned in the loftiest esoteric knowledge,
filled the scenes of the *Comedy* with real persons and portrayed real events
in the lives of the dead . . . And here we have a luminous proof of the fact
that the first fables were histories. (NS/817)

In his contention that the classical myths, however fabulous they
might appear to us, must nevertheless be considered as truthful in
their narration of past events, because their authors encoded in

---

[94] Bernard Knox, *Word and Action* (Baltimore: The Johns Hopkins University Press, 1979),
p. 15.

them the seminal experience gained through these events, Vico sought to bridge the polarity between mythology and history. He did this by showing that both are different yet equally 'true narrations' of events: in both cases people signify those, and only those, events which seem important to them. Thus, in the passages preceding the above conclusion, he sets out to counter 'the truth understood by Castelverto, that history must have come first and then poetry, for history is a simple statement of the true but poetry is an imitation besides'. As regards the historical authenticity and validity of ancient mythology, he says, we must remember that because 'men are naturally led to preserve the memories of the institutions and laws that bind them within their societies', and 'inasmuch as the poets came certainly before the vulgar historians, the first history must have been poetic' (NS/811–3). Furthermore, in Vico's view, the Greek authors themselves composed their mythology as poetic history: 'after Urania – the Muse defined by Homer as the Science of good and evil, or of divination, in virtue of which Apollo is the god of poetic wisdom of divination – they must have conceived the second of the Muses, Clio, the narrator of heroic history' (NS/533).[95]

In his attach on 'the truth understood by Castelverto' Vico in fact challenged some of the basic ideals of historiography in his time. For the leading Enlightenment historians held to Castelverto's conviction that since 'history is a simple statement of the true', ancient or primitive mythologies must be viewed as contrarious and worthless to their profession. As Gibbon said: 'I am ignorant, and I am careless, of the blind mythology of the barbarians'.[96] Vico opposed this notion by calling up Tacitus's example: in his *Germania* the Roman historian, the second of Vico's 'four authors', did take the mythology of the barbarians seriously. For he saw that the 'ancient hymns' of the Germans were 'the only style of record or history which they possess', a fact which required him, being their historian, to find out what such songs

---

[95] On the mythological infiltration of ancient historiography, see the well-known studies of Francis M. Cornford, *Thucydides Mythistoricus* (London: E. Arnold, 1907); Georges Dumézil, *The Destiny of the Warrior*, tr. A. Hiltebeitel (Chicago: The University of Chicago Press, 1970). For a revision of this view, see Moses I. Finley, 'Myth, Memory, and History', *History and Theory*, 4 (1965), pp. 281–302.

[96] On the ideological origins of these notions, see J. G. A. Pocock, 'Gibbon's *Decline and Fall* and the World View of the Late Enlightenment', in *Virtue, Commerce, and History* (Cambridge: Cambridge University Press, 1987), pp. 143–56.

mean.[97] Vico praises Tacitus for his insightful observations, and notes that these have been confirmed by modern studies of the American Indians, as well as of ancient Persian and Chinese traditions (NS/470). Vico's definition of mythology as a true narration of history can thus be interpreted as a polemical stance against the rationalists' hardened conception of history, as well as against their weak conception of mythology. His main methodological postulate, that 'all doctrines must start from the point where the matters of which they treat first began to take shape' (NS/314), when applied to the modern doctrine of history itself, formed a corrective or 'revisionist' method for his new historiography. Vico thus sought to liberate history from its rigid positivism by exposing it to the irrational impulses in its mythopoeic sources.

Generally speaking, Vico's new notion of what historical scholarship was all about grew out of his positive approach towards the so-called 'irrational' in human mind, society and history. In his view, the apparently irrational expressions of past or foreign cultures – those which his contemporaries tended to define, and so to discard, as myths – were, in fact, 'truthful narrations', which, however, had been created in a different key, according to a 'poetic logic' rather than a rational one. For the thinkers of the Enlightenment, the devout proponents of one eternal and universal Natural Law, the very idea that there could be a different, let alone 'poetic', 'logic of reality' must have seemed quite implausible if not sheer nonsense. They had absolute confidence in one and only one concept of reason – their own – as the sole constructive force of social reality. This dismissive attitude to the apparently 'irrational' was, as Hayden White has shown, particularly prevalent among the Enlightenment historians.[98]

Thus, for example, Bayle's portrayal of classical gods and heroes, hilarious as it was in its exposition of the sheer human characteristics of these legendary figures, was marred by his constant condemnation of their apparent immorality and irrationality; his 'enlightened' critical judgment of the dark

---

[97] Tacitus, *Germania* II.3, tr. M. Hutton, Loeb Classical Library (Cambridge, Mass.: Harvard University Press, 1970).

[98] Hayden White, 'The Irrational and the Problem of Historical Knowledge in the Enlightenment', in *Tropics of Discourse* (Baltimore: The Johns Hopkins University Press, 1978), pp. 135–49.

aspects in man blinded him, as it were, to some of the most creative impulses in pagan culture. Similarly, Voltaire worked out in his *Essay on the Manners of the Nations* a masterful study in comparative cultural history; and yet, he could not possibly accept that past cultures were perhaps not really immoral, but simply had different moral values. Inevitably, his absolute moral and rational standards affected his judgment of apparently irrational and immoral phenomena in history. In the article 'History' in the *Philosophical Dictionary* Voltaire poses the question, whether 'Temples, Festivals, Annual Ceremonies, and even medals are historical proofs', and then rules them out: 'One naturally tends to believe that a monument erected by a nation to celebrate an event is proof that it happened; yet if these monuments were not erected by contemporaries and if they commemorate some improbable deed, do they prove anything except that people have wanted to consecrate a popular opinion?'[99] Voltaire's intention here and in his other philosophical-historical essays was to undermine the ultra-traditional premises of nationalistic and religious historiography at the time. He was, in the words of a modern commentator, 'one of the great destroyers of accepted myths, and though one or two truths also get swept away in the process of destruction, the general effect is a salutary one'.[100] Vico, however, was interested in precisely these 'truths'. And therefore, while for Voltaire and his ilk festivals, annual ceremonies and similar 'popular opinions' were not valid historical 'proofs' that the event had 'really happened', for Vico, as we shall see, such 'vulgar traditions' did indicate that something had definitely happened, though not necessarily in the way it had been described.

It appears, then, that in as much as the scientific ideal of history in the Enlightenment was that of a true representation of reality, historical works which were not up to that standard were discarded as 'mythical' – a derogatory term which means 'false fictions' of reality. The Enlightenment historians were not yet ready to consider a third possibility, of which the classical myths were the prime example – that of 'true fictions' of reality. Whereas the Enlightenment historians shared Voltaire's conviction that

---

99 Voltaire, art. 'History', in the *Philosophical Dictionary*, in *The Age of Louis XIV and Other Selected Writings*, tr. L. H. Brumfitt (London: The New English Library, 1966), p. 327.
100 J. H. Brumfitt, Introduction to *The Age of Louis XIV*, p. xxi.

'History is the recital of things represented as true. Fable, on the contrary, is the recital of things represented as fiction', Vico, on the other hand, believed in and developed a whole theory of 'true fictions'. Having established the fact that human societies can exist only and insofar as they remember and consecrate those creative moments in which they came-into-being – 'men are naturally impelled to preserve the memories of the laws and institutions that bind them in their societies' (NS/201) – Vico could understand why, as a result, 'all barbarian histories have fabulous beginnings' (NS/202). These 'fabulous beginnings' were now understood by Vico as the 'master-key' to the subsequent history of the nation because they had actually determined it:

> Our mythologies agree with the institutions under consideration, not by force and distortion, but directly, easily, and naturally. They will be seen to be civil histories of the first peoples, who were everywhere naturally poets . . . These great fragments of antiquity, hitherto useless to science because they lay begrimed, broken, and scattered, shed great light when cleaned, pieced together, and restored. (NS/352, 357)

Now, in view of such seemingly pretentious declarations, it seems only fair to ask, whether Vico himself ever practised these notions in historical research, or whether his 'historical mythology' was, and perhaps was bound to remain, mere theory on his part with no or very little relevance for historical scholarship? This question begs a more general question, to wit, whether and to what extent Vico, who has been aptly described by one of his biographers as 'one of the most historically-minded men who ever lived',[101] was really a historian himself, or whether Arnaldo Momigliano is right in his verdict that 'Vico was isolated in his times partly because he was a great thinker but partly also because he was a worse scholar than his contemporaries'. According to Momigliano, Vico fails as a historian because 'the antiquarian movement of the eighteenth century passed him by'.[102]

This harsh judgment is as true as it is unfair. It ignores the fact

---

[101] Henry P. Adams, *The Life and Writings of Giambattista Vico* (London: G. Allen and Unwin, 1935), p. 174.

[102] Arnaldo Momigliano, 'Ancient History and the Antiquarian', in *Studies in Historiography* (London: Weidenfeld and Nicolson, 1966), p. 19. For a different, and much more favourable, view of Vico's contributions to historical scholarship, see the essays of Fausto Nicolini, *Vico storico*, ed. F. Tessitore (Naples: Morano, 1967).

that Vico knew, but consciously rejected, some of the principal methods and aims of antiquarian scholars like Scaliger, Muratori, or the French jurists. Above all, he opposed what Momigliano defines as the antiquarians' greatest contribution to historiography, namely the 'distinction between original and secondary sources'. Vico, in contrast, sought to show that secondary sources such as 'vulgar traditions', which have given 'the original meanings' of the primary sources 'improbable', 'obscure', 'scandalous', and 'incredible' interpretations – nevertheless 'must have had public grounds of truth', namely truthful messages 'by virtue of which they came into being and were preserved by entire peoples over long periods of time' (NS/149). In his historical inquiries Vico thus tried, as it were, to extend the range of historical truth from *Geschichte* to *Wirkungsgeschichte*, namely from what had originally happened to how it later was conceived to have happened. He subsequently turned his attention from real events in history to their mythical images. He assumed that historical myths which 'came into being and were preserved by entire peoples over long periods of time' are not simply political fabrications of origins and rights. They must be seen, rather, as dramatic narratives which explain the present situation of a social group in terms of a creative act which took place in its past. By continuously evoking this foundational act as the decisive moment of change in the history of the group, these narratives form a social consensus around it. For the social group, this original constitutive act, real or imagined, is always true. On these premises, he declared, he would work out a new theory of 'historical mythology' (NS/203), as well as, one might add, mythological history: the historical course of any nation or civilization was determined by its myths. As Vico put it in the *First New Science*:

For even the learned historians are obliged to narrate the vulgar traditions of the peoples whose histories they write, in order that they be accepted as truths by the vulgar and [thus] be useful to the states for whose continuous existence they are written, leaving the assessment of their truth to scholars . . . The reverence to which their antiquity entitles them is, however, ensured by the following maxim: that communities of men are led naturally to preserve the memory of those customs, orders and laws which hold them within this or that society. If all gentile histories have therefore preserved their fabulous origins . . . the fables must uniquely contain historical accounts of the oldest customs, orders and laws of the first gentile nations. This will be the guiding principle for the whole of this work.[103]

This positive appraisal of mythology as true history initiated, as it were, a new idea of historical criticism. As I shall argue in the next chapter, Vico differed most drastically from the Enlightenment historians in his conception of the 'critical' function of their work. For the latter, 'historical criticism' was a 'science' of knowing facts, an attempt to secure, through the rigorous analysis of textual and antiquarian evidence, one ultimate and objective truth about what had 'really happened' in history. Vico, in contrast, perceived historical criticism as an 'art' of recollecting meanings, i.e., an attempt to redeem from the evidence of the past many subjective truths and hidden or forgotten meanings, and so, as it were, to secure their tradition through history. And so, whereas all the other methods in this field sought to separate fact from fiction, the *New Science* alone devised a new hermeneutical method by virtue of which historians could explain under what conditions in human history fact and fiction necessarily merged into those 'true fictional' modes of comprehension and narration. Against the science of historical criticism in his time, which sought to separate the historical wheat from the legendary chaff in ancient narrations, Vico attempted to accommodate both by means of a new philological scholarship, which he termed, significantly, the 'new art of criticism' (*nuova arte critica*).

---

[103] Vico, *The First New Science*, pars. 92-3.

CHAPTER 4

The revision of history

For the history of civilization the perennial dream of a
sublime life has the value of a very important reality. And even
political history itself, under penalty of neglecting actual
facts, is bound to take illusions, vanities, follies, into account.
There is not a more dangerous tendency in history than that
of representing the past as if it were a rational whole and
dictated by clearly defined interests.

Johan Huizinga, *The Waning of the Middle Ages*, ch. 7

Vulgar traditions must have had public grounds of truth, by
virtue of which they came into being and were preserved by
entire peoples over long periods of time.

G. B. Vico, *The New Science*, par. 149

I

In recent scholarship on the Enlightenment it has become a
truism that this era must not be regarded as the 'Age of Reason',
but rather as the 'Age of Criticism'.[1] Whereas the former label has
acquired derogatory connotations, signifying, among other
things, the Enlightenment's naïve and destructive faith in the
omnipotence of reason, the latter label and the concept of
criticism appear to depict more accurately the cultural ideology
which motivated this movement.[2] Above all, however, the label
'Age of Criticism' is more accurate because it is compatible with

---

[1] For general reviews of the problem in modern historiography see George Boas, 'In
Search of the Age of Reason', in E. R. Wasserman (ed.), *Aspects of the Eighteenth Century*
(Baltimore: The Johns Hopkins University Press, 1965), pp. 1–19; M. S. Anderson,
Historians and Eighteenth-Century Europe (Oxford: Oxford University Press, 1979),
pp. 64–78.
[2] Cassirer, *The Philosophy of the Enlightenment*, p. 275; Paul Hazard, *European Thought in the
Eighteenth Century*, tr. J. Lewis May (Harmondsworth: Penguin Books, 1965), p. 19.

the way in which some of the leading thinkers of the Enlightenment saw their age. Thus, in the preface to the *Critique of Pure
Reason* Kant identifies his age as one of *Kritik* to which everything
must submit. Henceforth, nothing was to remain exempt from
'the test of free and open examination'.[3] And in the very similar
words of Edward Gibbon: 'All that men have been, all that genius
has created, all that reason has weighed, all that labor has
gathered up – all this is the business of criticism. Intellectual
precision, ingenuity, penetration, are all necessary to exercise it
properly.'[4]

The Enlightenment ideology of criticism was not immune to
criticism. This came mostly from those religious and political
conservatives, whose world-views and interests were undermined
by the iconoclastic fever of the age. The most notable protagonist
in this vein was Edmund Burke who contended that the French
philosophes had effectively demystified the divine sanctions of
traditional values and institutions, but had failed to replace these
prejudices with an alternative workable system of ethics. Modern
critics of the Enlightenment have repeated this allegation.[5]

Vico is unique among all these critics of criticism because he was
the first theorist to challenge seriously not only the practical
consequences, but also the theoretical premises of the Enlightenment ideology of criticism. Furthermore, his *New Science*, though
certainly inimical to the overtly critical ideology of the time, was
not, in itself, anti-critical in principle, as some interpreters have
taken it to be. Rather, he developed a different and contrary
theory of criticism, a constructive one, which he termed the 'new
art of criticism' (*nuova arte critica*). The main task of this section
will thus be to explain the terms and conception of this theory. My
contention is, that Vico's counter-Enlightenment strategy can best
be apprehended by looking at the way in which he interpreted the
meaning of, and resolved the tension between, the two definitive

---

[3] Immanuel Kant, *The Critique of Pure Reason*, tr. N. Kemp Smith (N.Y.: Saint Martin's
1965), p. 9.
[4] Edward Gibbon, *Essai sur l'étude de la littérature*, in *Miscellaneous Works of Edward Gibbon*,
ed. Lord Sheffield (London, 1814), IV, p. 38.
[5] In entitling his work *An Age of Crisis: Man and World in Eighteenth-Century French Thought*
(Baltimore: The Johns Hopkins University Press, 1959), Lester Crocker neatly subverted
the term Age of Criticism. He accuses the Enlightenment scientists of man that 'by
affirming what they perceived to be man's true place in the universe they loosed the
metaphysical moorings and set him adrift' (p. 471).

concepts of the age – the concepts of 'criticism' and 'tradition'. More specifically, I will concentrate on the use of these terms in the historiography of the Enlightenment, wherein the apparent contradiction between the two was most forcefully accentuated.

As a cursory glance at the titles of some well-known historical studies in the late seventeenth and early eighteenth centuries makes clear, the adjective 'critical' seems to have become the trade-mark of the history profession. Beginning in the late seventeenth century with Simon's *Critical History of the Old Testament* (1679) and Bayle's *Critical-Historical Dictionary* (1696) we see an ever-growing flow of studies of history, all claiming to be 'critical'. History, it seems, had to be, by definition, 'critical'; it remains to be seen, however, whether and to what extent criticism had to be 'historical', as far as these scholars were concerned.

The term 'criticism' itself owes its inception and most of its modern connotations to classical theories of literature. In classical Greece, the *kritikoi* were those participants in a conversation, discussion, or dialogue who explained why and on what grounds they made their judgments. 'Criticism' was most commonly used in debates on aesthetics, and it generally stood for that learned appreciation of a work of art, which was not based on purely subjective taste, nor on official dicta of 'authorities', but on sound objective norms of judgment like 'mimesis', 'sublimity', etc. In the sixteenth and seventeenth centuries, as for the various schools of classicism in the eighteenth century, the notion of 'criticism' was still confined to that literary connotative range. Its task was, in Dryden's words, to establish upon some absolute and timeless precepts of reason 'a standard of judging well' all literary texts.[6]

As against this, however, there was a growing awareness of the fact, that any literary evaluation inevitably involved historical considerations. Thus, when Francis Bacon made his famous distinction between the two traditions of knowledge, 'the one critical, the other pedantical', he defined the tasks of the critical as:

(1) concerning the true correction and edition of authors, (2) concerning the exposition and explication of authors, (3) concerning the times, which in many cases give great light to true interpretations,

---

[6] Quoted in René Wellek, *Concepts of Criticism* (New Haven: Yale University Press, 1963), p. 87.

(4) concerning some brief censure and judgment of the authors, and (5) concerning the syntax and disposition of studies.[7]

The task of seventeenth-century historians was, or ought to have been, the third one – the interpretation of literary texts in their historical context. Yet, this task was hampered by the more excessive demand of the fourth Baconian regulation, which demanded strictly rational criteria in the judgment of literary texts of the past. This restrictive trend was also evident in the historical scholarship of the time in which, as Marc Bloch has pointed out, 'the very word "criticism", which up to that time had connoted little more than a judgment of taste, [was then] passing to the almost new sense of a test of truth'.[8]

Criticism as a test of truth: this was precisely how thinkers like Spinoza, Simon, Bayle, Voltaire, Hume, or Gibbon conceived of their task as interpreters of historical texts, profane as well as sacred. They were intent not so much on explication as on testing the truths proclaimed by the ancient authors. As Descartes put it in a famous passage in his *Discourse on Method*:

Then, too, the mythical stories represent, as having happened, many things which are in no wise possible. Even the most trustworthy of the histories, if they do not change or exaggerate the import of things, in order to make them seem more worthy of perusal, at least omit almost all the more commonplace and less striking of the background circumstances, and the account they give of them is to that extent misleading. Those who regulate their conduct by examples drawn from these sources are all too likely to be betrayed into romantic extravagances, forming projects that exceed their powers.[9]

In so doing, Descartes helped demystify the art of history itself, turning it, as his faithful follower Bayle would ultimately define it, from a *tradition of stories* into a *science of facts*.

Now, the problem of tradition in historiography is simple yet tricky: is tradition a medium-of-truth or an obstacle-to-truth? And this is an old – perhaps the oldest – problem in this field. It is already evident in Thucydides's famous comments against Herodotus, who claimed that his task is not to pass judgment on stories that he had heard from the Egyptians, only to relate them

---

[7] Bacon, *The Advancement of Learning, The Philosophical Works*, III, pp. 413–14.
[8] Marc Bloch, *The Historian's Craft*, tr. P. Putnam (New York: Vintage Books, 1953), p. 82.
[9] Descartes, *Discourse on Method*, in *Descartes' Philosophical Writings*, p. 97.

faithfully. To this Thucydides replies, that the main problem of historiography is that 'men accept from one another hearsay reports of former events, neglecting to test them just the same'.[10] These remarks make clear that the tension between criticism and the loyalty to tradition is as old as the profession itself; furthermore, they suggest that, from the outset, historians have been acutely aware of the paradox inherent in their task – to relate traditional stories in a critical way. Indeed, the subversive aspect of this task is already intimated in the original Greek term for 'historian', which means an 'eyewitness', the one who obtains truth about what happened not merely by repeating 'what they say' (this is, literally, an act of 'mythmaking'), but rather by examination of witnesses and through enquiry into the actual causes of what happened.[11] In their original and ideal sense, then, both terms – 'history' and 'criticism' – were, or ought to have been, tautological. History, it was believed, could achieve real knowledge of events 'as they really happened' if, and only if, it were critical of tradition.

In the two centuries between the Renaissance and the Enlightenment the anti-traditional polemics and tactics of historians greatly increased. It was, above all, in the Enlightenment's professed animosity towards the traditional in all its guises, that we can detect the crucial difference between the two epochs, or rather, as I shall argue, between their opposing conceptions of historical criticism: whereas the Humanists in the Renaissance were still enchanted by the very idea of 'tradition', and in their works sought to restore the message of the classical culture as faithfully as possible, the Enlightenment historians regarded tradition, any tradition, as false, and not just because it was antique, hereditary, arational, etc. As Ernst Cassirer has noted: 'As a purely philosophical movement the Enlightenment disproved much more easily of its heritage than Humanism within the sphere of merely scholarly research'.[12] Above all, the thinkers of the Enlightenment argued, the very act of tradition was false because it could not possibly be 'critical': the age of criticism

---

[10] Thucydides, *History of the Peloponnesian War*, i.xx, Eng. tr. C. F. Smith, Loeb Classical Library (Cambridge, Mass.: Harvard University Press, 1919).

[11] R. G. Collingwood, *The Idea of History* (Oxford: Oxford University Press, 1946), pp. 25–31.

[12] Cassirer, *The Philosophy of the Enlightenment*, p. 235.

consists in doubt, and the act of traditionalism in faith, and the two cannot be held together.[13] As one modern scholar has put it, while for the adherents of tradition, historical inquiry into the past had to preserve tradition because it was the medium of truth, for the critical historians it seemed that 'tradition (that is to say, documents of the past and their accepted interpretation) puts itself between us and the past in the same way as it puts itself between the mind and the object of proof. It renders or may render impossible the true knowledge of the past.'[14] Thus, during the eighteenth century 'historical criticism' and 'traditionalism' came to signify not just different ideals of historical scholarship, but contradictory ideals of life.

Yet, however useful this clear-cut contrast of 'historical criticism' and loyalty to 'tradition' may have been for the reassessment of records of the past, it turned out to be a major stumbling block to full historical understanding. For the one problem these historical critics were not yet ready, or able, to tackle was, how to account for the way in which common-sense conceptions and traditions are also constitutive of social reality. It was, as Hans-Georg Gadamer has argued, precisely this dogmatic approach to poetic tradition as 'opposed' to rational enlightenment – rather than as necessary and complementary to it – which hampered the philosophers' view of social reality and their missionary task in transforming it. As long as the champions of reason were oblivious to the poetic constitution of their own modes of thought, to the inevitable conditioning of their social experience by historically transmitted conventions; as long as their 'critical' activity was confined to what Gadamer calls 'the disrepute of prejudices through the enlightenment',[15] they could not properly realize the 'historicality' of their own reason, that is the way in which every understanding of reality, theirs included, is necessarily permeated by traditional notions and terms. Therefore, though the philosophical historians of the Enlightenment are commonly credited

---

[13] The argument that the main task of the Enlightenment was to oppose 'traditionality as such' is forcefully reiterated by Franco Venturi, 'The European Enlightenment', in *Italy and the Enlightenment: Studies in a Cosmopolitan Century*, tr. S. Corsi (London: Longman, 1972), pp. 1–32.

[14] Emile Bréhier, 'The Formation of Our History of Philosophy', in *Philosophy and History, Essays Presented to Ernst Cassirer*, ed. R. Klibansky and H. J. Paton (Oxford: Oxford University Press, 1936), p. 161.

[15] Hans-Georg Gadamer, *Truth and Method* (London: Sheed & Ward, 1975), p. 250.

by modern historians of anthropology with having 'invented' the rules and methods of this profession, they in fact lacked a genuine anthropological sense. They could not yet grasp that most essential idea in modern anthropology that 'the really important thing to know about a society is what it takes for granted'.[16]

Vico intentionally construed his 'new art of criticism' against both the 'old', uncritical theories of history, which simply accepted and transmitted tradition's stories and values, and against the new, ultra-critical theories of history which totally discarded tradition. 'Vulgar traditions', he contended, are indispensable to all societies, as well as to those who study them, because it is always in and through such collective patterns of thought that people construe their social reality. For Vico, traditions were not an obstacle but a medium of 'historical truth' – a means of making and discovering this truth. Yet, what precisely was this 'truth' that he was looking for? What, in other words, was the subject matter of historical literature? As I shall now argue, it was in the special nature of his conception of historical truth that Vico diverged most radically from the philosophical historians of the Enlightenment.

For the latter the answer was simple: History deals in facts, only in facts and nothing but the facts – and therefore the historian must seek only the truth of facts. The most forceful exponent of this view was Pierre Bayle. In his *Critical-Historical Dictionary* he states that because 'truth' is 'the soul of history, it is an essential thing for a historical composition to be free from lies; so that though it should have all other perfections, it will not be history, but a mere fable or romance, if it want truth'. Other kinds of literature such as philosophy, theology, or poetry were concerned with other respective truths – moral, religious, or aesthetic, and needed other criteria of composition and evaluation; but history, being the simple narration of facts, must be practised and criticized according to absolutely scientific criteria and methods which rule what is real and what is not, and can thus help us to decide what really happened, or could have happened, and what must be deemed as mere fable. Historians must be philosophers endowed with what Bayle called 'Historical Talent' – which is

---

[16] A. L. Kroeber and C. Kluckhohn, 'General Features of Culture', in *Man and Contemporary Society* (New York: Columbia University Press, 1955), I, p. 197.

basically a talent for disengagement from personal and from other people's views, and especially from 'religious zeal, which prompts us to cry down what we think to be true'.[17] In his numerous commentaries on pagan or Judaeo-Christian historians Bayle noted that most of them were equally, and fatally, prompted by religious and nationalistic sentiments; the distinctly critical aim of his historical dictionary was to substitute the various truths that these authors erroneously believed to detect in and through historical events, with what he, guided solely by the universal standards of rationality, knew to be the sole truth of these events – that they had merely happened. His critical-historical method of interpretation was an exercise in distinguishing between the subjective intentions of the author of the text, or its 'meanings', and the objective events as they really happened, and which alone merited the title of 'truth'.[18]

Bayle derived this distinction between meaning and truth in historical literature from Spinoza's *Theological-Political Treatise*. Spinoza's main argument in that work is that the authors of the Old Testament primarily composed it for political purposes, seeking only to inculcate piety and obedience to their particular God, and therefore we must not even seek in it any truths – whether religious, natural, or historical. The nature and standards of truth were not to be deduced from scriptural descriptions, but solely from natural reason:

Scripture does not explain things by their secondary causes, but only narrates them in the order and the style which has most power to move men, and especially uneducated men, to devotion; and therefore it speaks inaccurately of god and of events, seeing that its object is not to convince the reason, but to attract and lay hold of the imagination.[19]

A valid interpretation of a Biblical text consists in the elucidation of the intentional message that its authors, bound as they were by the mental, linguistic, natural and historical conditions which prevailed in their times, could possibly have sought to convey in it. This message which, in Spinoza's view, was political, not metaphysical, and therefore particular and not universal, is entirely

---

[17] Pierre Bayle, *Historical-Critical Dictionary*, quoted in Hayden White, *Metahistory* (Baltimore: The Johns Hopkins University Press, 1973), p. 49.
[18] Elisabeth Labrousse, *Bayle*, tr. D. Potts (Oxford: Oxford University Press, 1983), pp. 50–1.
[19] Spinoza, *Theological-Political Treatise*, tr. R. H. M. Elwes (N.Y.: Dover, 1951), p. 91.

contained in, and largely confined to, the verbal sense of the
words, namely to the words as spoken to and meant to be understood by the multitude of believers: 'Scriptural interpretation
proceeds by the examination of Scripture, and inferring the intention of its authors as a legitimate conclusion from its fundamental
principles'.[20] Spinoza thus urges the interpreter to look for and
'work not on the truth of passages, but solely on their meaning',
namely to examine them 'solely by means of the signification of
the words, or by a reason acknowledging no foundation but
Scripture', and to remember all along that 'it is one thing to
understand the meaning of scripture and the prophets, and quite
another thing to understand the meaning of God, or the actual
truth'.[21] The latter can be obtained by a higher kind of knowledge,
which is not at all dependent on the Bible, nor on any historical
sources, but is purely natural-philosophical:

The truth of a historical narrative, however assured, cannot give us the
knowledge nor consequently the love of God, for love of God springs
from knowledge of Him, and knowledge of Him should be derived from
general ideas, in themselves certain and known, so that the truth of a
historical narrative is very far from being requisite for our attaining our
highest good.[22]

Spinoza thus believed that we can obtain historical truth from
ancient narratives, but he drastically qualified the value of that
truth. An historical truth about events, 'however assured', was only
circumstantial – it could merely attest to the fact that certain
events had indeed happened; as such, however, this truth was of
only secondary or peripheral value to the other, and much more
valuable, truth – that which could explain, by referring to the laws
of God or Nature which rule Man, why and how these events had
really happened.

Vico's intellectual debt to Spinoza and to other practitioners of
the historical-critical method of interpretation was immense,
though never explicitly acknowledged.[23] Vico's main achievement

---

20 Spinoza, *Theological-Political Treatise*, p. 100.
21 Spinoza, *Theological-Political Treatise*, p. 170.
22 Spinoza, *Theological-Political Treatise*, p. 61.
23 Vico's knowledge and usage of Spinoza have been much discussed. Noteworthy dis-
    cussions include Frederic Vaughan, *The Political Philosophy of Giambattista Vico* (The
    Hague: Martinus Nijhoff, 1972), and James C. Morrison, 'Spinoza and Vico', *The Journal
    of the History of Ideas*, 41 (1980), pp. 49–68. These commentators interpret Vico's *New*

in historical criticism – 'The Discovery of the True Homer' – is quite clearly modelled on Spinoza's discovery of the true Moses. Spinoza (following Ibn Ezra) not only ruled out Moses as the author of the *Pentateuch*, but attributed its composition to the entire Hebrew people, noting that as 'histories' they must have been 'compiled from various writers without previous arrangement and examination', so that 'the events therein recorded as having happened in old time' must be treated as oriental mythologies.[24] In a similar vein Vico claimed that the *Iliad* and the *Odyssey* were not written by Homer himself, who in fact had never even existed, but rather were compiled by the many Greek peoples (which together must thus be considered 'the true Homer'). Such similarities abound. More than anything else, however, Vico owes to Spinoza his main heuristic principle – that the meaning of the text is immanent and must be derived from its historical context. Vico simply applies Spinoza's rule that 'our knowledge of Scripture . . . must be looked for in Scripture only'[25] to Homer: 'we are obliged . . . to discover the truth, both as to his age and as to his fatherland, from Homer himself' (NS/788). Spinoza's stricture against any metaphorical or mystical allegorization of Biblical passages is echoed in Vico's call for 'stripping off the mystical interpretations' of Homer's works, in order to 'restore to the fables their original historical meanings [*loro natii sensi storici*]; and the naturalness and ease, free of violence, subterfuge, or distortion, with which we were able to do so, show that the historical allegories which they contained were proper to them' (NS/846).

Yet, for all these apparent similarities in the methical interpretation of such historical sources, there is one cardinal difference in their respective approaches to critical evaluation: For Spinoza, as well as for Bayle and the entire Enlightenment historiography, to know the 'truth' about an event of the past meant to know it as a 'clear and distinct case', that is to say, to have its naked facts stripped of all the vulgar layers with which tradition

Science along the methodological rules set forth by Leo Strauss in his *Persecution and the Art of Writing* (Glencoe, Ill.: Free Press, 1952), and accordingly come to the conclusion that, as in the case of Spinoza (in Strauss' view), so too in the case of Vico we must interpret his pronouncements on dangerous topics like religion and politics as a deliberately obscure, and ultimately subversive, 'art of writing' designed to escape and defeat the 'persecution' of the Spanish and Papal Inquisitions in Naples.

24 Spinoza, *Theological-Political Treatise*, p. 128.
25 Spinoza, *Theological-Political Treatise*, p. 99.

has wrapped them. Vico's conception of 'historical truth' was radically different from this common, quasi-Cartesian view. For him 'historical truth' was inseparable from its 'fabulation', since this, he believed, attests to the way in which people not only perceived the events – but also created them. Vico's *new art* of criticism can thus be seen as consciously antithetical to the *new method* of criticism: he sought to overcome the latter's convenient distinction between what had really happened (truth) and what people merely believed to have happened (meanings) by suggesting that in historical reality the meanings that people have spun around real events have themselves become eventual, that is to say they constitute this reality to such an extent that these meanings cannot be reduced to the dichotomic categories of 'false' and 'true'. The duty of 'historical criticism', as Vico would ultimately conclude, is not to judge tradition as false just because it offends our standards of veracity, rationality, beauty, and so forth; rather, it must be an effort to understand and interpret its truth in and on the terms of those who wrote it, to grasp its common sense. By means of this new, so-called positive or redemptive 'art', in which we are called upon to appreciate historical traditions as 'truthful', even though and especially when they strike our modern sensibilities as being 'vulgar' – Vico believed to have overcome what he regarded as the negative kind of historical criticism, namely, the Cartesian-Enlightenment exercise in pure intellectual judgment of these and any traditions.

In this, Vico was heading in the same theoretical direction as his nineteenth-century successors. Because, as R. G. Collingwood has noted, the truly modern contribution of nineteenth-century historians towards a new science of history, was their new conception of 'historical evidence'. For historians in the Enlightenment, data of the past were trustworthy 'evidence' only after their factual authority and rational veracity had been approved by modern standards of truth. Myths, legends, folk-tales etc. were considered worthless as 'historical evidence', and therefore useless to science. As against this positivistic-mechanical approach to data – the new historians adopted a hermeneutical approach, one that claimed, as Collingwood put it, that 'if in some source you found a statement which for some reason could not be accepted as literally true, you must not on that account reject it as worthless . . . the important question about any statement contained in a source is not whether it is true or false, but what it means'. Collingwood duly notes that Vico was 'the first person to make this point'.[26] And, indeed, this is precisely the point that Vico was making in his 'new art of criticism'.

In his *Autobiography* Vico traces the evolution of his distinctly hermeneutical (in all but name) conception of criticism in his life and writings. He duly pays homage to other critics of criticism. He is particularly indebted to Tommaso Cornelio, the central figure in the Neapolitan *Academy of Investigators*, who, Vico declares, 'had found little or no pleasure in criticism – perhaps because he had observed that . . . critics never attain to the virtues of a language because they are always pausing to note the defects in others'. Following Cornelio's example Vico too resolved 'to read the Latin authors completely free of notes, entering into their spirit by means of philosophical criticism'. It was 'for all these reasons', he adds, that he 'lived in his native city not only a stranger but quite unknown'. Later on, when he came to write the *New Science* he first moulded it in what he terms '*forma negativa*', that is according to the common 'critical' fashion of the day, expounding 'the improbabilities, absurdities and impossibilities' of past authors; but, he says, eventually he 'decided that this negative form of exposition, though intriguing to the imagination, is repugnant to the understanding, since by it the human mind is not enlarged'.[27] Vico thus set out to write his *New Science* in an alternative fashion, in a distinctly 'new critical' one, the main aim of which was to counter the fashionable negative method of criticism with a positive art of criticism. This new kind of positive criticism was worked out for the first time in Vico's *New Science* of 1725. His work, he states, has 'two practical aspects':

One is a new art of criticism [*nuova arte critica*], which serves as a torch by which to discern what is true in obscure and fabulous history. The other is, as it were, an art of diagnosis which, regulated in accordance with the wisdom of mankind, gives the stages of necessity or utility which belong to the order of human things and hence provides the principal end of

---

[26] R. G. Collingwood, *The Idea of History*, p. 260 (see also p. 77). In the same vein, Marc Bloch compares the historian to a magistrate, who 'knows that his witnesses can lie or be mistaken. But he is primarily interested in making them speak so he may understand' (*The Historian's Craft*, p. 90).

[27] Vico, *The Autobiography*, pp. 133–4, 166.

this Science, which is recognition of the indubitable signs of the state of the nations.[28]

This is an opaque yet eminently revealing statement. For our purposes it is particularly important, since in it Vico completes, as it were, his long struggle towards a redefinition of the concept and task of historical criticism. Whereas in his first work, *On the Study Methods of our Time*, he still praised the achievements of the 'new critical method' of Descartes and his followers, and claimed that it was 'common to all the sciences and arts', he soon began to doubt its applicability to the human studies. Already in that work he posits the 'topical art' of knowledge (that is, knowledge of human actions by intuitive-imaginative grasp of motives) over against the 'critical method' of knowledge, that which guarantees only mechanical-physiological processes. From his second work, *On the Most Ancient Wisdom of the Italians* onward, Vico gradually developed his new conception of 'criticism', turning it from a rigorous 'new method' of explaining causes into a subtler 'new art' of understanding meanings. In that work he argued and sought to prove that in the study of social affairs the 'topical' method is superior to the 'critical' one, as it dispenses with the latter's high-minded 'clear and distinct ideas' (which were known, if at all, only to 'few philosophers'), and enables us instead to discover the truly authentic and common ideas of 'the people', in as much as these are implied in their most typical turns of phrase.

Now, when we turn to the above-quoted declaration, it is clear that in it Vico perceives the 'new critical' task of his distinctly *new* Science in essentially therapeutic and even 'redemptive' terms; there is a certain implicit connection between the two practices of the *New Science*, that is between the 'new critical' and the 'diagnostic' arts of observation. Vico, always attentive to the etymological meanings of words, here tacitly exploits the terminological affinity between 'criticism' and 'crisis'; he refers to an old and forgotten usage of the term in the medical profession, wherein 'to criticise' meant to take care of and cure a body in a 'critical' condition. Vico envisages the 'new art of criticism' of his Science to be just such a curative treatment of modern society. What he means by this strange formulation is probably this: that the philological ('new critical') observation of ancient myths in a

---

[28] Vico, *The First New Science*, par. 391, *Selected Writings*, pp. 154–5.

nation is imperative for the sociological ('diagnostic') observation of its moral and social condition. All the more so because these conditions are determined by myths.

Vico's basic attitude to tradition was certainly motivated by his conservative religious and political sensibilities. He was well aware of the mythical heritage embedded in the institutions of Catholicism and Monarchism. For theologians and historians in Vico's time the problem of tradition, which had been thoroughly debated, though not resolved, at the Council of Trent, was still a lively issue. And even though Vico himself did not get directly involved in this ongoing debate between the Protestant and the Catholic reformers about the validity of tradition, he was certainly aware of it, and in his own way responded to it – from entirely different perspectives. A brief schematic summary of this debate will help us to put Vico's notion of tradition into the right intellectual context.

The theological debate on the problem of tradition at the Council of Trent failed to reach any satisfactory conclusion.[29] The pro-Catholic resolution, which stated that 'This truth of the Bible is contained partly in written books, partly in unwritten traditions' was unacceptable to the Protestant polemicists, who based their entire ideology on two 'modern' principles, which they appropriated for their own purposes – the principles of individualism and rationalism. They rejected as heretical two fundamental Catholic principles: (a) that the Christian doctrine was only partly revealed in the Biblical text; and (b) that it could (and did) develop in history by means of oral and practical traditions. These reformers opposed, then, not only the affirmations of the Christian community of tradition, but any idea of divine revelation not made directly to the individual reason. In order to counter the Catholic claim about 'the infallibility of oral traditions' Protestant theologians devised a new heuristic method of 'scriptural rationalism': whereas Catholic apologetics maintained that religious truth had been revealed gradually and mysteriously, principally through saints and magistrates, over 1,000 years of ecclesiastical

---

[29] For two illuminative expositions of this problem from opposite religious views, see Yves. M.-J. Cognar, *Tradition and Traditions* (London: SCM Press, 1966), and Heiko Oberman, 'Quo Vadis, Petre? Tradition from Irenaeus to Humani Generis', in *The Dawn of the Reformation* (Edinburgh, T&T Clark, 1986).

development, the Protestant polemicists insisted on the immediacy and perspicuity of this truth, which in principle allowed every man to discern it in the Scriptures, simply by means of his natural rational capacities. They dismissed the Catholic attempt to extend Revelation to secondary and non-verbal means, to unwritten traditions, as a cunning device of the Church magistrates to gain control over the minds of simple believers. The Calvinists, in particular, denounced the notion of tradition as too all-embracing and thus incompatible with the principle of personal responsibility: they held that each man had to accept the responsibility for finding the truth for himself, and, more generally, that man must be freed from human authority in order to become more submissive to divine authority.

As we can see from these brief remarks, the dispute about the function of 'tradition' in Christianity hinged on a crucial disagreement with regard to the constitution of religious knowledge itself. The Protestant attempt to recover the pure timeless essence of Christianity by stripping it off its later, merely traditional elements – i.e. the Hellenic, patristic, medieval, and all other accretions of a thousand years of doctrinal development – was, in the final analysis, an attempt to separate religion from history; whether it was an attempt to reduce Christianity to its Hebraic prophetic and apocalyptic elements, as in many millenarian sects; or to its clear philosophical principles, as in Socinianism – the message was clear: the Christian doctrine was pure and complete already – and only – in its original primitive form. Any historical change in it was therefore seen as its degeneration and corruption. The Protestants thus rejected all later additions, interpretations, and other modifications of this pure text as being merely man-made 'authorities' rather than God-given truths. Ultimately, then, like most other disputes in this long warfare, the dispute about the validity of tradition was, in fact, a dispute about the legitimacy of the Church itself: whereas the Protestants saw the Church as being merely a spiritual notion of Christians, the sole duty of which was to be a custodian of the sacred Scripture, not an arbiter of Christian morality, the Catholics, on the other hand, perceived the Church to be a real historical society which united the past and the present, and all religious groups and sects, in one living tradition. Vico's innermost historicist sensibilities, I think, were rooted in these deep Catholic convictions.

Vico did not so much believe tradition, as he believed in tradition; that is, although he accepted in principle the Catholic idea of tradition as a medium-of-truth he did not think that everything taught by tradition was true. Rather, like some enlightened (and quite unorthodox) Catholic thinkers in his time – Simon, Mabillon, or Montfaucon – Vico held to 'tradition' but was not a 'traditionalist', if by that term we mean a servile follower of past authorities.[30] He retained the most essential Catholic conviction that the 'truth' – in religion as well as in all other fields – is not just God-given but also man-made. For him tradition was primarily a category of awareness of history and its effects on man. And so, unlike and against the critical-historical scholars of the age who, as a rule, disapproved of the very idea of traditional knowledge which was seen to be based on collective faith rather than on individual reason, Vico upheld this notion for precisely those reasons. He maintained that popular traditions, fabulous and credulous as they might be, must not be discredited for this reason as irrational and untrue. He argued, instead, that

Vulgar traditions must have had public grounds of truth, by virtue of which they came into being and were preserved by entire peoples over long periods of time. It will be another great labor of this Science to recover these grounds of truth – truth which, with the passage of years and the changes in languages and customs, has come down to us enveloped in falsehood. (NS/149–50)

The phrase 'public grounds of truth' is a rather rough translation of the Italian original – *publici motivi del vero*. The term *publici motivi* indicates more clearly what Vico regards as the main force in the social construction of reality, to wit, the popular impressions and interpretations of reality which, being the essential lessons of the collective-historical experience, are continuously recorded, reassessed, reaffirmed and transmitted by the common people in such 'vulgar traditions' as linguistic phrases, myths, popular rituals and plays and so on. Such popular traditions are maintained because they embody and convey to the members of the community important messages, symbolic and practical codes of behaviour: they teach them, in fact, what it

---

[30] Jaroslav Pelikan draws this crucial distinction: 'tradition is the living faith of the dead; traditionalism is the dead faith of the living', *The Vindication of Tradition* (New Haven: Yale University Press, 1984), p. 65.

means to be a member in a community. Through exemplary tales they elaborate essentially social concepts such as shame, pride, embarrassment, humiliation and the like, and thereby teach them what they must feel and think and do in everyday situations. Vico implies that those who live in a community, like those who study it, must always be aware of the 'public motives (of what is commonly regarded as) the true' in it. These 'public grounds of truth', Vico surmises, are more likely to be found in poetic metaphors than in rational conceptions, in works of art rather than in authoritative histories, in popular 'customs' rather than in official 'laws'. Above all, these truths are to be gleaned from the mythological lore of tradition. The new critical historian should no longer be confined to the scientific task of discovering what actually happened, to the reconstruction of external events by verification of sources, objectivity in the assignment of causes, etc.; he must go beyond the boundaries of the discipline and concentrate, instead, on mental events, on hopes and dreams and events that might have happened – and in a way, did happen – in as much as entire groups of people wanted and actually believed them to have happened.

Vico's vindication of tradition in terms of 'judgment without reflection' has much in common with modern attempts to demonstrate the value of the collective and pre-rational modes of thought in all spheres of culture. Over the last decades scholars in the humanities and the social sciences have become increasingly attentive and responsive to the lessons of the Romantics, Nietzsche and Freud, Weber and Durkheim, Wittgenstein and Gadamer. Much as these thinkers differ from one another in their concrete treatments of tradition (and personal commitments to it), they all seem to agree with Vico that the primary task of any inquiry in any field of knowledge is to clarify what Vico had termed its 'public grounds of truth', namely the particular socio-historical conditions and underlying 'structures of consciousness' in which its categories have been formed and processed. In their respective ways, all these thinkers and their followers have taken an anti-rationalistic 'turn' and come to criticize the Enlightenment ideal of pure reason not only as impossible in itself, but also as fundamentally misconceived: the Cartesian-Kantian beliefs in the universality and necessity of reason or in the sovereignty of the autonomous rational subject have been criticized as impervious to the contingency and conventionality of the social rules and criteria within which all processes of knowledge formation occur. For these anti- or post-Enlightenment thinkers, no act of cognition is or could ever be so pure as to allow a direct and immediate perception of the objects by the mind, since, they argue, the imperial *a priori* is always embedded in empirical conditions, and absolute truth-claims are always made in a contingent social reality, performed in different language-games, and thus always subject to specific 'forms of life'.

These modern apologies for tradition, therefore, differ radically from the classical conservative apology – as put forth for example by Edmund Burke – in one crucial aspect: they all view (and justify) 'tradition' as a dynamic, open and critical process of learning from past experience, not merely as a repetitive and uncritical imitation of it. For them, loyalty to tradition is not as an act of resignation from personal responsibility and submission to higher authority, but rather as an act of heightened awareness on the part of the individual with regard to his social world and history, an awareness which may lead him to even greater responsibility for and participation in maintaining social practices. In Gadamer's view,

That which has been sanctioned by tradition and custom has an authority which is nameless, and our finite historical being is determined by the fact that always the authority of what has been transmitted – and not only what is clearly grounded – has power over our attitudes and behaviour . . . A tradition is constantly an element of freedom and history itself.[31]

For Gadamer, as for Vico and the Romantics, this awareness of our being-in-tradition, is or at least ought to be decisive for the way we understand and interpret our human world. Gadamer acknowledges his debt to Vico's notion of *sensus communis* and reiterates his claim that, since human beings made their civil world by using their poetic capacities and traditions, the interpretation of this world must be more 'aesthetic' than 'scientific'.[32] Awareness of tradition thus ultimately implies a 'hermeneutical turn' for the 'modern historical sciences', which, Gadamer says, have hitherto made 'what has grown historically and has been transmitted

---

[31] Gadamer, *Truth and Method*, p. 249.   [32] Gadamer, *Truth and Method*, p. 16.

historically an object to be established like an experimental finding – as if tradition were an alien and, from the human point of view, as unintelligible, as an object of physics'.[33]

This opposition to the Enlightenment ideal of knowledge has undermined some of its principal cultural ideals as well, leading, on the whole, to a much more positive appreciation of such concepts as 'community', 'virtues', 'myth', 'metaphor', or 'prejudices', all of which have likewise fallen into disrepute. These and similar concepts, which thinkers from Bacon to the Enlightenment (and to modern positivism) regarded as destructive to the growth of knowledge, have now been recognized as constitutive of it. In the same vein the concept of 'authority' has also been reappraised: whereas radical critics of traditional authority have consistently attacked the a-rational norms and forms by which it secured obligation to the family, the church, and the state, modern conservative theorists have attempted to show that social life must necessarily be based on such primary emotional commitments of the individual to his natural, religious, and political communities. How to maintain traditional authority in a secular age? This was the topical issue of the age at large, and, in my view, was also the most crucial 'political' issue in Vico's life and writings. His aim was to offer a new theory of authority (*autorità*) based on his new theory of myth, such as would clarify the essential fictive nature of all forms of authority by exposing their poetic 'coming into being'.

The opening lines of the *New Science* affirm that this indeed was the major theme in Vico's work. There Vico makes clear both his aim and method of inquiry. He declares that in this work he employs 'a new art of criticism' by which

philosophy undertakes to examine philology (that is, the doctrine of all the institutions that depend on human choice; for example, all histories of the languages, customs, and deeds of people in war and peace) . . . Our Science may thus be considered a *philosophy of authority*. For by virtue of new principles of mythology herein disclosed as consequences of the new principles of poetry found herein, it is shown that the fables were true and trustworthy histories of the customs of the most ancient peoples. (NS/7) (emphasis added)

33 Gadamer, *Truth and Method*, p. xxi.

II

In his classic essay *Science as a Vocation*, Max Weber conceded that because the emotional level of modern man has not yet advanced as far as the intellectual one, there is an imminent danger that the demythologization of political power might end up in its remythologization. The main problem concerning myth-making in politics, Weber thought, is that because of the new professional ethos in the humanities and the social sciences, modern political scientists no longer deal with questions of 'ultimate and most sublime values', i.e., with those metaphysical questions to which the old myths had given an answer. Therefore, Weber observed,

We live as did the ancients when their world was not yet disenchanted of its gods and demons, only we live in a different sense. As Hellenic man at times sacrificed to Aphrodite and at other times to Apollo, and, above all, as everybody sacrificed to the gods of his city, so do we still nowadays, only the bearing of man has been disenchanted and denuded of its mystical but inwardly genuine plasticity. Fate, and certainly not 'science', holds sway over these gods and their struggles . . . Many old gods ascend from their graves; they are disenchanted and hence take the form of impersonal forces. They strive to gain power over our lives and again they resume their eternal struggle with one another.[34]

It seems, then, that the historical process of rationalization, described elsewhere by Weber as 'the disenchantment of the world', has indeed demystified the world of nature, but less effectively so the world of the polity. Modern man may thus be said to have become quite disenchanted with, yet not sufficiently enlightened about, the origin and nature of political power. Much like Plato and Machiavelli, then, Weber too came to the rather pessimistic conclusion, that a society, even if it is governed by 'philosophers' or 'scientists', still needs that which alone can give it cohesion: a shared and implicit knowledge of its origins and ends, a secret unity of tradition as embedded in its historical heritage.

Following Weber, modern social scientists have become increasingly concerned with the crucial problem of maintaining political

---

[34] Max Weber, 'Science as a Vocation', in *From Max Weber*, ed. H. Gerth and C. Wright Mills (New York: Oxford University Press, 1946), pp. 148–9.

'authority' in modern 'disenchanted' society, with what Weber has defined as 'the probability of securing obedience to definitive commands from a relevant group of people' through the evocation of its 'belief in legitimacy'. It is now a commonplace that in order to understand any political culture we must examine how it conceives, expresses, and justifies the right to use 'power', by what subversive means its ruling class evokes voluntary compliance and submission. In recent discussions on the nature of authority political scientists have been more and more concerned with the specific ceremonial means – rites, feasts, hymns, myths, etc.– whereby dominant hierarchies are created and maintained (and also overturned).[35] 'If authority is to be defined at all', Hannah Arendt reminds us, 'it must be in contradistinction both to coercion by force and persuasion by argument'.[36]

The problem of maintaining distinctly 'traditional authority' in the 'enlightened state' is by no means new. It became particularly acute in the eighteenth century, as liberal and radical critics threatened to (and eventually did) discredit the older hybrid notions of hierarchical authority – primarily those of nature (family), religion (church) and ancestry (aristocracy). The 'modernist' attack on the traditional forms of authority had some immediate personal repercussions, particularly among those who were equally committed both to the philosophical ideals of the Enlightenment and to the political traditions of elitism. The case of Edward Gibbon, as recently analyzed by Lionel Gossman, is a poignant illustration of the point.[37]

According to Gossman, the one major impression which pervaded Gibbon's life and work was precisely the desecration of all forms of traditional authority. Gibbon, like many conservatives at the time, was acutely aware of the fact, that a perfectly legitimate authority – one that is (in Gossman's words) 'absolutely original, self-authorizing, self-contained, indifferent because independent

---

[35] The exemplary study in this field is Ernst Kantorowicz, *The King's Two Bodies: A Study in Medieval Political Theology* (N.J.: Princeton University Press, 1957); for more recent studies, see *Rituals of Royalty: Power and Ceremonial in Traditional Societies*, ed. D. Cannadine and S. Price (Cambridge: Cambridge University Press, 1987).

[36] Hannah Arendt, 'What was Authority?', in *Authority*, ed. Carl J. Friedrich (Cambridge, Mass.: Harvard University Press, 1958), p. 82.

[37] Lionel Gossman, *The Empire Unposses'd: An Essay on Gibbon's Decline and Fall* (Cambridge: Cambridge University Press, 1981).

of any other, requiring neither justification nor recognition of itself as dominion over another'[38] – had become impossible. This realization tormented Gibbon on all levels of experience: as an obedient son, as a would-be believer, as a conservative politician, and, above all, as a philosophic historian: What should the conscientious historian do once he realizes, as Gibbon did, that all the traditional forms of authority – paternal, religious, or political – were, in the final analysis, means of domination, idealized fictions of origins, rights, duties, and order, all made up to legitimize the use of sheer physical power? Gibbon's dilemma with regard to the traditional authorities in his own life and society was aggravated by the realization that it was his own chosen profession, historiography, which literally 'authorized' such fictions of legitimacy. Having recognized the fact that every political authority consists of historical myths, Gibbon, the enlightened historian and conservative politician, faced a serious dilemma – whether to expose or to sustain these myths. Ultimately, as Gossman shows, Gibbon opted for the common conservative solution: he supported the causes and forces of tradition, believing that for the majority of mankind and for the time being, 'fictitious authority' – the only possible one – was better than no authority at all. In the famous opening lines of the work, while describing the Antonine rule over the Roman empire as 'the period in the history of the world, during which the condition of the human race was most happy and prosperous', Gibbon observes that what delayed the disintegration of Roman society already at this stage was precisely that ability – to hold on to certain ideal fictions of order: 'The *image* of a free constitution was preserved with decent reverence; the Roman senate *appeared* to possess the sovereign *authority*, and devolved on the emperors all the executive powers of government'.[39] Gibbon thought that every society depends on such protective political beliefs, as these render it immune from what he called the 'leakage of reality' – namely, the eruption of irrational and anarchic forces from within.[40] Gibbon, however, never fully resolved the tension

---

[38] Gossman, *The Empire Unposses'd*, p. 26.

[39] Gibbon, *The Decline and Fall of the Roman Empire*, I, p. I (emphasis added).

[40] Gibbon's notion of 'leakage of reality' is brilliantly analyzed by Peter Brown, 'Gibbon's Views on Culture and Society in the Fifth and Sixth Centuries', *Daedalus*, 105 (1976), pp. 73–88.

between his enlightened philosophical ideals and conservative political beliefs.

In his devout yet non-dogmatic religious beliefs, and in his political advocacy of the monarchist cause in Naples and elsewhere (he admired the 'popular commonwealth' of England), Vico was an early exponent of such enlightened conservatism. Yet the fact that Vico held to certain political ideals can hardly qualify him as a political theorist. Indeed, any attempt to characterize his thought as 'political' is still liable to cause controversy. Croce's drastic declaration that Vico 'was really an a-political man' still reverberates in the modern Vichian scholarship. The political classification of Vico is difficult, mainly because in his theoretical and 'occasional' (i.e. commissioned) writings there is very little to suggest that he had any real knowledge or interest in contemporaneous political matters. Croce's verdict that 'there was nothing in him of the combative spirit of an apostle, propagandist, agitator, or rebel, which characterized many of the philosophers of the Renaissance' and that on most important political issues of the time he 'remained silent and apparently ignorant' is still, with all due respect to recent counter-claims, quite correct.[41]

On Croce's terms, Vico appears indeed to have been a totally aloof and a-political thinker. If, on the other hand, we adopt a broader view of politicality, such as that suggested by Piovani, according to which we must pay attention not only to Vico's explicit statements on 'immediate problems' but also to 'those forms of sensibility' which reveal his links to the contemporary political struggles, then we may find that many seemingly a-political topics in the *New Science* were, in fact, quite significant to the major political lore of the age.[42] Following this line of thought, Giuseppe Giarrizzo, the leading 'political' interpreter of Vico, has shown that Vico was very much aware of Naples' acute social problems, especially those concerning the agrarian and municipal rights of the baronial aristocracy;[43] Vico, however, tended to reflect on such problems through the prism of classical scholarship. His philological concerns must not be viewed, thus, as apolitical as they seem; rather, as Pietro Piovani has brilliantly

41 Benedetto Croce, *La filosofia di Giambattista Vico* (Bari: Laterza, 1947), pp. 288–9.
42 Pietro Piovani, 'Apoliticality and Politicality in Vico', in *Vico's Science of Humanity*, p. 402.
43 Giuseppe Giarrizzo, 'La politica di Vico', *Quaderni contamporanei*, 2 (1968), pp. 63-134.

observed: 'The "philological" interest in the genesis of things pays
homage to their greatness, yet progressively strips them of their
superficial glitter. In the childhood of mankind, glimpsed at its
beginnings, there is nothing which does not become diminished
in some way. The genetic way of knowing is a critical process.'[44]
Vico's 'philosophy of authority' bears this out most clearly:
believing that 'the nature of everything born or made betrays the
crudeness of its origin' (NS/361) Vico sought to expose the essentially mythopoeic nature of political reality. An examination of his
theory of 'authority' may thus show us to what extent Vico's social
and political views were informed and articulated by his basic
mythopoeic view of human nature.

In accordance with his general division of human nature and
history into three different yet consequtive and complementary
stages of growth – the god-like, the heroic, and the human – Vico
distinguishes three kinds of socio-political authority, through
which, he claims, each society must progress:

The first was the authority of property, in virtue of which those from
whom we derive title to property were called *auctores* . . . This authority
had its source in divine government from the time of the family state, in
which divine authority must have been vested in the gods, for it was
believed, fairly enough, that everything belonged to the gods . . . Afterward in the heroic aristocracies in which the senates were the seat of
sovereignty (as they are in the aristocracies of our own time), authority
quite properly was vested in these reigning senates . . . Finally the
commonwealth passed from popular liberty to monarchy, and there
ensued the third kind of authority, which is that of credit or reputation
for wisdom; and hence the authority of counsel, in respect of which the
jurisconsults under the emperors were said to be auctores. Such also
must be the authority of senates under monarchs, who have full and
absolute liberty to follow or not to follow the counsel their senates give
them. (NS/945–6)

In this passage and throughout his work Vico repeatedly exploits
the etymological meanings implied in the term 'authority', which
he correctly derives from the Latin term *augere* (to add), in order
to relate the act of original (political) 'annexation' to the act of
sanctioning it through (poetical) 'authorship'.[45] He uses these

---

[44] Piovani, 'Apoliticality and Politicality in Vico', p. 406.
[45] Eric Partridge, *Origins: A Short Etymological Dictionary of Modern English* (New York: Macmillan, 1966), p. 132.

terminological affinities to emphasize the historical concomitance between both forms of exploitation. This etymological duality in the term, he believed, indicates its dialectic nature in socio-historical reality: it reveals, as it were, the poetic character of all political institutions, as well as the political implications of poetry.[46]

Now, Vico's mythopoeic assertions had, or at least could have had, immediate political repercussions in his own life and times. Because, beyond its historical allusions to ancient Rome, the above-quoted passage is one of the most revealing statements of a sensitive and critical observer about the political situation in Kingdom of Naples. Here, Vico makes clear his predilection for enlightened despotism (though in the more moderate form of constitutional monarchy), but he does it in a way which is rather ambivalent – and dangerous. By analyzing the natural-historical growth of the royal authority in the ancient pagan world he exposes, as it were, the essential characteristics of royal authority as such. And what he strongly implies is that every political authority – from the earliest theocracy, through the various forms of aristocracy, and up to the most enlightened monarchy – is inevitably mythical. For Vico, as for modern historical materialists, the original act, the *nascimento*, of any political authority, however, subliminal in appearance, was the brutal usurpation of the common 'property'. Vico thought, as Gibbon did after him, that the establishment of any 'authority' is initially no more than an acquisition of right by might, a seizure of power which is subsequently covered-up by fabrication of rights.

The Kingdom of Naples in the first half of the eighteenth century thrived on such myths of authority.[47] The ruling families prided themselves on their Roman or even Etruscan origins. Heroic figures and scenes from classical mythology inspired the

---

46 This was noted by Erich Auerbach in 'Giambattista Vico und die Idee der Philologie', repr. in *Gesammelte Aufsätze zur modernen Philologie* (Bern: Franke Verlag, 1967), p. 233. Eric Havelock has rightly suggested that the ancient relationship of poetics and politics was rooted in the mnemotic consciousness of public life, *Preface to Plato* (N.Y.: Grosset & Dunlapp, 1971), pp. 125–37.

47 For contemporary accounts of these foundational myths, see Giovanni Antonio Summonte, *Historia della città e regno di Napoli* (Naples, 1601–43), 1748 ed., I, pp. 1ff.; a popular collection of legendary tales, which was widely read (because erroneously ascribed to the famous historian Giovanni Villani), was *Cronaca di Partenope*, ed. Antonio Altmura (Naples: Fiorentino, 1974).

decorations of the royal palaces and municipal buildings, and pagan gods and heroes were widely celebrated in national feasts and popular shows in this otherwise very Catholic city. Vico was well-versed in this lore. He was occasionally commissioned to write ceremonial orations or apologetic biographies which customarily alluded to the mythical heritage of the town. These were particularly important in political controversies over legitimacy of new rulers, which were replete with local legends and myths of the remote past. During Vico's life-time there occurred two drastic changes of royal rule over the city and Kingdom of Naples: first, in 1707, after 200 years of rule by the Spanish viceroys, the Kingdom was taken over by the Austrian viceroys; and then, in 1734, the Kingdom was conquered by Charles of Bourbon, who reinstated Naples' political independence. Through that period political life in Naples was deeply affected by constant disputes about the ancestral origins, the rightful historical claims, and the legal criteria of legitimacy of the Gallispanti and the Habsburgian contenders to the crown. And thus, when the Bourbons established themselves in Naples, it was Vico who was chosen to deliver the laudatory speech, in which he equated the new ruler with Aeneas, the mythological founder of the town.[48] And, as a recent study on the royal Bourbon palace in Caserta has illustrated, the new rulers were determined to live up to these mythical images.[49] Subsequently, in 1735 Vico was appointed a Royal Historiographer, an appointment which further required him to combine mythological and historical enquiries, to establish, in fact, the integral continuity between what he elsewhere called 'the obscure and fabulous times' and 'the historical times'.

It is also important to note, as Rafaelle Ajello and others have done, that the monarchical disputes in Naples were entangled with the oscillation of republican sentiments in the Kingdom.[50]

---

[48] The *laudatio* to the Bourbons is in *Opere di G. B. Vico*, ed. F. Nicolini (Bari: Laterza, 1911–41), VIII, pp. 122–4; Vico also composed some mythological verses, written in a commonly dense and elaborated Baroque style. See, for example, *Giunone in danza*, in *Opere*, V, pp. 318–45.

[49] George L. Hersey, *Architecture, Poetry, and Number in the Royal Palace at Caserta* (Cambridge, Mass.: MIT Press, 1983).

[50] Rafaelle Ajello, *Il preilluminismo giuridico*, vol. 2, *Il problema della riforma giudiziaria e legislativa nel Regno del Napoli durante la prima metà del secolo XVIII* (Naples: Jovene, 1965). See also Pier Luigi Rovito, *Respublica dei togati: Giuristi e società nella Napoli del seicento* (Naples: Jovene, 1981).

Towards the end of the seventeenth century there emerged a class of civil servants (*ceto civile*), mostly lawyers (*togati*) who struggled to wrest control of the municipal affairs from the hands of the established feudal nobility (*nobili di sedile*). These reformers were also critical of the papal curia. In their attempt to secure municipal autonomy from both baronial hegemony and papal suzerainty, they naturally turned to and supported the royal authority. For most of his life Vico belonged to the ranks of these civil reformers. But when this movement turned in the 1730s towards more secular and republican politics, Vico, by then already old and ever more wary of the 'critical spirit', drew back to his life-long conservative ideals.

In that respect he belonged, like his great teachers Gravina and Muratori, to the mainstream of the *umanesimo meridionale*. The 'southern humanism' of the Spanish-Austrian era was, as Francesco Tateo has shown, committed to the 'feudal' rather than to the (northern) 'republican' notions of authority.[51] Its adherents conceived of their state in organic-historical and holistic terms, and regarded its institutions as truly spontaneous and collective creations of the people. They duly espoused strict loyalty to the age-old hierarchical and especially monarchical authorities. To these southern humanists the northern states seemed artificial and agonistic, ruined by competitive individualism. Above all, the northern states lacked any real authority, because their princes were all illegitimate, usurpers, often *condottieri* who owed nothing to their local traditions. It was here, then, in Vico's attempt to explain and justify the monarchical authority in Naples over against both aristocratic and democratic claims – that his general theory of the mythopoeic origins and constitution of political authority proved particularly relevant to the immediate political problems of the time.

Now, as I have already noted, Vico rarely addressed these or any other political issues of his time directly. He did, however, comment on them in his own way, through seemingly apolitical investigations into ancient and primitive societies. The problem of authority was the object of just such a study. In what follows I shall therefore investigate this problem in the specific context and form

---

[51] Francesco Tateo, *Umanesimo meridionale* (Bari: Laterza, 1981).

in which Vico discussed it – that is, in his interpretation of Roman history through its mythology.[52] Thus, what will be offered in the following pages, is a political interpretation of Vico's own political interpretations of Roman mythology.

In the first half of the eighteenth century, the science of politics in general, and the problem of authority in particular, were commonly discussed in Roman terms and examples.[53] Rome was the 'common fatherland' of the nations (*Roma communis patria*), a repository of historical cases which exemplified almost every possible kind of political rule and transformation. Vico modelled his entire 'natural law of the gentes' – his famous cyclical order of *corsi e ricorsi* – on Roman history. The complete course of Rome inspired and exemplified the 'ideal eternal history traversed in time by the history of every nation in its rise, development, maturity, decline, and fall' (NS/349). His depiction of the Roman *eroi* and *bestioni* was modelled, implicitly at least, on their Neapolitan counterparts, the *nobili* and the *lazzaroni*, and surely there were many parallels and lessons to be drawn between the two epochs. In his numerous *Versi d'occasione* Vico drew many analogies between current Neapolitan affairs and well-known Roman examples, and thereby challenged his audience to view their own life and history as prefigured in the annals of Roman history. In his inaugural lecture *On the Study Methods of Our Time*, Vico lamented the decline of humanistic studies in general and of the 'noble and most important branch of studies, the science of politics' in particular; in order to regain that kind of knowledge, he urged his audience, the law students, to pay close attention to Roman political history: 'I would have the jurist study the origin, the consolidation, the growth, the culmination, and the dissolution of a great polity like the Roman Empire. Let him draw a parallel between the Roman Empire and the monarchic system of our age, in order to investigate whether the same beneficial effects

---

[52] Vico's debts and contributions to Roman scholarship are clarified by Santo Mazzarinno, *Vico, L'Annalistica e il Diritto* (Napoli: Guida, 1971), and by Pietro Piovani, 'Il debito di Vico verso Roma', *Studi Romani*, VII (1969), pp. 1–17. On Vico's indebtedness to Tacitus see Santino Caramella, 'Vico, Tacitus, and Reason of State', in *Vico: An International Symposium*, pp. 29–37.

[53] The transition of political Roman terms and examples (or political 'paradigms') from the Renaissance to the eighteenth century is a major theme in J. G. A. Pocock's magisterial *The Machiavellian Moment* (N.J.: Princeton University Press, 1975).

spring from both of them.'[54] It seems then that in Naples, as in other enlightened yet despotic regimes of modern Europe, Rome was not only the ideal, but probably the only possible ground on which to discuss openly the rather acute problems concerning the rightful origins and constitution of monarchical authority. For Vico, the evolution of Roman authority contained some essential lessons applicable to all societies. Its most intriguing aspect was the transition from Republicanism to Caesarism, a transition which was definitely conservative, and yet, in Vico's view, a necessary and, as such, a most enlightened one.

Vico was aware of the fact that in ancient Rome, the political term *auctoritas*, as distinct from the legal term *potestas* (power), implied a certain kind of legitimacy to rule, or the right of a person or group to counsel and command on 'natural' ground: either by virtue of personal qualities and achievements, or by genuine 'popular' consent and demand. He was particularly attentive to the distinctly 'traditional' criteria which the Romans used to determine whether a person or a group was entitled to rule, to literally 'augment' Roman affairs. For the Romans, he contended, everything depended on the testimony of the ancestors, that is on certain foundational acts performed *in illo tempore* and preserved in religious and national lore, so that only he who could prove to act according to these prescriptive examples was truly 'authorized' to rule. And so, when Cicero maintained that 'although the people have the power, the Senate has the authority', he was reiterating thereby the common Roman view, that although the people are the only rightful source of public control in the state, the people themselves handed over this power to those whom they found best qualified to use it.[55] In this case power was granted to the senatorial oligarchy which kept the foundational tradition most faithfully. Cicero could thus declare: 'the people's constant need for the advice and authority of the conservative upper class [*optimates*] is what holds the state together'.[56] Later, in the transition from republic to empire during the period

---

[54] Vico, *On the Study Methods of Our Time*, pp. 33, 66; on Vico and Roman Law, see Max H. Fisch, 'Vico on Roman Law', in *Essays in Political Theory Presented to George E. Sabine*, ed. M. R. Knovitz and A. E. Murphy (Ithaca, N.Y.: Cornell University Press, 1948), pp. 62–88.

[55] Cicero, *De Legibus*, 3.12.38, tr. C. W. Keyes, Loeb Classical Library (Cambridge, Mass.: Harvard University Press, 1943).

[56] Cicero, *De Legibus*, 2.12.

of 'principate' there emerged a new concept of 'authority', that of 'the best citizen' (*optimus civis*) who, by virtue of his personal pre-eminence, also became 'the prime citizen' (*princeps*). In their early and ideal form, Augustus' resolutions (*constitutiones*)attracted, as he himself remarked, and as later writers also noted, respect and obedience by virtue of the sheer 'authority' of his personality. Theodor Mommsen took this example as the definitive notion of what 'authority' was all about: it is, he said, 'more than a counsel and less than a command; rather a counsel with which one could not properly avoid compliance'.[57] Such ancient examples and apologies for oligarchic-monarchic rule were adopted and further developed (or exploited) by the modern enlightened conservatives in the eighteenth century. Augustan Rome was a source of inspiration and imitation to the opponents of radical republicanism. Vico, like other enlightened conservatives at the time, sought to revive the ancient notion of 'principal authority' (*auctoritas principis*) as exemplified by Augustus in Rome, and use it as a necessary corrective measure to the incremental or 'senatorial authority' (*auctoritas patrum*), which was the ideal of the republican reformers. And as we shall now see, it was precisely this political interpretation of ancient Roman poetics which, in turn, helped him decode the poetics of modern Neapolitan politics.

The problem with the republic, as both its ancient and modern critics knew, was its vulnerability to corruption. Its military success inevitably led to material excess, and thereby to individual opportunism uncontrollable by law. Such moral, political, and economic shifting within the republic were liable to ruin the equality on which it rested. In fact of this danger, so ran the conservative argument, a strong central personal authority was required, one who would fend off both democratic anarchy and aristocratic oligarchy, in short – a monarch. As Montesquieu observed: 'No authority is more absolute than that of a prince who succeeds a republic, for he finds himself with all the power of the people, who had not been able to impose limitation on themselves'.[58] Vico reached similar conclusions, though, quite typically,

---

[57] For a philosophical analysis of the history of the term and conceptions of *auctoritas* from the Roman period to modern times, see Leonard Krieger, art. 'Authority', in the *Dictionary of the History of Ideas* (New York: Charles Scribner's Sons, 1973).

[58] Montesquieu, *Considerations on the Causes of the Greatness of the Romans and Their Decline*, tr. D. Lowenthal (N.Y.: The Free Press, 1965), p. 138.

here as elsewhere in his work, he seems to have derived these philosophical conclusions from philological inquiries into the etymological-literal meanings of the original terms under discussion. In this way, for instance, he deals with the concept of Republic, which means the 'public good' (*res-publica*). In his view, men in the popular republics do not gain more of the 'public good' than men in the monarchies, in fact they fare even worse, because the 'public good' in the monarchies is identified by some powerful magnates with their own 'private goods', who therefore seek to manage and to defend it most efficiently, and so, however inadvertently, end up keeping it for all to enjoy it (NS/950). In the republics, on the other hand, the 'public good' is divided to 'as many minute parts as there are citizens making up the people who have command of it' (NS/951), a fact which causes constant conflicts and eventual disintegration. Vico added to these philosophico-philological considerations some Roman illustrations:

Since in the free commonwealths all look out for their own private interests, into the service of which they press their public arms at the risk of ruin to their nations, to preserve the latter from destruction a single man must arise, as Augustus did in Rome, and take all public concerns by force of arms into his own hands, leaving his subjects free to look after their private affairs and after just so much public business, and of just such kinds, as the monarch may entrust to them. Thus are the peoples saved when they would otherwise rush to their own destruction. (NS/1004)

In his search for the integrative authority of Roman society Vico was as much influenced by Livy and his most notable modern interpreter Machiavelli. The latter emphasized above all the unifying function of archaic Roman religion and other conservative traditions. 'The observance of religious teaching', he declared, guarantees 'the greatness of republics'. He further observed that 'one can have no better indication' of political decline and imminent fall than 'to see divine worship little valued'.[59] Machiavelli made it clear, however, that in Rome and elsewhere, religious practice should have nothing to do with religious truth and morality: his sole concern was with the

---

[59] Machiavelli, *Discourses on the First Decade of Titus Livius*, in *The Chief Works and Others*, tr. A. Gilbert (Durham, N.C.: Duke University Press, 1965), pp. 225, 226.

political utility of 'religion', with the way it had been used by judicious Roman magistrates and priests 'in inspiring the people, in keeping men good, in making the wicked ashamed'.[60] This pragmatic argument was reiterated and much enhanced in the eighteenth century, most forcefully by Montesquieu and Gibbon.

In his treatment of the formation of political 'authority' Vico was likewise utterly pragmatic rather than moralistic. In his account of the evolution of civil and political institutions he may well be seen as 'Machiavellian': he concentrates on the mechanism-of-power, not its intrinsic value; he does not ask whether this or that form of control and manipulation is more just, but rather which is most efficient and generally beneficial. Furthermore, like some modern historians, sociologists, and anthropologists of the state, Vico too realised that the crucial question in politics is not *who* governs, but *how and by what means* he or she legitimizes this fact. Hence, his interest in the practical and ceremonial aspects of government, his attention to symbolic gestures which point to divine origins, to the invention of super-natural traditions, and to similar ritual means of divination by which the rulers have always tried to consecrate their terrestrial authority.

In ancient Rome, as in modern Naples, during times of religious decline, the only traditional authority which could still incite compliance without exerting either coercive power or rational conviction was the *mythical* authority of the *princeps* or 'enlightened despot'. And in modern Naples, just like in Augustan Rome, this authority consisted of political myths of origins and rights. In his Roman enquiries Vico sought to trace the mythopoeic formation of this authority from its brutal inception up to its most exalted and perfect phase – the enlightened despotism of Augustus – and thus, ultimately, to justify it. As Vico himself has noted (NS/352–8) he based his entire 'philological' reconstruction of Roman history on his 'new art' of reading its constitutive myths. Vico knew that these heroic fictions, or partial fictions, which had stimulated and inspired the Romans for many generations, and have been extensively retold by European writers and

---

[60] Machiavelli, *Discourses*, p. 224.

artists ever since, had hardly if ever been used by modern historians in such a radical way. He nevertheless believed that by virtue of his 'new critical art' these 'great fragments of antiquity, hitherto useless to science because they lay begrimed, broken, and scattered, shed great light when cleaned, pieced together, and restored' (NS/357). He was thoroughly convinced that his 'new critical art' would yield new, exciting discoveries, and justly so, because his 'historical mythology' was indeed innovative, and opened onto fascinating, intriguing, new historiographic horizons.

Though many scholars of Roman mythology before him had noted the real political issues of these literary fictions, Vico was the first scholar who realized that Roman mythology not only embodied important ideological concepts in certain personages and in their actions, but also captured the more complex aspects and dynamics of socio-political reality in the portrayal of the *relations* between them. Roman mythology, in other words, was not just an arbitrary assemblage of separate gods and heroes, invented and stock-piled at random by the Romans as they went along. Rather, he reasoned, Roman mythology was a careful even if unconscious composition of some permanent and many chthonic deities, an elaborate network of figures and events set-up along-side and over against each other in a meaningful pattern. Or, as modern students of myth would have it, Roman mythology was a 'structure' of functional relationships, displaying, in its totality of figures and affairs, a coherent and well-structured pantheon. In this imaginary society, then, mutual relations between gods and heroes reflected and illuminated class-relations in Roman society. The most obvious example was, of course, the division of the Roman gods into those of the *gentes maiores* and those of the *gentes minores*. Vico promptly concluded that this mythological division reflected the real social division in Rome (NS/317). The fact that Roman mythology, in contrast to the Greek, was totally free of any family relationships (as there are no sons, brothers, etc. among its deities) was a further proof as to the strict class-differentiation found therein.

According to Vico, Roman political history from its inception had been determined by one basic pattern of class-struggle, in which the patrician families sought to control the belligerent and heterogeneous masses of the plebs:

The first cities were founded on orders of nobles and troops of plebeians, with two contrary eternal properties emerging from this nature of human civil institutions . . . that the plebeians always want to change the form of government, as in fact it is always they who do change it, and that the nobles always want to keep it as it is. (NS/609)

This class-struggle was the key to all subsequent events in Rome (but not, as Marxist interpreters of Vico would have it, always and in all places).[61] In the beginning Rome was only a small settlement of a few clans of war-lords, a nuclear society in which each *pater familias* ruled his own family despotically. Then, it became a meeting-place, or *asylum*, for the natives and wandering refugees from other settlements in Latium. The latter were taken in by the founding families as servants and labourers; their 'status roughly approximated that of the slaves who came later with the taking of prisoners in war' (NS/18). More commonly they were regarded (and treated) as sub-human creatures, *bestioni*, and Vico interprets various theriomorphic myths as relating to them:

The heroes or nobles, by a certain nature of theirs which they believed to be of divine origin, were led to say that the gods belonged to them, and consequently that the auspices of the gods were theirs also. By means of the auspices they kept within their own orders all the public and private institutions of the heroic cities. To the plebeians, whom they considered to be of bestial origin and consequently men without gods and hence without auspices, they conceded the use of natural liberty. (NS/414)

Vico rejected and ridiculed the notion that there was ever a Golden Age in Roman history, the ideal Republic in which the people enjoyed true civil liberties and equal opportunities to participate in its policy-making. This notion had an enormous impact on ancient and modern historians, and was instrumental in the formation of early modern ideologies of Republicanism. Vico was surely familiar with Machiavelli's *Discourses* on Livy's *History of Rome*, in which the Florentine thinker advanced the theory that the Roman republic attained its 'dominant position' because it possessed 'so much *virtú*'. The definition of *virtú* in the *Discourses* is essentially republican: it consists in the willingness of

---

[61] Arnaldo Momigliano rightly doubts whether Vico could be taken as a Marxist *avant le lettre*. He notes that while 'Vico's interpretation of history certainly relies on class struggle', he did not establish this notion as a general law-of-history. 'Roman "Bestioni" and Roman "Eroi" in Vico's Scienza Nuova', *History and Theory*, 5 (1966), p. 19.

the citizen 'to advance not his own interests but the general good, not his own prosperity but the common fatherland'.[62] Machiavelli further notes that it was principally due to the exemplary *virtuoso* activities of Rome's founders Romulus and Numa and their patrician successors that such republican notions were 'kept up in that city for many centuries', and it was for that reason that he was seeking to revive them for men in his own time.[63] Vico appreciated Machiavelli's historicist strategy, but he rejected both his historical interpretations and political conclusions. Like other conservative thinkers at the time, he delighted in undermining the historical validity of the Livian-Machiavellian model 'period of Roman virtue'. In fact, Vico's sarcastic commentaries on Livy's work must be read as a direct refutation of Machiavelli's interpretation. Singling out Livy's depiction of that age as '*nulla aetas virtutum feracior*',[64] Vico ironically asks

What did any of the [the Patricians] do for the poor and unhappy Roman plebs? Assuredly they did not increase their burdens by war, plunge them deeper in the sea of usury, in order to bury them to a greater depth in the private prisons of the nobles . . . Precisely because the nobles of the first peoples considered themselves heroes and of a nature superior to that of their plebeians, they were capable of such misgovernment of the poor masses of the nations. For certainly Roman history will puzzle any intelligent reader who tries to find in it any evidence of Roman virtue where there was so much arrogance, or of moderation in the midst of such avarice, or of justice or mercy where so much inequality and cruelty prevailed. (NS/668)

The plebeians had to endure this kind of dehumanization for many generations. Vico rightly observed that their 'underdeveloped minds' were not yet able to promote their own heroic claims and divine traditions over against those of the masters. Throughout the long political strife in Rome, going back to primeval times, each class articulated its unique social identity over against that of the other by appealing to the common mythological heritage.[65] The most powerful argument for authority in

---

62 Machiavelli, *Discourses*, p. 218.
63 Bruce James Smith, *Politics and Remembrance: Republican Themes in Machiavelli, Burke, and Tocqueville* (N.J.: Princeton University Press, 1985), pp. 26–101.
64 Livy, *History of Rome*, 9.16.19.
65 In his study of Roman myths, Michael Grant observes that the struggle between the *optimates* and the *populares* was one of the main causes for the later resurgence of myths: 'For this struggle was convulsing the Roman state during the later second and first

Rome was the patrician appeal to the *mos maiorum*, to the divine origins of their historical rights. This common appeal to and control of the auspices, Vico saw, had always served the aristocratic cause. In the early stages of Rome and thereafter its mythology was the main common ground on which both parties really converged, or, more precisely, battled for supremacy. The Roman class-struggle over political rights was thus essentially one between and about mythical claims. And since ancient rome was so immersed in and ruled by its myths, the true ruler in Rome was the one who ruled its myths.

Some of Vico's most penetrating observations pertain to the mental-historical process (which we would nowadays term the formation of class-consciousness), in which the plebeians formed their own counter-tradition within the common national culture. Vico shows how the plebeians first revolted against their own self-image as inferior species by nature, or, to use the Marxian term, against their own 'false consciousness', by inventing their own mythical heroes and precedents. He praises the 'prophetic insight' of Phaedrus, the Roman popularizer of Aesop, who first made this point. Vico quoted approvingly this passage from Phaedrus' *Book of Fables*:

> Attend me briefly while I now disclose
> How the art of fable telling first arose.
> Unhappy slaves, in servitude confined,
> Dared not to their harsh masters show their mind,
> But under veiling of the fable's dress
> Contrived their thoughts and feelings to express . . .
>   (NS/425)[66]

Vico further noticed that in Roman mythology there are numerous cases in which we find distinctly patrician gods, like Mars, Vulcan, or Venus (which originally 'were three divine characters signifying the heroes'), assuming plebeian roles (NS/579-81). This case of 'double fables or characters', he explains, occurred in that early and most crucial phase of the class-struggle, when the plebeian myth-makers were strong enough to

---

centuries BC, and the historians of that period were only too glad to employ the mythical past in order to display their own current partisanship' (*Roman Myths* (London: Weidenfeld and Nicolson, 1971), p. 37).

[66] Phaedrus, *Liber Fabularum*, 3.34–38.

challenge the patrician 'monopoly' over the political-cultural heritage of Rome. They were not yet able, as it were, to counter these patrician gods and heroes with their own made-up figures, so instead they attempted to confiscate these patrician idols for their own political cause. Vico is very careful to distinguish, in each particular case, between the original patrician version and the subversive plebeian one. For Vico such a discovery corroborated his basic assumption that the structure of Roman mythology, with and through its multilateral tales, mirrored the versatile political structure of Roman society.

Yet, for all their resilience and ingenuity in this mythical warfare, the plebs wanted to be recognized as 'human beings', which means, in practical terms – to be granted certain basic civil rights, primarily the right to possess and to inherit land. Here the plot thickened, as the plebs became increasingly more aware of the disadvantages implied in their – and in any – mythical claims for rights. Vico shows how

with the passage of the years and the far greater development of human minds, the plebs of the peoples finally became suspicious of the pretentions of such heroism and understood themselves to be of equal human nature with the nobles, and therefore insisted that they too should enter into the civil institutions of the cities. (NS/1101)

He then goes on to reconstruct the later history of Rome as a continuous, and largely successful, struggle of the plebs to secure their hard-won mythical rights by permanent legislation. This reconstruction consists of a highly original, albeit extremely idiosyncratic, account of the establishment of common (plebeian) legal rights over against exclusive (patrician) mythical claims. First the plebs managed to acquire the right to limited ownership of land in exchange for military service (*lex Poetelia*); and then the right to full ownership of land (set forth in The Twelve Tables); and lastly the right to lawful marriage and inheritance (as Vico wrongly interpreted the law of *Connubium*). Now, while Vico's specific interpretations of these and other legal cases in Roman history have been severely criticized as being rather fatuous, his more fundamental heuristic principle, namely that in primitive societies laws serve primarily the lower classes, because they secure their rights better than myths and customs, must be regarded as one of his most seminal contributions to modern sociology.

Reflecting on the Roman example, he established this general socio-political precept:

The weak want laws; the powerful withhold them; the ambitious, to win a following, advocate them; princes, to equalize the strong with the weak, protect them. This axiom [clarifies the nature of] . . . the heroic contests in the aristocratic commonwealths, in which the nobles want to keep the laws a secret monopoly of their order, so that they may depend on their choice and that they may administer them with a royal hand. (NS/283–4)

Vico observed that the conflict between the continuing patrician mythmaking and the new plebeian legislation was inevitable, and potentially destructive to the whole Roman system. The fact that Rome survived indicated to him where its success, and the ultimate secret of its 'authority', lay. The greatest Roman achievement, he concluded, was its judicious mythical legislation, that is to say, the way in which its magistrates and jurisconsults prudently resolved the tension between myth and law – by turning the one into the other.

There are, he declared, 'three proper reasons for the distinction which the Roman law attained in the world':

the magnanimity of the plebs in wanting to share the civil rights and laws of the fathers; the strength of the fathers in keeping those rights within their order; and the wisdom of the jurisconsults in interpreting the laws and extending their utility little by little as new cases demanded adjudication. (NS/281)

Vico's general argument here follows Machiavelli's provocative assertion that, paradoxically, it was the conflict between patricians and plebeians which made the Roman state both free and powerful. For Machiavelli this dissension was 'an evil necessary to the attainment of Roman greatness', as it forced both rival parties to 'keep watch over the other' and to adopt an extremely careful legislative policy, such as curbed their sectarian interests by appealing to their common sense of *res republica*.[67]

Much like Machiavelli, Vico too thought that ultimately it was this practical legislation informed and guided by mythical-religious norms which made Rome great. Authority in Rome belonged not to a class or order but to 'persons of experience, of

---

[67] Machiavelli, *Discourses*, p. 199. As F. E. Adcock notes, the Roman class struggle was 'not so much a cleavage of sentiment as the working out of a more lasting unity of the Roman people' (*Roman Political Ideas and Practice* (Michigan: Ann Arbor, 1959), p. 27).

singular prudence in practical matters, and of sublime wisdom in intellectual matters' (NS/941). The crucial qualification for an authority was 'credit or reputation for wisdom . . . in respect of which the jurisconsults under the emperors were said to be *auctores*' (NS/946). Their true genius as 'authors', he argues, was to create new laws out of the old myths, to accommodate, as it were, the same old traditional values to their new political legislation. In that respect, they proved themselves much wiser than the Greek philosophers (or, by implication, the modern rationalists). Whereas the Greeks 'advanced immediately to the highest refinement' and thus 'hastened the natural course which their nation was to take . . . the Romans, on the other hand, proceeded at an even pace in [the development of] their customs' (NS/158). Elsewhere Vico argues that the Romans were able to maintain civil peace and religious tolerance all over the empire, because their jurisconsults appealed to 'the common sense of the human race, on which the consciences of all nations repose', that is 'they established their principles of justice on the certainty of the authority of the human race, not on the authority of the learned' (NS/350; cf. NS/1003).

Ultimately, then, the Roman jurisconsults were successful because they readily admitted the indispensability of mythical sanctions to political order, and sought to restore this mythical base even in enlightened times. Vico could thus conclude:

In conformity with such natures, ancient jurisprudence was throughout poetic . . . It introduced so many empty masks without subjects, *iura imaginaria*, rights invented by imagination. It rested its entire reputation on inventing such fables as might preserve the gravity of the laws and do justice to the facts. Thus all the fictions of ancient jurisprudence were truths under masks, and the formulae in which the laws were expressed . . . were called carmina, or songs . . . all ancient Roman law was a serious poem, represented by the Romans in the forum. (NS/1036–7)

Vico was well poised to observe that even in its later stages, ancient rome was still largely conditioned by its constitutive myths. The impact of mythical images, rites, and traditions was stronger and lasted longer than the actual 'mythical age'.[68] As he remarks

---

[68] On the Machiavellian origins of the Vichian view of politics as a process of 'human ascent' from, and by virtue of, 'passion, force, and authority' see the insightful comments of Benedetto Croce, 'Machiavelli and Vico', in *Philosophy, Poetry, History: an Anthology of Essays*, tr. C. Sprigge (London: Oxford University Press, 1966), pp. 655–70.

elsewhere, such forms of 'poetic speech . . . continued for a long time into the historical period, much as great and rapid rivers continue far into the sea, keeping sweet the waters borne on by the force of their flow' (NS/412). More concretely, Vico observed how

As the savagery of the times began to abate, as private violence began to be forbidden by judiciary laws, and all private forces were becoming united in the public force called civil sovereignty, the first people, by nature poets, must naturally have imitated the real forces that they had previously employed to preserve their rights and institutions. And so they have made a fable of natural emancipation and created from it the solemn civil conveyance represented by the handing over of symbolic knot, in imitation of the chain whereby Jove had bound the giants to the first unoccupied lands, and by which they themselves had later bound thereto their clients or famuli. With this symbolic emancipation they consecrated all their civil translations by *actus legitimi*, which must have been solemn ceremonies of peoples still mute. (NS/1030)

On the basis of Vico's inquiry, one could easily come to the logical conclusion, that much like in ancient Rome, there must always be in any political association a ruling class which uses a set of established mythical forms (legendary tales, emblems, rites, ceremonies, etc.) to exemplify the fact that it 'holds the power' legitimately. Vico may well have believed that all our political ideas and institutions, then and now, are such *acta legitimi*, that is that they have all evolved from, and still consist in, such 'poetical' images of legitimate exercise of power. These fables of power, Vico adds, are 'marvellously sublime', and literally so, since they transform physical desires and real acts of power into mere symbolic exercises of this power, thereby neutralizing their potential destructive effects. Ultimately, the truly great achievement of the Roman jurisconsults was to create such substitutive fables of power in their laws, and thus to construe a judicial system which retained enough mythical awe to evoke compliance. For Vico, as indeed for most European monarchists at the time, Augustan Rome epitomized the ideal government, because it was an absolute yet sufficiently enlightened and constitutionalized regime, officially ruled by a hereditary (i.e. Caesarian) and awe-inspiring monarch (in all but name), yet practically governed by judiciously sceptical senators and magistrates. Vico repeatedly elevated Augustan Rome to a universal model of a well-governed state:

Now in free commonwealths if a powerful man is to become monarch the people must take his side, and for that reason monarchies are by nature popularly governed: first through the laws by which the monarchs seek to make their subjects all equal; and then by that property of monarchies whereby sovereigns humble the powerful and thus keep the masses safe and free from their oppressions . . . the very form of the monarchic state shall confine the will of the monarchs, in spite of their unlimited sovereignty, within the natural order of keeping the peoples content and satisfied with both their religion and their natural liberty. For without this universal satisfaction and content of the peoples, monarchic states are neither lasting nor secure. (NS/1008, 1104)

It might be argued that in such statements Vico agrees with the classical republican theorists (Polybius and Cicero) and the modern ones (Machiavelli), for he too implies that because of the imminent danger of corruption in the commonwealth it needs a 'mixed government', one in which the people would still be directly involved and effective. Yet Vico, like so many intellectuals in Naples, deeply distrusted both the baronial aristocrats and the common people of the town, and sought to dislodge both of them from positions of power. Whereas Machiavelli held 'popular liberty' in high esteem, and regarded it to be the ultimate condition and guarantee for political achievements ('Experience shows that cities have never increased in dominion or riches except while they have been at liberty'),[69] Vico was rather disdainful: in his vocabulary, the term 'natural liberty' stands for anarchy, signifying passionate and unruly behaviour. He accuses 'the tribunes of the plebs at Rome' that they 'provoked civil wars in their commonwealths and drove them to total disorder. Thus they caused the commonwealths to fall from a perfect liberty into the perfect tyranny of anarchy or the unchecked liberty of the free peoples, which is the worst of all tyrannies' (NS/1102). And so, while Machiavelli goes on to celebrate the justness of the people's cause over against the cause of both the Roman monarchs and the patricians (it is 'very marvellous to observe what greatness Rome came to after she freed herself from her kings'),[70] Vico prefers law and order and opts for the Hobbesian solution, the one which ensured the stricter central rule of a monarchical authority, based on general tacit consent.

---

[69] Machiavelli, *Discourses*, p. 328.   [70] Machiavelli, *Discourses*, p. 329.

For Hobbes defines authority literally as 'authorization' – 'no man is obliged by a covenant of which he is not author' – and seeks to show how such authority may best be achieved in the sovereign agreement, or 'covenant', in the ratification of hereditary monarchy, which is the modern substitute for the mythical *Leviathan*. Vico too was sensitive to, if not appreciative of, the new liberal conception of authority, the one which stressed the voluntary and spontaneous commitment of the subjects to their own chosen rulers: 'The body politic is most fortunate, indeed, where the rigorous observance of the law binds the citizens together like the worship of an unknown god'.[71] But, again like Hobbes, he subverted the democratic meaning and implication of this commitment for he sought to show that in any free and heterogeneous society there should always be a central authority which is capable not only of evoking such voluntary and spontaneous commitments, but also of controlling and integrating them. Vico goes so far as to argue that the ascension of a strong monarch like Augustus is the best providential remedy against the inevitable corruption of commonwealths:

To this great disease of cities . . . Providence ordains that there be found among these peoples a man like Augustus to arise and establish himself as a monarch and, by force of arms, take in hand all the institutions and all the laws, which, though sprung from liberty, no longer avail to regulate and hold it within bounds. (NS/1103–4)

Vico well knew that the monarchic option, even in its most perfect realization in Augustan Rome, let alone in the modern constitutional monarchies, was not good in itself. And even though in his public lectures and occasional verses he often celebrated the achievements of the modern polity, and generally believed that 'in Europe, where the Christian religion is everywhere professed, inculcating an infinitely pure and perfect idea of God and commanding charity to all mankind, there are great monarchies most humane in their customs' (NS/1092) – he was wary of its vulnerability to what he called the 'great disease of the cities': the emergence of individualistic and materialistic norms. He realized that as the urban citizens in the modern 'popular states' have become more enlightened they are 'no longer prompted by religious sentiments as formerly', and therefore 'prone to ill-doing' (NS/1101). The best remedy against this kind of civil crisis is a traditional monarchy. For commonwealths in crisis, he adds, there are only two other possible remedies, both of them much worse than monarchy – slavery to 'better nations', and total and final deterioration into the archaic anarchy of the state of nature:

But if the peoples are rotting in that ultimate civil disease and cannot agree on a monarch from within, and are not conquered and preserved by better nations from without, then providence for their extreme ill has its extreme remedy at hand. For such peoples, like so many beasts, have fallen into the custom of each man thinking only of his own private interests and have reached the extreme delicacy, or better of pride, in which like wild animals they bristle and lash out at the slightest displeasure . . . By reason of all this, providence decrees that, through obstinate factions and desperate civil wars, they shall turn their cities into forests and the forests into dens and lairs of men. In this way, through long centuries of barbarism, rust will consume the misbegotten subtleties of malicious wits that have turned them into beasts made more inhuman by the barbarism of reflection than the first men had been made by the barbarism of sense. For the latter displayed a generous savagery, against which one could defend oneself or take flight or be on one's guard; but the former, with a base savagery, under soft words and embraces, plots against the life and fortune of friends and intimates. Hence peoples who have reached this point of premeditated malice, when they receive this last remedy of providence and are thereby stunned and brutalized, are sensible no longer of comforts, delicacies, pleasures, and pomp, but only of the sheer necessities of life. And the few survivors in the midst of an abundance of the things necessary for life naturally become sociable and, returning to the primitive simplicity of the first world of peoples, are again religious, truthful, and faithful. (NS/1106)

The hypothetical tone of this oration cannot disguise Vico's very real fears of the imminent dangers inherent in the culture of modernity. Like later enlightened conservative critics of the Enlightenment – Burke, Tocqueville, Burckhardt – Vico too identified this cultural ideology with the message of individualism. And he saw, as the latter would see, that without some communal restrictions – without a certain *sensus communis* – the essentially positive message of self-fulfilment was liable to degenerate into libertarian feats of egotism and social atomism. Unlike the latter critics, however, who would opt for rational and, as such, distinctly modern, political solutions (Burke's enterprise economism of *laissez faire*, Tocqueville's American model of democracy, Burckhardt's ethnic-civic humanism) – Vico's 'remedy' through 'sensual barbarism' is distinctly classical, and is akin to both the ancient Biblical or Stoic catastrophic solutions, as well as to their modern versions in Rousseau's or Machiavelli's 'cultural primitivism'.

According to a well-known definition of this cultural ideology, it consists in 'the discontent of the civilized with civilization, or with some conspicuous and characteristic feature of it. It is the belief of men living in a relatively highly evolved and complex cultural condition that a life far simpler and less sophisticated in some or in all aspects is a more desirable life.'[72] Vico could have found the same sentiments and ideas in Machiavelli's famous passage in the *Discorsi*, where, after discussing the merits in the roughness (*rozzezza*) of tribal life, the Florentine author concludes:

It is a well-established fact that the life of all mundane things is of finite duration. But things which complete the whole of the course appointed them by heaven are in general those whose bodies do not disintegrate, but maintain themselves in orderly fashion so that if there is no change; or, if there be change, it tends rather to their conservation than to their destruction. Here I am concerned with composite bodies, such as are states and religious institutions, and in their regard I affirm that those changes make for their conservation which lead them back to their origins [*le riducano inverso i principii loro*]. Hence those are better con-stituted and have a longer life whose institutions make frequent renovations possible, or which are brought to such a renovation by some event which has nothing to do with their constitution, for it is clearer than daylight that, without renovation, those bodies do not last.[73]

Machiavelli's *Discorsi* are presented as commentaries on Livy's first ten books, the books in which the Roman historian sought to reconstruct Rome's earliest history out of its mythological sources. And as Machiavelli well notes, Livy was very careful not to refute these sources. In the preface to his work Livy says that 'Such traditions as belong to the time before the city was founded, or rather was presently to be founded, and are rather adorned with poetic legends than based upon trustworthy historical proofs, I propose neither to affirm nor to refute'. Livy acknowledges that 'it

---

[72] Arthur Lovejoy and George Boas, *Primitivism and Related Ideas in Antiquity* (Baltimore: The Johns Hopkins University Press, 1935), p. 7.

[73] Machiavelli, *Discourses*, pp. 459–60.

is the privilege of antiquity to mingle divine things with human, and so to add dignity to the beginnings of things', and declares that 'to such legends as these, however they shall be regarded and judged, I shall, for my own part, attach no great importance'. And if, these reservations not withstanding, Livy goes on to recall these 'poetic legends' the reason for doing so lies in the knowledge that these tales have become part of the Roman ideology, that is to say constitutive elements of the matters to which, he says, 'I would have any reader give his close attention – what life and morals were like; through what men and by what policies, in peace and in war, empire was established'.[74] For Machiavelli the Livian message was clear: The duty of the enlightened philosopher-philologist in the modern state is not to subject its sacred beliefs and rites to sceptical rationalism just because they are 'mythical', but precisely the opposite: he must guard them and, furthermore, consistently and actively recall them.

'To recall the people to their *acme* or perfect state' – these are already Vico's words, and they form the central practical message of his *New Science*. This message is thus expressed in a short Conclusion to the work which he wrote in 1731, but never published – the *Pratica della Scienza nuova*.[75] In that draft he sought to show in what way and to what purpose his *New Science* could actually be used:

This entire work has so far been treated as a purely contemplative science concerning the common nature of the nations. It seems for this reason to promise no help to human prudence toward delaying if not preventing the ruin of nations in decay. It consequently seems to be lacking in the practice that all those sciences should have which are called 'active', as dealing with matters that depend on human choice. That practice can easily be derived from the contemplation of the course the nations run. Instructed by such contemplation, the wise men and princes of the commonwealths will be able, through good institutions, laws, and examples, to recall the people to their *acme* or perfect state. The practice of the science that we as philosophers can offer is such as can be completed within the academies. What is requires of us is that, from these human times of acute and intelligent minds in which we are born, we should here at the end look back to the picture that was placed at the

74 Livy, *History of Rome* 1.3–6, tr. B. O. Foster, Loeb Classical Library (Cambridge, Mass.: Harvard University Press, 1919).

75 Giambattista Vico, *Practice of the New Science*, tr. T. G. Bergin and M. H. Fisch, in *Vico's Science of Humanity*, pp. 451–4.

beginning. And it requires that the academies, with their sects of philosophers, should support not the corruption of the sect of these times but the three principles upon which this Science has been founded. These are: that there is divine providence; that human passions must be moderated since they can be; and that our souls are immortal. And [they must uphold] this criterion of truth: that we must respect the common judgment of men – the common sense of mankind – which God, who does not allow himself to be forgotten even in the most abandoned nations, never rouses to more vigorous reflection than when they are most corrupt. The reason for this is that so long as the peoples keep to good customs, they do decent and just things rather than talk about them, because they do them instinctively, not from reflection. (NS/1405–6)

Like his illustrious predecessors in antiquity and the Renaissance, Vico too, it seems, held to the age-old view, that any nation is basically conditioned by, and can best be understood through, its foundational myths. His commentary on the myth of Aeneas illustrates this point. Both the Roman jurisconsults and Vico himself employed it in their respective conservative political strategies. In the *New Science* Vico quotes approvingly Samuel Borchart's opinion, according to which Aeneas 'never set foot in Italy' (NS/772). But that, he realized, was not the main issue in this or indeed in any other political myth. After all, even Vico himself recited this same myth in his welcoming oration for the Bourbon king in Naples! Bochart, like other 'old' critical historians, may have found the historical truth *about* the myth, but he did not really come to grips with the historical truth *of* the myth. That is, he did not treat it as a *vera narratio* of the Roman, as well as – Vico might well have thought – the Neapolitan people. For Vico, the pertinent question was not whether Aeneas had ever existed, let alone set foot in Italy, but rather, why this myth had been created and preserved by the Italians for so many generations. According to his reconstruction of the myth, the story about Aeneas' arrival was an invention of the Greek colonists in Latium, and the Romans came to know it when they later conquered and destroyed the colony. The very fact that this myth survived into Roman culture was, for Vico, an historical proof that there must have been a Greek colony in Latium. Vico further noted that although the Romans must have been familiar with this myth since 451 BC, they revived and appropriated it only about 280 BC, during the war against Pyrrhus, when they became interested in Greek culture.

The crucial significance of this myth for the Italians lies in its Hellenic origin, namely that it enabled the Romans – brutish and inferior people as they knew themselves to be – to trace their origin to a much older and nobler culture than their own. The elevation of Aeneas to the status of the legendary founder of Rome, which reached its peak in Vergil's great epic, thus gave expression to the Romans' innermost 'necessities and utilities' – to secure a perfectly civil origin and unity for their tradition.[76]

To sum up: Vico used his Roman inquiries and examples to argue, against the republican reformers, that Rome's original political strength is not to be found in any mysterious spark of moral *virtus*, believed to have been embedded in its peoples, but rather in the historical construction of its politico-mythical 'authority'. What made the Romans so supreme were not rational ideas and moral ideals, but rather their poetic capacity to 'imagine' and to 'believe'. 'The threefold labor of great poetry', Vico reiterates time and again, has always been

(1) to invent sublime fables suited to the popular understanding; (2) to perturb to excess, with a view to the end proposed; (3) to teach the vulgar to act virtuously . . . Of this nature of human institutions it remained an eternal property, expressed in a noble phrase of Tacitus, that frightened men vainly 'no sooner imagine than they believe' [*fingunt simul creduntque*]. (NS/376)

This precisely was the achievement of the Roman jurisconsults, and this, presumably, was also what Vico hoped to achieve in Naples. Ultimately, it appears, the task of the enlightened conservative man of letters in Naples, much like that of the judicious jurisconsult in Rome and of the king-philosopher in Plato's Republic, was not to break nor to blindly propagate the myths of the state, but rather to sustain and make the people increasingly more aware of them. Or, in the words of Leszek Kolakowski, he must realize that

---

76 As Georges Dumézil has shown, in Roman as well as in any other traditional society 'The function of that particular class of legends known as myths is to express dramatically the ideology under which a society lives; not only to hold out to its conscience the values it recognizes and the ideals it pursues from generation to generation, but above all to express its very being and structure, the elements, the connections, the balances, the tensions that constitute it; to justify the rules and traditional practices without which everything within a society would disintegrate' (*The Destiny of the Warrior*, tr. A. Hiltebeitel (Chicago: The University of Chicago Press, 1970), p. 3).

values inherited under a binding function of authority are being inherited in their mythical form; they are not being inherited as information about social or psychological facts (that this or that happens to be thought valuable) but precisely as information regarding what is or is not a value. The idols of the tribe govern in an inescapable manner: a complete emancipation from them springs from a tyranny of another illusion. Universal godlessness is utopia. Myths that teach us that something simply is good or evil cannot be avoided if humanity is to survive.[77]

III

Reflecting on the failure of modern scholars to understand the true 'authoritative' nature of the Roman state, Vico concluded that this had been caused by a certain intellectual fallacy, common among philologians who reason only 'grammatically' and philosophers who reason only 'rationally' – and not, as it were, historically. Modern interpreters of Roman literature, he argued, have commonly failed to realize that whereas verbal forms of certain political terms have remained the same since ancient times, their modern connotations have radically changed. Hence the failure to interpret the original meaning of certain key-words, and the tendency to read into them 'ideas proper to their own refined and learned minds' and enlightened times (NS/666). In particular, the interpreters

were left in obscurity by failure to define the three words 'people', 'kingdom', and 'liberty'. Because of these words it has been commonly but erroneously believed that the Roman people from the time of Romulus had been composed of citizens both noble and plebeian, that the Roman kingdom had been monarchical, and that the liberty instituted by Brutus had been a popular liberty. And these three undefined words have led into error all the critics, historians, political theorists, and jurists, because no present commonwealth could give them any idea of the heroic ones, which were of a most severely aristocratic form and therefore entirely different from those of our time. (NS/105)

The conceptual anachronism he points out here typified for Vico what he took to be a common fallacy in the human sciences, stemming from 'the conceit of the scholars, who will have it that what they know is as old as the world' (NS/127).

---

[77] Leszec Kolakowski, *The Persistence of Myth*, tr. A. Czerniawski (Chicago: The University of Chicago Press, 1989), p. 25.

Now, as the passage above indicates, Vico thought that political theorists in particular have been prone to this 'conceit of the scholars', because, in their quest for ideal solutions to concrete social problems – they have become too obsessed with abstract terms, general theories, and timeless models: 'Philosophy contemplates reason, whence comes knowledge of the true; philology observes that of which human choice is author, whence comes consciousness of the certain' (NS/138). The failure of political theorists to understand the nature of political 'authority' was then symptomatic of the failure of all philosophers to understand the creative mechanism of 'human choice', to grasp the a-rational yet reasonable (or, in Vico's term 'common-sensible') process of decision-making in which human beings literally 'authorize' their social world and its rules by 'imagining and believing' their own fictions. 'The philosophers', he concludes, 'failed by half in not giving certainty to their reasoning by appeal to the authority of the philologians' (NS/140). They failed, in short, to understand the true nature of man – that he is an 'author': he is indeed a sovereign maker of his civil world, yet he makes it as an artist, not as a scientist or an engineer, producing it by his poetic rather than rational capacities. Vico urges them to take a philological turn similar to that which he recommends for the theologians, who, he says, must realize that their task, 'the knowledge of God . . . does not have its end in metaphysic taking private illumination from intellectual institutions and thence regulating merely her own moral institutions, as hitherto the philosophers have done' but, instead, in a new kind of metaphysic, a practical-historical one, such that 'should know God's providence in public moral institutions or civil customs, by which the nations have come into being and maintain themselves in the world' (NS/5). Similarly, the new science of politics must be more philological than philosophical; that is to say, more practical and interpretive than conceptual and deductive. The enterprise of political theorists is not to look for general structures which presumably determine human activities, but rather to understand these structures and activities as embodied in practices, or 'civil institutions', which are constantly repeated and transformed as they are carried out by the agents engaged in these practices. Vico's new science of politics was, accordingly, thoroughly 'philological', that is to say, his investigations were largely interpretive, not determinative or predictive as in the more positivistic sciences of man in his time, and mostly in a very literary fashion, consisting almost entirely in one 'persistent great effort' – to discover how all our 'civil institutions' have been constituted by mythologies.

This basic mythopoeic conception of human nature and society informed Vico's method of interpretation in all the spheres of life. Inasmuch as all civil institutions are largely conditioned by their mythopoeic make-up, he decreed that the science of politics, like any other science in the New Science, must ultimately be that of interpretive poetics. The logic and operation of myth in constraining, and not determining, human activities – as can be seen, most clearly, in the formation of the conative emotions, or inhibitions, of the three 'principles of humanity' – thus became paradigmatic for all other civil and political institutions. I regard this assertion – that modern society largely consists in, and must be interpreted through, its myth-historical poetics – to be Vico's most important contribution to the modern science of politics. He tried to work out this new science of politics by diverting his attention from superficial words to their underlying images, from singular high-minded philosophical theories to the collective myths and other 'vulgar traditions' through which such theories have always been processed and authorized.

From his earliest orations to the last paragraphs of the *New Science* Vico constantly urged political theorists and leaders to deal not so much with political theory as with 'political wisdom', such as had been exemplified by the Roman *jurisprudentia*. Already in the *Study Methods of Our Time*, while discussing the different legal systems in the classical world, Vico says that the Roman system was superior to the Greek one because its lawmakers were primarily practitioners, and not just theoreticians, of justice: while in Athens 'the philosophers displayed the relationship of the philosophy or doctrine of right to the state, justice, and the laws' in ideal theoretical terms, without any concern to the practical norms and habits of their society, in Rome, by contrast, 'the philosophers were themselves jurisconsults, in the sense that they turned all their wisdom to the practice of law. That which, in Greece, was taught by the philosophers, in Rome was learned by political practice itself (*ipse usu reipublicae*].'[78]

---

[78] Vico, *On the Study Methods of Our time*, pp. 47–70.

In the *New Science* this observation becomes a theorem: Instead of the rigid imposition of norms, laws, and theories on political reality (which marks both the most primitive and the most enlightened ages of mankind) jurisprudence 'looks to the truth of the facts themselves and benignly bends the rule of law to all the requirements of the equity of the causes' (NS/940). In attending 'to the smallest considerations of the justice which is called for by cases when the facts are fully specified' (NS/951) the Roman jurisconsults taught all jurists a universal lesson in adjudication: that in judging the various cases in the state they always gave priority to immediate practical considerations over timeless and merely theoretical ideals. As a rule, Vico says, the Roman jurisconsults sought to 'justify their views as to what is just by appealing to the sect of their times [*setta de' loro tempi*]' as do indeed all the enlightened emperors, then as now, who 'when they wish to give a reason for their laws or for other ordinances issued by them, say that they have been guided by the sect of their times . . . For the customs of the age are the school of princes' (NS/979).

In appealing to the 'customs of the age' the Roman juris-consults established a pragmatic criterion of judgment which, in Vico's view, was right and applicable not only in civil and political legislation, but in all other spheres of human affairs. As a rule, he believed, the philosophical, moral or aesthetic norms of any society must be accorded with its *costumi del secolo*: there simply are no ready-made and universal norms of truth, justice, or beauty which can be applied to all societies at all times. The belief that such norms exist and that they possess them caused 'entire nations and all scholars' to pass all kinds of anachronistic judgments on other – and their own – cultures. This was also

the inexhaustible source of the errors about the principles of humanity that have been adopted by entire nations and by all scholars. For when the former began to take notice of them and the latter to investigate them, it was on the basis of their own enlightened, cultivated, and magnificent times that they judged the origins of humanity, which must nevertheless by the nature of things have been small, crude, and quite obscure. (NS/123)

Vico supplies numerous examples of such conceitful judgments of historical sources, the most notable of which (in his view) were those of the Homeric epic and of the Twelve Tables. In so doing, however, Vico was not just seeking to expose such rather simple misconceptions. He was primarily interested in exposing the rationalistic fallacy underlying them all. Political thought, he believed, must be based on prudential, and not on merely theoretical, principles.

Vico inherited the concept of *prudentia* from a long humanistic-rhetorical tradition of philosophy of action. The concept had its roots in the Aristotelian notion of *phrónesis*, or practical knowledge, such as was crucial for the activity of the citizen in the city. Aristotle duly noted that in the mundane affairs of social life man acquires certain prudential rules of right and wrong behaviour, which require an awareness of the specific moral norms and social forms of life of the community. The notion that social life inevitably consists in moral flexibility was taken over and further advanced by theorists of civic humanism from Cicero to Machiavelli. In their different ways, these thinkers realized that civil life requires and produces a unique kind of moral knowledge, one that consists in a pragmatic interpretation, and not theoretical application, of the law. Machiavelli identified this knowledge with the *virtuoso* qualities of citizens – and principally rulers – in the city, who must always seek to secure civic glory and greatness in a world governed by contingency and irrationality. It is easy to see that Vico largely concurred with this pragmatic attitude to political morality.

Furthermore, his predilection for the *prudentia* of the Roman jurisconsults over the *theoria* of the Greek metaphysicians was not confined solely to legal and political issues: for him, their 'wisdom . . . in interpreting the laws and extending their utility little by little as new cases demanded adjudication' (NS/281) exemplified the ideal of operative knowledge in all the fields of humanity: they all had to be pursued in similar fashion; that is to say, primarily as *interpretive* arts of revision. And the rule of interpretation in each case must be precisely that of the Roman jurists who did not apply an abstract principle of justice to all the cases but tried to find the principles which informed the practices of the age. These principles are often patently a-rational, but this, in Vico's view, does not mean that they are false and wrong because, as he points out in *The Study Methods of Our Time*, 'prudence seeks out in human actions the truth as it is, even when it proceeds from imprudence, ignorance, desire, necessity, or chance'.[79] In this way, then, by depicting Roman *jurisprudentia* as the perfect 'wisdom' in civil life, Vico managed to regain philosophical legitimacy for *prudentia*, that is for that practical knowledge which in the *New Science* he calls *coscienza* and elevates to the status of new scientific knowledge, a truly *scienza nuova*.

Thus, inasmuch as he urged political theorists to get down from the heights of philosophical ideas, theories, and models and go back to the basic 'human ideas', Vico's conception of what politics is or should be all about is as sceptical and pragmatic as that of most enlightened conservatives, then and now. His call to subject political theory to the authority of concrete social traditions rather than to that of abstract individual reason is redolent of what modern conservative theorists like Michael Oakeshott claim – that political knowledge must be based on socially-grounded customs rather than on abstract reason. In a famous essay Oakeshott argues against the liberal ideal of 'rationalism in politics' because it projects a kind of political knowledge which is both much too theoretical and merely 'technical', such that 'is susceptible of formulation in rules, principles, directions, and maxims' and may therefore be learned and 'applied' from a book. Oakeshott suggests instead that politics is a practical and essentially traditional knowledge which 'can neither be taught nor learned, but only imparted' to the student by his master or social institutions, by way of 'initiation into the moral and intellectual habits and achievements of his society'. It involves 'an entry into the partnership between past and present, a sharing of concrete knowledge' – the knowledge produced and preserved by tradition.[80]

Vico's 'new art of criticism' of interpreting political theories and institutions through their mythological narratives and other 'vulgar traditions' may thus be said to have completed his revision of the Enlightenment's theory of history, the theory to which he himself had adhered in the early stages of his career. We should remember that, in his first inaugural lectures, while he was still under the spell of Descartes, Vico dismissed classical philology as

---

[79] Vico, *On the Study Methods of Our Time*, p. 34.
[80] Michael Oakeshott, 'Rationalism in Politics', in *Rationalism in Politics* (London: Methuen, 1962), pp. 10, 32.

amounting to knowing 'no more than did the potter, the cook, the cobbler, the summoner, the auctioneer of Rome'. During the next decade his attitude had been completely reversed, and he came to lament the fact that 'the study of languages is today considered useless, thanks to the authority of Descartes, who says that to know Latin is to know no more than Cicero's servant girl knew'.[81] It was principally against this latter view that he then began to develop his 'new art of criticism', recognizing, as it were, that to know what the common people in Rome knew is the hardest thing of all, that it is indeed much harder to know what Cicero's servant girl knew than to know what Cicero himself knew. For the master's thoughts, at least, had been written down, but those of his servant girl seem to have sunk into oblivion. Surely, her 'human ideas' must have been much simpler and poorer than the very 'Roman' ideas of Cicero's class; and yet, from Vico's point of view, in order to know what the Roman magistrates and philosophers thought up in their high-minded terms it was important to find out what the common people in the *forum* perceived in their common-sensual terms. Cicero's 'principles of metaphysics, logic, and morals', like those of Socrates, must have 'issued from the market place'. Similarly, his bold – and really outrageous – renderings of Solon or Romulus to being merely the 'poetic characters' of their peoples in Athens and Rome, bizarre as they might seem to us, were ingenious and constructive: they helped establish new 'higher critical' standards in historical scholarship, according to which all the great men in history, their ideas and deeds could be dissolved into the common mentality of their peoples. In so doing Vico may be said to have shifted the focus of modern historians from the mere recording of external deeds performed by great men toward the analysis of the inner modifications which regularize common human behaviour. His 'history of human ideas' fulfilled this duty, insofar as it refrained from dishing up the clear and distinct ideas of the philosophers, and elaborated instead on the collective psychological realities through which such ideas have been construed. In his view, the common social practices of the people precede and determine even the most unique ideas of individual philosophers:

---

[81] Quoted in Max H. Fisch's Introduction to *The Autobiography of Giambattista Vico*, p. 37.

Now, because laws certainly came first and philosophers later, it must have been from observing that the enactment of laws by Athenian citizens involved their coming to agreement in an idea of an equal utility common to all of them severally, that Socrates began to adumbrate intelligible genera or abstract universals by induction . . . we thus conclude that these principles of metaphysics, logic, and morals issued from the market place of Athens. (NS/1041, 1043)

In his historical investigations, then, Vico did not deal with heroic achievements of individuals and their world-views, the common stuff of the Renaissance tradition in cultural history, but rather concentrated on the attitudes of ordinary people toward everyday life. And he was not interested so much in their conceptual ideas as in their sensual images of life, death, marriage, work, sex, family, and so on. What was needed, Vico rightly saw, is a new kind of philology, a truly New Science, that would enable us to recover those common-sensual and truly 'human' ideas from the high-minded and mostly authoritative sources of the past.

This, then, was the radical innovation in Vico's 'historical mythology' – that mythology was thereafter perceived as neither a-historical nor anti-historical but as counter-historical. 'Counter-history', as defined by one modern scholar, consists in the 'belief that the true history lies in a subterranean tradition that must be brought to light'. It is thus 'a type of revisionist historiography, but where the revisionist proposes a new theory or finds new facts, the counter-historian transvalues old ones'.[82] This formulation conveys quite accurately, I think, the main idea of Vico's task in retrieving egregious and incongruous mythology for normative historiography. He rightly reasoned that if the common people in those ancient civilizations could express themselves at all, they must have done so in their own lower idioms and alternative modes of communication. Heretic beliefs, revolutionary movements, rebellious heroes, and other subversive forces, he saw, have found no recognitions in the official literature, but they have left their traces in such counter-historical accounts as fables, folk-tales, festivals, and the like. Such also were the mythologies of the nations which, according to Vico, often narrate those forbidden 'true stories' which have been systematically suppressed or

---

[82] David Biale, *Gershom Scholem: Kabbalah and Counter-History*, rev. edn (Cambridge, Mass.: Harvard University Press, 1982), pp. 7–8.

omitted from their official, homogeneous 'histories', 'philosophies', or 'religious creeds'. The essential 'critical' task of the
historian is not to discard but rather to redeem those rudimentary
versions of 'the true' from their oblivion in that 'night of thick
darkness, enveloping the earliest antiquities'.

Vico justly considered the discovery of the 'poetic logic' of
history to have been 'the master-key of this Science', because it was
this discovery which enabled him to show how 'this human world,
the world of civil society' evolved from its mythological origins; by
grounding history in mythology he managed, as it were, to fulfil
his initial and most important methodological postulate in which
he decreed that 'theories must take their beginning from that of
the matters of which they treat' (NS/314). In my final concluding
comments I shall ask whether, and to what extent, this new
scientific, exceedingly revisionist, historiographical task, has been
recognized and fulfilled by modern scholars.

Conclusion

Vico disconcerts. Two hundred and fifty years after his death he continues to baffle his admirers as he did in his lifetime – and in his death. As can be read in his own *Autobiography*:

When the hour for Vico's funeral rites had been set, almost all the professors were eager to pay this last tribute to their deceased colleague and came to his house to accompany the remains. The Confraternity of Santa Sophia, of which Vico had been a member, were to carry the coffin as they regularly did for their deceased members. When the Confraternity arrived at his house, they began to murmur that they would not allow the professors of the University to bear the pall. The professors on the other hand contended they had the right to that honor, and adduced many precedents. Meanwhile the corpse was carried down into the courtyard of the house and laid on the bier, which bore the arms of the Royal University. Hereupon there began a great uproar between the members of the Confraternity and the professors of the University, neither side being willing to yield to the other, and both showing in the presence of the dead how far human weakness and pride can go. As no amicable understanding could be reached, the Confraternity, with small regard for human decency, decided to take their leave, abandoning the corpse where it lay. The professors alone were unable to carry out the funeral rites, and the corpse had to be carried back into its old dwelling.[1]

According to Max H. Fisch, the Marquis of Villarosa compiled this report and published it in 1818 in his authorized continuation of Vico's *Autobiography* while 'drawing heavily on the oral Vico tradition' in Naples, hence its 'gossipy character'.[2] Assuming, as we must, that this then is not really the history of what had actually happened, but only a story, the question arises: what are we to

---

[1] Vico, *Autobiography*, p. 207.
[2] M. H. Fisch, Introduction to the *Autobiography*, p. 18.

make, if at all, of such a story? What kind of a story is it – is it tragic or comic? True or false?

These queries as to the deeper meaning of what is patently only a vulgar tradition may seem frivolous, but I think they are important, especially in view of the theory I have expounded in this study: that 'vulgar traditions' must have had 'common grounds of truth'. In this case, I would like to suggest, the vulgar tradition about Vico's death contains the truth about Vico's life. For the contest between the professors and the priests over the right to bury Vico was really, and quite literally, about the right to appropriate him: to whom did Vico really belong – to the Professors or to the Priests? Or, to rephrase the question in Vico's own terms, the contest here was similar to the one in which Vico himself participated, that of the Ancients and the Moderns over Homer, and which he summed up in his Discovery of the True Homer: now the contest was, as it were, about The Discovery of the True Vico. And if I may be allowed to pursue this analogy a little further, I would add that the same principles and methods which led Vico to his discovery of the True Homer must be applied in the discovery of the True Vico. Vico, we recall, discovered the True Homer through the myths of Homer as well as those about him, and ultimately identified him with the 'Greek peoples', with 'what they say', *mythologein*, about him. In the same vein, we must discover the True Vico through the myths he interpreted, and those which interpret him – like the one quoted above concerning his posthumous legacy. Furthermore, just as Vico realized that Homer could not be discovered by either the Moderns or by the Ancients, because his wild mythical world and poetry were so alien to their moral and aesthetic norms, and therefore concluded that only he himself, with his new science of mythology, could discover Homer as he truly was – so too must we realize that Vico could not be known, and therefore could not be duly owned after his death, by either the professors or the priests, and for exactly the same reasons: for in his profession – both as an academic and as a believer – Vico dealt with issues which were much too archaic and anarchic for the common scientific standards by which his admirers judged him. His *New Science* was new in the strongest sense of the term, an entirely different kind of science in its premises and methods, in its medium and message – in short, it was not just another science but a science of the other. This, then, is the ultimate reason why the first contenders for Vico's legacy, like so many who came afterward, failed to get hold of it, or at least, as I see it, this is the ultimate meaning of the story: for in exposing the myths that preceded and constituted all scientific theories, Vico defied any such claims and attempts to appropriate him to any scientific theory, and this he is still doing.

And this indeed is the strongest impression we are left with upon completing this study of Vico's *New Science*: that this is a science that aims at what lays before and beyond the sciences, that deals with the 'human condition' itself, with the basic ways and means by which human beings have made up their civil world; that is to say not with their later scientific ideas and theories but with their primal and most common beliefs and practices, with what Vico called their 'philology' rather than with their 'philosophy', in short – with life itself. And it is for this reason that this work had commonly been more successfully appropriated by poets and free thinkers than by professors and priests. For, on the whole, they were more attentive to his new scientific medium and message, and more responsive to its mythopoeic expressions and interpretations. The modern scholars, on the other hand, have generally tended to treat his work in the more disciplinary measures of their sciences, as presumably did those professors and priests who came to bury him, and have likewise failed to put him to rest. This attitude is particularly inadequate, and even unfair, in the case of Vico, who was probably the first major theorist who revolted against the Cartesian methodology and Enlightenment ideology of critical-rational scientism. Alasdair MacIntyre has been one of the most forceful critics of this excessive scientism in our modern culture, especially in ethics, and he has rightly invoked Vico's name and words in his attempt to refute it, noting that

it was Vico who first stressed the importance of the undeniable fact, which is becoming tedious to reiterate, that the subject matters of moral philosophy at least – the evaluative and normative concepts, maxims, arguments and judgments about which the moral philosopher enquires – are nowhere to be found except as embodied in the historical lives of particular social groups and so possessing the distinctive characteristics of historical existence . . . Morality which is no particular society's morality is to be found nowhere.[3]

---

[3] Alasdair MacIntyre, *After Virtue: A Study in Moral Theory*. sec. rev. edn (London: Duckworth, 1985), p. 265.

The affinity between MacIntyre's views and Vico's is more profound, and touches what I regard to be Vico's major discovery – the mythical constitution of society. Although MacIntyre does not elaborate on Vico's theory of myth, and does not refer at all to such key notions as 'true narration' or 'poetic characters', it seems safe to infer that these notions are compatible with, and may even have inspired, his own narrativist theory of human life in society and history. Some of Vico's most profound insights about the indispensability of myth to modern society are clearly explicated by MacIntyre; his theory merits, therefore, some further elaboration.

In his works MacIntyre largely reiterates the common conservative charge against the Enlightenment thinkers, namely that by promoting individual rights and reasons over against all forms and norms of traditional practices, they subjected all cultural virtues to radical relativism. What makes his historical inquiry so original, and uniquely Vichian, is his claim that in order to survive modern society must regain a new sense of tradition, or, to use his terms, to reassert its narrative constitution. According to MacIntyre, the basic rule of life is that 'man is in his actions and practices, as well as in his fictions, essentially a story-telling animal. He is not essentially, but becomes through history, a teller of stories that aspire to truth.' What he means by this is that we live out and understand our life (and those of others) according to certain narratives which lay out for us basic precedents, rules and prescriptions for moral action in social situations. A successful life depends on whether those who live it possess and exercise 'the virtues', which are those qualities which their society has predetermined as crucial for that sort of life, or 'role' in life, which they seek to discover and to fulfil. According to MacIntyre, each society defines for its members these 'roles' through the typical heroes of its traditional stories. 'Hence', he says, 'there is no way to give us an understanding of any society, including our own, except through the stock of stories which constitute its initial dramatic resources. Mythology, in its original sense, is at the heart of things. Vico was right and so was Joyce.'[4]

Indeed, Vico was right and so was Joyce – in his interpretation

---

[4] MacIntyre, *After Virtue*, p. 216.

of Vico. Joyce's remarks on Vico's historical theories are now well-known and much discussed: 'I would not pay overmuch attention to these theories', Joyce said, 'beyond using them for all they are worth, but they have gradually forced themselves on me through circumstances of my own life'.[5] Joyce scholars have given various answers as to what these 'circumstances' were, and detected many venues in which Vico's theories have indeed 'forced themselves' into his work. It seems to me that Joyce was responsive to Vico because he saw in Vico's 'great effort' to forge a new science of history by means of imaginative philology, rather than by realistic philosophy, that pattern of quest which was closely related to his own struggle for a new art of literature. In their major works both authors managed to liberate themselves from scientific history which dwells on mere factuality – be it antiquarianism in Vico's time or positivism in Joyce's – by turning to that narrative mode which has always been considered subversive of normative scientific history – namely, mythology. Out of their common disillusionment with the contemporaneous scientific modes and narrative styles of history-writing in their times grew a new science of historical mythology in the case of Vico and a new art of literary mythology in the case of Joyce. Joyce himself supplied the main clue to this hypothesis: late in his life, when he was asked by the Danish writer Tom Kristensen how to understand his work, Joyce advised him to read the *New Science*. 'But do you believe in the *New Science*?', asked Kristensen, to which Joyce replied: 'I do not believe in any science, but my imagination grows when I read Vico as it doesn't when I read Freud or Jung'.[6] As I see it, Joyce preferred Vico to these and all other theorists of myth-in-history precisely because Vico was less 'scientific' than they were in the reduction of history to myth. Though he believed that human beings made their history by myth, Vico – and Joyce after him – did not interpret all human history as being so rigidly determined by mytho-logical patterns of thought, but only as incited and constrained by them, forever moved and moving by

---

[5] *The Letters of James Joyce*, vol. i, ed. Stuart Gilbert (N.Y.: Viking Press, 1966), p. 241. I have examined Joyce's 'circumstances' in my 'Mythology and Counter-History: The New Critical Arts of Vico and Joyce', in *Vico and Joyce*, ed. D. P. Verene (N.Y.: State University of New York Press, 1987), pp. 32-47.

[6] Quoted in Richard Ellmann, *James Joyce*, rev. edn (Oxford: Oxford University Press, 1982), p. 693.

their forceful images and narratives – seemingly forwards, but in fact always inwards and backwards.

Thus, having recognized in Vico the discoverer of myth for history and the redeemer of history through myth, Joyce set out to fill the same role in and for literature. It was through their innovative use of mythology, then, that they literally made history anew. For both realized that myths, being the creative interpretation of common collective experience, also shaped that experience to the extent that it was impossible, or at any rate futile, to purge historical narratives from their mythological fictions. They both realized that as human beings we all live through mythological history; they both knew that as scholars and artists all they can – and must – create is 'historical mythology'.

Vico himself defined the historical task of his work as the interpretation of history through its *repilogamenti della storia poetica* (NS/679ff.). This is a rather ambiguous phrase, the English translation of which – 'epitomes of poetic history' – does not adequately convey its performative and reflexive aspects. Edward Said's translation of 'repilogamenti' as 'recapitulations' is, I think, plausible and instructive.[7] The recapitulation of poetic history is an exercise in what I have called the 'revision' of history. Its aim is to retrieve by recognition those truths which, so to speak, had been suppressed by the prosaic history of civil society, yet preserved in its poetic history: the 'vulgar' truths of the common people in their everyday life, their beliefs, hopes, and dreams, which, as Frances Yates once put it, 'are as much a part of history as the terrible events which falsify them'.[8] By postulating that 'theories must start from the point where the matter of which they treat first began to take shape' so that 'the first science to be learned should be mythology or the interpretation of fables', Vico taught us how and where to reveal these 'true narrations', referring us back to the mythopoeic origins and transformations of all our theories. And what Vico prescribed to all theories, must be applied to his own theories and those concerning him: they too must be referred back to their own mythopoeic origins and transformations. As, I trust, my interpretation of the story of his death

---

[7] Edward Said, *Beginnings: Intention and Methods* (N.Y.: Basic Books, 1975), p. 356.
[8] Frances Yates, *The French Academies of the Sixteenth Century*, Studies of the Warburg Institute (London, 1947), p. 199.

has just shown: what seemed at first sight to be only a 'gossipy' story, no more than a 'vulgar tradition', a myth about Vico's death, has turned out to be the 'true narration' of Vico's life, works, and enduring legacy.

Index